THE
AMERICAN
PEACE MOVEMENT

Ideals and Activism

SOCIAL MOVEMENTS PAST AND PRESENT

Irwin T. Sanders, Editor

THE
AMERICAN
PEACE MOVEMENT
Ideals and Activism

Charles Chatfield

with the assistance of
Robert Kleidman

Twayne Publishers • New York
Maxwell Macmillan Canada • Toronto
Maxwell Macmillan International • New York Oxford Singapore Sydney

The American Peace Movement: Ideals and Activism
Charles Chatfield, with the assistance of Robert Kleidman

Twayne Publishers
Macmillan Publishing Company
866 Third Avenue
New York, New York 10022

Maxwell Macmillan Canada, Inc.
1200 Eglinton Avenue East
Suite 200
Don Mills, Ontario M3C 3N1

Macmillan Publishing Company is part of the Maxwell Communication Group of
Companies.

Copyediting supervised by Barbara Sutton.
Typeset by Compset, Inc., Beverly, Massachusetts.

10 9 8 7 6 5 4 3 2 1 (hc)
10 9 8 7 6 5 4 3 2 1 (pb)

The paper used in this publication meets the minimum requirements
of American National Standard for Information Sciences—Permanence
of Paper for Printed Library Materials, ANSI Z39.48-1984. ∞™

Printed and bound in the United States of America.

Library of Congress Cataloging-in-Publication Data
Chatfield, Charles, 1934–
    The American peace movement : ideals and activism / Charles
Chatfield with the assistance of Robert Kleidman.
        p.   cm.—(Social movements past and present)
    Includes bibliographical references and index.
    ISBN 0-8057-3851-7 (hc).—ISBN 0-8057-3852-5 (pbk.)
    1. Peace movements—United States—History.   I. Kleidman,
Robert.   II. Title.   III. Series.
JX1961.U6C45   1991
327.1'72'0973—dc20   91-39672
                                                      CIP

327.172
C 492 o 1992

Contents

v

Illustrations

Preface

A generation of scholarship on the peace and antiwar movement in the United States has produced numerous detailed studies and a comprehensive narrative, Charles DeBenedetti's *The Peace Reform in American History*. Until recently, however, sociologists have not included the peace reform in social movement theory, despite the resurgence of interest in this field that accompanied organized opposition to the Vietnam War and nuclear weapons. This book is an attempt to inform narrative history with sociological insights and to ask not only what this reform movement has attempted and accomplished but also how it has functioned. It interprets the peace movement in terms of social process.

In this respect, recent sociology provides useful tools of analysis. It is particularly helpful for the interpretation and comparison of discrete social movements. Organized effort to secure peace and oppose war can be studied as a social movement in the sense that Charles Tilly defined it: "a sustained *interaction* in which mobilized people, acting in the name of a defined interest, make repeated broad demands on powerful others via means which go beyond the current prescriptions of the authorities."[1] Tilly's emphasis on the word *interaction* points to the dynamic relationships among those people who organize for change as well as between them and the government or society they seek to alter. Going beyond this level, social theorists like Max Weber, Jürgen Habermas, and Alain Touraine have tried to relate social movements to long-term changes in the structure of society; the larger their focus, however, the more generalized their analyses have been. It is perhaps not unfair to say that they have leaped from the study of historic movements to the theory of history.

This study lies on the intermediate level of historical narrative. It is cast in the form of a story. Partly, this is to make it most accessible to the general reader. But this form also enables us to relate continuity to change—continuity in the overall goals and ideals of the sequence of peace and antiwar movements, and changes in the organization of those movements, the society in which they functioned, and the world they addressed. Framing the study in this way helps us to assess the roles, frustrations, and achievements of the peace reform over time.

Although cast in narrative form, the chapters that follow are informed by analysis of (1) historic foreign policy issues and differing interpretations of national interest; (2) peace movement constituencies in relation to the elements of the public they sought to mobilize; (3) the organization, leadership, and strategies of each specific movement; (4) the politics of coalition and factionalism; and (5) the results of the movement, insofar as they can be known. The Conclusion reflects on the story in terms of social movement theory.

I deeply appreciate Robert Kleidman's assistance. Although a historian by training, I am particularly interested in social process. Kleidman, a sociologist at Cleveland State University, has a penchant for grounding analysis in primary sources and historical context. Moreover, his comparison of the Emergency Peace Campaign of the 1930s, the campaign against atmospheric nuclear testing of the 1950s, and the nuclear freeze movement of the early 1980s complements my own studies of the peace movement during World War I and the interwar period, and of the antiwar movement in the Vietnam era. My colleague introduced me to resource mobilization theory and made available his Ph.D. dissertation, "Organizing for Peace: Neutrality, the Test Ban, and the Freeze" (University of Wisconsin, 1990) while it was still in progress. He also carefully critiqued each chapter of this volume.

Although most of this book draws upon our own work, chapters 1 and 4 are based on historical studies that, although not all indicated in the notes, are accessible through standard bibliographies. Both of us are deeply indebted, even for chapters grounded in our primary research, to a wealth of scholarship in our respective fields. In particular, I owe a great debt to Charles DeBenedetti, whose untimely death left me with the responsibility for completing his *An American Ordeal: The Antiwar Movement of the Vietnam Era* (Syracuse University Press, 1990).

The staff of Twayne Publishers has been very congenial and helpful, notably Athenaide Dallett in proposing this project, Irwin T. Sanders and John Martin in their judicious suggestions and Larry Hamberlin in rigorous copyediting.

I am ever indebted to my wife, Mary, for her inspiration and understanding.

November 1990

In the months following the composition of this preface, the United States engaged Iraq in a major war. The Persian Gulf crisis had been a salient issue since August 1990, but military preparations and even congressional authorization for warfare had been framed in such a way that the political system was not a venue for debate on the war itself. So brief and militarily successful was the war and, therefore, so strong was the administration's credibility, that no significant public opposition evolved. In some postwar assessments one can discern a failure to distinguish between an antiwar campaign and the peace movement. The proper lesson to draw, I suggest, is that military success is not tantamount to political purpose, and that the absence of an antiwar campaign does not obviate the importance of continuing public pressure for peace-oriented foreign policy.

April 1991

Abbreviations

ADA	Americans for Democratic Action
AFSC	American Friends Service Committee
APS	American Peace Society
AUAM	American Union against Militarism
CALC	Clergy and Laity Concerned
CEIP	Carnegie Endowment for International Peace
CIA	Central Intelligence Agency
CLW	Council for a Livable World
CND	Campaign for Nuclear Disarmament
CNVA	Committee for Non-Violent Action
C.O.	conscientious objector
CORE	Congress of Racial Equality
CPS	Civilian Public Service
CPU	Church Peace Union
CSFW	Coalition to Stop Funding the War
EPC	Emergency Peace Campaign
FCNL	Friends Committee on National Legislation
FOR	Fellowship of Reconciliation
FPA	Foreign Policy Association
IFOR	International Fellowship of Reconciliation

LEP	League to Enforce Peace
LNA	League of Nations Association
LNNPA	League of Nations Non-Partisan Association
MFS	Mobilization for Survival
NAG	National Action Group
NCCEWVN	National Coordinating Committee to End the War in Vietnam
NCPW	National Council for Prevention of War
NPC	National Peace Conference
NSBRO	National Service Board for Religious Objectors
NWFC	Nuclear Weapons Freeze Campaign (or Clearinghouse)
NYPS	New York Peace Society
PAC	political action committee
PSR	Physicians for Social Responsibility
SANE	National Committee for a Sane Nuclear Policy
SALT	Strategic Arms Limitation Talks
SDS	Students for a Democratic Society
SNCC	Student Nonviolent Coordinating Committee
SPU	Student Peace Union
UCS	Union of Concerned Scientists
UPU	Universal Peace Union
UWF	United World Federalists
VMC	Vietnam Moratorium Committee
VVAW	Vietnam Veterans Against the War
WILPF	Women's International League for Peace and Freedom
WPF	World Peace Foundation

WPP	Woman's Peace Party
WRI	War Resisters International
WRL	War Resisters League
WSP	Women Strike for Peace
YMCA	Young Men's Christian Association

For Mary

The November Mobilization, 15 November 1969, brought some half million people to Washington, D.C., in protest of the Vietnam War. It was the climax of three days of peaceful but dramatic events organized by the New Mobilization Committee and the Vietnam Moratorium Committee. *Swarthmore College Peace Collection; courtesy of Theodore B. Hetzel*

Introduction

Washington, November 1969

> *People who dare to challenge authority are thus the basis of collective action, social movements, and cycles of protest. Movement organizations are groups that attempt to harness the energies of these people to broader ideological goals. They use collective action to gain a following, enunciate their goals, and demand responses.*[1]

The nation appeared to be in motion, although its direction was not clear, as students climbed aboard three chartered buses, left the campus of a college in southwestern Ohio, and headed eastward on Interstate 70. It was dark by the time they reached Pennsylvania. Ahead of them and behind were the lights of other buses from the upper Midwest (in Michigan the demand for chartered coaches outran the supply). At Breezewood, where they paused for refreshment before heading southward toward Washington, people milled about the terminal. Dawn broke in Maryland to reveal a seeming convoy driving onto the nation's capital. Well inside the city, the buses filed up Constitution Avenue to the Washington Monument, let off their passengers in the chill morning air, and turned right to park near the tidal basin in sight of the domed Jefferson Monument. Back on the Mall, the students rubbed the sleep out of their eyes and found themselves part of a mass of humanity headed toward the Capitol and the largest demonstration in the nation's history to that time.

Behind them rose the gray shaft of the monument, beyond it the Lincoln Memorial, and across the Potomac the Pentagon. Further on and out of sight were the swelling Appalachian mountains and Ohio hills from which the students had come. Leading to their trek were four years of turmoil over a war in Vietnam.

Only a month before, citizens across the country had declared a moratorium, a one-day suspension of business as usual, in order to wrestle with the issues of that war. The conflict was rooted in Cold War policy dating from at least 1955, when the United States undertook the task of building a nation in South Vietnam in an effort to contain communism in Southeast Asia. In the process, American foreign policy became committed to a regime that was increasingly repressive and tenuous, its legitimacy challenged within the South and from the North. Conflict had escalated into full-fledged although undeclared war in 1965, when President Lyndon Baines Johnson authorized sustained bombing in North Vietnam and followed that with combat troops in the South. Three years later the bombing and ground fighting had only engaged both sides more fully in a frustrating stalemate that took an enormous toll on the people of Vietnam and the morale of America.

A fresh offensive at the outset of the Tet lunar year in 1968 had revealed both the dimensions of the tragedy and the persistence of communist strength, eventually leading the Johnson administration to set a ceiling on its military commitment. The new president, Richard M. Nixon, had promised to bring peace without abandoning the South Vietnam regime, and war had ground on. Opponents of the war had organized the public demonstrations that began with a fall moratorium on 15 October 1969, when citizens from every walk of life—business and labor leaders, scholars and clergy, students and housewives, civic officials and members of Congress—had conducted rallies, prayer vigils, teach-ins, leafleting, discussions, and debates from the East Coast to the West. Even some soldiers in Vietnam had participated in the solemn outpouring of disillusion and discontent.

President Nixon had counterattacked at the end of the month with a public address that rallied patriotic support and put his opponents on the defensive. In turn, he had driven together the two major wings of the antiwar movement, the moderate and liberal organizers of the national moratorium and the more radical and pacifist coalition preparing for a massive November mobilization in Washington. The lines thus tightly drawn, antiwar dissidence was focused on the capital. That was the drama toward which the students from Ohio had been drawn.

It began on the Thursday evening before their arrival, when demonstrators began to process from Arlington Memorial Cemetery, across the Memorial Bridge, up Constitution Avenue—briefly in the glare of floodlights in front of the White House—to the Capitol. The line of vigil stretched four miles. Each person carried a candle and wore a placard with the name of an American citizen killed in action or a Vietnam village destroyed during the war. Well over 40,000 people walked through the night, all day Friday, and through that night, finally slipping their placards into makeshift coffins at the foot of the Capitol building. It was toward that location that the Ohio students walked on Saturday morning.

By noon they were part of a crowd of perhaps half a million people filling the Mall from the west portico of the Capitol to the Washington Monument. After invocations and speeches they all poured into Pennsylvania Avenue, a broadly representative though largely young citizenry that included even men on active military duty. American flags were sprinkled among signs protesting the war. Demonstrators were massed between lines of civilian marshals. They walked to Fifteenth Street, where they turned southward, passing the White House grounds, onto the gentle slope west of the monument. There, huddled in small clusters against the cold, the gathering crowd listened absently to interminable speeches amplified from a platform at the foot of the hill, as marchers filed into the Mall throughout the afternoon.

What did these demonstrators have in common that drew them from not only Ohio but Wisconsin and Michigan to the west and from cities along the Atlantic seaboard? Part of the "peace movement" or the "antiwar movement," how were they related to other contemporary and historic social movements in America? Who were these people? What brought them together?

If anyone really paid attention to the speakers it was not the president, who, the White House advised, was watching Saturday football. Not that anyone on the Mall said anything new—that was not the point of the demonstration, after all—nor that they agreed on anything except that the war was utterly wrong and must be ended immediately. The speakers' roster had been arduously negotiated, in fact, so that it would include a wide range of viewpoints acceptable to the sponsors.

Beyond the pale of the coalition sponsoring the mobilization were small groups of militant radicals, including the Weathermen. Already some of them had threatened to disrupt the plans for orderly protest and had engaged in a confrontation with police at Du Pont Circle. On Saturday, during the speeches a few militants moved through the crowd with signs promoting a rally after the official demonstration—a confrontation at the Justice Department on behalf of the "Chicago Eight," a group of men on trial for allegedly having conspired to incite violence at the 1968 Democratic national convention. The picketers, like the speakers, were mostly tolerated by the crowd. Only the songs of familiar folk artists like Pete Seeger and Peter, Paul, and Mary made the program at all palatable to the chilled audience. At the close of the afternoon, and as doves were released into the sky, thousands of voices joined the cast of *Hair* in the rhythmic chant, "All we are saying / is give peace a chance."

The crowd dispersed, most of them to board the buses just off the Mall to the south. The original plan was for them to meet their buses at designated churches in downtown Washington, but in order to reach those sites people would have had to cross the triangle of federal buildings where the Justice Department was located and where the unauthorized rally had been planned. Fearing trouble there, the organizers had tried to move people away from it. Trouble there was, provoked by a small group of militants. A few hundred people were caught up in violence that spilled outward from the Justice Department. Tear gas filled the federal triangle and wafted into the downtown area. It stung the eyes of confused demonstrators, including a few of the Ohio students whose bus had not gotten revised directions that morning.

What was going on here? What did the organizers of the mobilization and the militant minority think they were doing? Furthermore, who negotiated the terms of the demonstration? Why was it necessary to negotiate a roster of speakers, after all? What was the relationship of the mobilization to the earlier moratorium? Who was in charge here?

It was early Sunday morning before the remaining Ohio group was collected and on their bus for the long ride back to campus. The coverage of the rally was full and fair, and the postdemonstration violence was minimized. Somehow it seeped into the students' minds that they had been part of a historic event; perhaps that was the hope that had lured them in the first place. Now they were headed back to college life as usual, to friends who would have known the past 12 hours only from news coverage, to career-tracking courses seemingly unrelated to this weekend. Was this more than an interlude for them? For the nation?

The organizers of the demonstration could congratulate themselves on the success of the event itself. But their coffers were depleted, factionalism disrupted their ranks, activists turned to other agendas or dropped out, and government war policy seemed to roll on as though nothing had happened. What was the point of all this effort? Was the movement more than a gesture?

This book explores questions raised by the November 1969 mobilization. Organized public opposition to the war in Vietnam crested in November 1969, but that single, highly visible wave of protest can only be understood in relation to the crosscurrents generated by the war from at least 1965 to 1973. In turn, opposition to the Vietnam War was part of a social movement organized to influence American foreign policy for peace and against war.

A social movement involves a sustained effort to change policy and the rationale on which it is based by mobilizing people around a specific cause. Thus we may speak of a civil rights, a women's, or an environmental movement. If the cause is peace itself, then it is proper to speak of a peace movement. Since the goal of peace is defined in different ways from time to time, though, it is possible to think in terms of several stages of the movement or even, given significant qualitative differences in those stages, of successive movements. In either case, the mobilization of people is done by specific groups, organizations that claim to represent constituencies for a social cause. People may be moved directly by the claims of organizations or indirectly by the historic context of which those groups are a part.

Organizations may be ongoing and formal, or occasional and ad hoc. The peace movement has included both types. Its lasting organizations have been based on long-term goals and values. Periodically, those values have been translated into issues around which large groups of people could be reached or mobilized, or through which peace organizations could relate to underlying changes in public attitudes. Issue-oriented campaigns are the way in which long-term goals are transformed into specific, immediate objectives. Thus, the November 1969 mobilization was organized by a group that campaigned for immediate American withdrawal from Vietnam. Other organizations—that which sponsored the previous month's moratorium, for example—tried to mobilize their own constituencies and the public at large to end the war and, by extension, to seek a different kind of peace than the government envisioned. It was an episode in a 150-year-old peace movement and, so distinct was its cause and organization, it was an antiwar movement. It was also one of several contemporaneous campaigns for social change. Accordingly, it tapped deep currents in the evolution and structure of American society. It raised critical issues that apply to other peace mobilizations.

Who Was Involved?

The questions Who were these people? and What brought them together? point to the shifting constituencies for peace and antiwar activity and the interests or ideas that bonded them, however tenuously and briefly. Who if anyone but themselves did they represent? What did they want? To what other actors in the national drama did they relate?

Most studies of social movements focus on class, racial, and gender-based groups. The participants in the mobilization were not predominantly from the working class or racial minorities, however, and the movement was not rooted in gender inequalities (although it was affected by them). It was decidedly middle class, and it included many college students. The middle-class character of the peace movement was a problem for activists trying to forge ties with important deprived constituencies. It created a quandary for analysts, too. Some of them dismissed it as symbolic behavior. That could explain some forms of protest, but it does not account for ongoing and often routine peace advocacy. Nor does it help to explain the effect of merely expressive actions on attempts to mobilize people for change. It is necessary to identify factors that led people to adopt alternative views on foreign policy. Almost certainly, the major consideration was a shared outlook, or worldview, and motivating ideals. What peace advocates had most in common was what they believed and felt.

Were the participants in the November 1969 mobilization representative of the national public? Most demonstrators probably were not even members of the organizations that sponsored the event. They were visible evidence of a constituency that those groups claimed to represent. Many peace groups maintained their opposition to war for decades, attempting to get their message to various sectors of the public. Sometimes, as in the fall of 1969, they won a popular response. In other cases, as during most of the Vietnam War, they faced apathetic or hostile public opinion. Accordingly, the rally raised questions about the relationship between peace constituencies and the public.

What Was Going On?

The question What was going on here? points to strategies of action. Some of them were so much taken for granted that they were usually not associated with the movement. These included providing information about international issues and policy choices, and even sponsoring international exchanges for the purpose of better understanding among people, on the assumption that a more informed public would make choices less likely to involve war. Similarly, methods of conflict resolution were taught in schools and civic groups in the hope that people would use the alternatives to violence in which they were being trained. More closely related to the peace movement were various ways of witnessing for personal ideals, notably conscientious objection to military service. The movement both propagated this approach and defended the right of individuals to exercise it. Some peace advocates openly declared their refusal to participate in the war in the hope that such war resistance would inhibit nations from fighting. This became an antiwar strategy when it was employed collectively in wartime, as it was during the Vietnam War.

The movement also experimented with many forms of political action designed to mobilize people for campaigns on specific policy issues. These included socially sanctioned actions such as using personal influence, lobbying decision makers, and mobilizing public opinion. Demonstrations were one way to mobilize people, although there were others, such as petition and letter writing, advertising, introducing and supporting legislation, and helping to elect friendly political leaders. There were also forms of action not always sanctioned by the political system, such as nonviolent direct action. Generally, activists who broke specific laws in order to make a political or moral point nonetheless subjected themselves to the legal process. In a crisis of authority like the Vietnam War, that condition could break down, as it did in the rally at the Justice Department. Flaunting law compromised other movement strategies, however, which suggested the importance of relating various ways of seeking public influence to one another.

Who Was in Charge?

The question Who was in charge here? points to the forms of organization attempted over a century and a half of peace advocacy. People did not just happen to show up at the same time and place with similar signs and banners, after all. An action like the November 1969 mobilization had to be organized. Who if anyone was calling the shots? On what basis and for what purpose? Was there any connection between the organization of protest in one era and another—between opposition to the Vietnam War, for instance, and the formation of the nuclear freeze movement a decade or so later?

Some level of formal organization is necessary in order to recruit members, make the flow of resources routine, and direct action. The development of centralized structures, with information and decisions made mainly in a national office, was natural as the peace groups reached out from one region of the country to another, targeted national policies, and related to an international movement. Insofar as their long-term goal included participation in decision making (in organizational as well as national policy), though, they encountered pressures for decentralization.

Professional leadership, because of its strategic position, access to funds, knowledge, and skills—often because of its very dedication to the cause—tended to formulate and establish policy. To what extent did it thereby minimize organizational democracy, lose touch with local vitality, or alienate grass-root activists? Did such leaders tend to become conservative and susceptible to co-optation by elites because of the importance they attached to their positions or, perhaps, the organization itself?

In order to form a broad social movement, specific organizations must work together. In the fall of 1969 the media pictured the Nixon administration as confronted by an antiwar "movement" at the seat of power, but on closer inspection the so-called movement dissolved into a loose, temporary grouping of discrete and very different organizations and individuals.

Behind every peace campaign in the twentieth century there has been a coalition of organizations. Some of those groups were formed during or before World War I and endured the lowest ebbs of public support and state tolerance. Others, like those sponsoring the 1969 mobilization and moratorium, emerged in connection with the large-scale, temporary mobilization of public opinion in response to a perceived policy crisis. These crisis mobilizations represented the ephemeral cooperation of groups with diverse histories, structures, ideologies, strategies, and tactics. There was a trade-off for cooperation, though. Although resources and influence could be multiplied, the identities and agendas of participating groups could be threatened. Coalitions typically dissolved, either when tensions among various factions grew too sharp of when crisis passed or the foreign policy issue was resolved. They often left behind new organizations and constituencies. The history of peace and antiwar mobilizations is in large part the story of a succession of coalitions.

What Was the Outcome?

The question Was the movement more than a gesture? points to the role of organized peace activists in American society and their relationship to U.S. foreign policy. Were their actions accurately portrayed in the media or correctly perceived by the public? What difference have they made?

In the last analysis, we must ask whether or not peace and antiwar campaigns have been anything more than idealistic, expressive gestures. Many specific foreign policy initiatives were proposed and promoted by peace advocates, who often worked directly with decision makers or lobbied the government; but as those programs were institutionalized, their origins in the movement were forgotten. Achievements were obscured also by changes in the international system, since one generation's solution to the problem of conflict did not always address the next generation's challenge. As innovative as was the League of Nations, for example, it was not designed for the world of the 1930s. Accordingly, the value of policies and programs designed to deal with earlier conflicts was eclipsed by the rise of later ones.

Meanwhile, citizen peace efforts widened and deepened the public debate on critical issues. Rarely has foreign policy been initiated in the public arena, although there have been cases of this (such as the proposal for an association of nations), but the perceived degree of public support often has set the perimeters of policy. The movement against the war in Vietnam opened up one of the most prolonged postwar debates in foreign policy history, a debate that in some form continued on issues of intervention in Nicaragua and elsewhere. In this sense, peace and other public-interest movements broadened the arena of decision making and therefore the distribution of political power.

In all these areas—the substance of policy, the decision-making process, and political accountability—the effect of specific movements is hard to trace. Foreign policy is a complex and often hidden process; the varied peace movement itself represents only a portion of public opinion; the interaction between public opinion, movement activity, and elites is complicated; and external factors such as the conduct of other nations intervene.

In any case, peace efforts affected activists themselves. Even if they did not achieve their immediate goals, peace advocates accumulated a repertoire of organizations, proposals, individual skills, analyses, and changed attitudes. They thus achieved subtle and far-reaching effects, including their impact on the next wave of mobilization and even on other movements. Social movements often provide storehouses of analyses, strategies, visions of possible futures, and skilled leadership for successive waves of mobilization and, in this way, they may well contribute to the capacity of a society to change.

Social movements are part of a multifaceted, political process involving power, resources, ideas, organizations, individuals, and a variety of actions that take place in settings that range from the Oval Office to the streets, from the Congress to the workplace, from the ballot box to the school and home. Citizen effort for peace and against war is the oldest continuously organized social movement, and it is one of the most diverse. If its impact is ambiguous and difficult to assess, that is largely because it has become an integral part of the American political process.

The first National Arbitration and Peace Congress (1907) epitomized the established peace groups organized at the end of the peace movement's first century. The Carnegie Hall program, reproduced in part here, gathered an elite that believed in the influence of ideas backed by prestige. It presents quite a contrast with the increasingly political mobilization of the following 80 years. *Swarthmore College Peace Collection*

Chapter One

The First Century of Peace Reform, 1815–1914

For over a century and a half the American peace movement has promoted a peaceful world and advocated positive alternatives to the use of mass violence. Sporadically, it has been marked by antiwar activism and protest. It has been, therefore, a movement of both advocacy and dissent. It could not be otherwise as long as warfare remained a legitimate instrument of national policy.

War is Janus-faced. It is destructive, sometimes enormously so, but it is rationalized in terms of high ideals and lofty motives—often peace itself. Whatever political and economic interests may motivate warfare, they are identified with national institutions and values. Warfare is double-faced, also, because it is an either-or conflict between two groups, each of which regards the other as an enemy.

Peace, as the object of an organized social movement, also has two visages. On the one hand, it has been viewed as a principle that absolutely precludes engaging in violence, as in an individual's renunciation of war.* On the other, peace has been the goal of preventing organized

*This position often is denoted as *pacifism,* especially in England and the United States. The word was coined early in the twentieth century to designate the broader tradition of peace advocacy. Its definition was narrowed during World War I, although it is still used in the original way, especially in Europe. This text follows the chronology of usage by employing *nonresistance* through its account of the nineteenth century and thereafter using *pacifism,* usually with an adjective such as *absolute* or *liberal,* for the renunciation of war altogether, whether as a moral imperative or in conjunction with political activism.

violence that could be justified under some conditions. These two aspects of peace have led its advocates to realign periodically over the merits of specific wars. An absolute test of ethical commitment and a relative social ideal: this dual import of "peace" is derived from the ancient Roman world, which produced Janus himself, the mythological god and patron of beginnings and endings for whom January is named.

Important leaders in the early Christian church condemned warfare, and there are records of Christians who refused military service under the Roman Empire. They responded out of absolute loyalty to Christ and his teaching as they understood it. As the church became ever more integrated with the imperial government from the fourth century on, though, the ethical rejection of all violence became discontinuous until the Protestant Reformation. At that time several Christian communities included the repudiation of violence among the tenets that distinguished them. They did not sanction violent coercion, but neither did they challenge the coercive power of government, and they are therefore known as *nonresistant* sects, or "peace churches." These included the Mennonites, the Brethren, and the Society of Friends (Quakers), although the heritage of Friends included both the individual rejection of violence and the promotion of social peace.

As Christianity became the official church of the Roman Empire, however, leaders such as Saint Augustine had developed the view that, although peace is a primary value, war might be justified under certain conditions. Codified in the late Middle Ages, this position has become known as "just war" theory.* It remained dominant with the Reformation and the rise of modern nation-states in Europe through the eighteenth century, and it was extended to the new world.

Since nonresistants were among those who migrated to America, the republic that emerged along the Atlantic coast inherited both their absolute commitment to nonviolence and the far more prevalent view that warfare may be warranted in the pursuit of a just peace. Washington, Franklin, Jefferson, and other early national leaders repeatedly expressed their abhorrence of war, although they regarded it as sometimes unavoidable. The American Revolution coupled national independence

---

*"Just war" is misleading, although it is so widely used that it cannot be avoided. A more appropriate term would be *"justified* war," because it is assumed that warfare may be justified under certain conditions even though war, like any other social institution, is not in itself "just." The merit of any war is therefore conditional and relative. The notion that a war is absolutely "just" is what gives force to a crusade.

with democratic ideals and provided an impetus for social reform through voluntary societies. "The peace reform"[1] was one of many movements for social change before World War I, and it attracted constituencies to each of the two facets of peace. Before the Civil War it gained special vitality from the advocates of absolute nonresistance. Subsequently it achieved significant breadth from reformers who, although they did not rule out the possibility of justified war, sought to avoid or at least mitigate that last resort by altering the international system. A hundred years of peace activism preceded the dramatic coalitions and divisions of the twentieth-century peace and antiwar movement.

A Moral Crusade, 1815–1865

Every war conducted by the United States in the nineteenth century elicited organized protest and outright opposition: the War of 1812, the Mexican-American War of 1846, the Civil War, and the Spanish-American War of 1898 (as it was extended to the Philippines). Government policy was challenged along with patriotic rhetoric and the rationale for fighting. Although in each case some individuals repudiated war itself, public protest focused on political and in some cases sectional issues. The circumstances differed, and war resistance was impelled by circumstance. Antiwar activity was not governed by a consistent worldview or ideology, and it did not extend in organized form beyond specific conflicts.

Organized peace activity in the United States, by contrast, began as a religious and humanitarian response to the devastating Napoleonic Wars, which Americans knew as the War of 1812. In the preceding century there had been a so-called Great Awakening of religious piety and also a growing confidence in the force of reason and natural law—the Enlightenment. Each current of thought touched different segments of society, but together they emphasized the value, freedom, and responsibility of individuals, and the possibility of personal and social progress. It was essentially this ethos, then, that initially brought peace advocates together.

Organizational Impulses   The peace reform began with the formation of two societies in 1815.[2] The New York Peace Society was founded in August, the project of former Connecticut merchant David Low Dodge and a small group of clergy and businessmen. Without knowing of the New York venture, Noah Worcester founded the Massachusetts Peace Society in December. Soon other small local societies were scattered through the country, but these two especially illustrated the orientations and limited constituency of the first 50 years of peace reform. It was no accident that the movement began when it did, for its ethos had been sharpened by a generation of warfare.

Dodge was a rigorous Presbyterian whose study of scripture led him to a thoroughly nonresistant position: the kingdom of Christ, to which one owed primary allegiance, was "not of this world."[3] Shortly after the Peace of Ghent (1815), he published a small book, *War Inconsistent with the Religion of Jesus Christ.* It opened by cataloging the ways that war violates humanitarian values, but its central theme was that "all who love our Lord Jesus Christ in sincerity cannot but ardently desire that wars may cease. . . . If so, would they not immediately renounce everything that leads to wars and fightings and embrace everything which would promote that glorious reign of righteousness and peace?"[4] On this basis Dodge and his friends founded their peace society. Anyone who would promote peace and pay dues could join, but the executive committee and real involvement was limited to absolute nonresistants. Of about 30 original members, some were clergy, others were philanthropic businessmen and merchants. The membership never exceeded 60 and declined after only a couple of years.

Worcester had fought at Bunker Hill and served in the Revolutionary army. Later he was ordained as a Unitarian minister, and in this pastoral role he too subjected warfare to biblical scrutiny. During the War of 1812 he worked out his thinking in the little classic *A Solemn Review of the Custom of War* (1814). The treatise opened on a religious note, but its indictment of war broadened to humanitarianism: "for war is in fact a heathenish and savage custom, of the most malignant, most desolating, and most horrible character."[5] Christians should be converted to peace, Worcester agreed, but also there should be a confederation of nations and an international court whose decisions would be enforced by moral sanctions. In the next generation the book was published in a dozen editions and distributed abroad. It became the basis for the Massachusetts Peace Society, which recruited all "friends of peace," whatever their differences on the merits of specific wars. Although Worcester himself probably was close to Christian nonresistance, he insisted that differences in moral judgment should be subordinated to the task of abolishing war as an institution.

Thus broadly framed, the Massachusetts Peace Society attracted a few respected religious and lay leaders, including Harvard University's president and some faculty members as well as local businessmen and

William Ladd (1778–1841), founder and president of the American Peace Society, was a tireless writer, and traveler for peace. He proposed a world organization that would include a world court and binding international law. *Swarthmore College Peace Collection*

politicians. They responded to a growing confidence in the possibility of human betterment that fed such diverse causes as Christian evangelism, temperance, educational and prison reform, treatment of the insane, better conditions for workers and women, and the antislavery movement. Peace appeared to be a worthy if distant goal, especially in the light of the recent war. Unlike most philanthropic groups then, the society was open to women. Like other cause-oriented groups, it was loosely organized. Indeed, it was mainly an extension of Worcester himself. Its program, modeled on the familiar proselytizing of religious societies, consisted mainly of spreading the word through occasional lectures, a journal, tracts, and its founder's book. With affiliated branches, the society attained perhaps 1,000 members by 1823, but membership was nominal and declined sharply in the next five years.

By that time peace reform had attracted the energies of Alan Ladd, who gave it an enduring organizational base. Robust and genial, a former sea captain who had a Harvard degree, Ladd had taken up farming in Maine during the War of 1812. Early in the 1820s he became active in the tiny Maine Peace Society. Allying himself with Worcester, he toured the Atlantic coast to get support for a national organization, which he founded in 1828 as the American Peace Society (APS).[6] Its constitution, written by Worcester, avoided doctrinal arguments by opening the society to all those who wanted to abolish war. In the first year that amounted to only 300 members. A fledgling among reform groups, the society then had only 5 percent of the funds available to the American Temperance Society. Its income grew sixfold in the following decade, and the distribution of tracts increased 60 times by 1842, the year Ladd died.

Lectures and literature: persuasion was the hallmark of early reformers of all kinds. They were out to engage the minds of men and women who, they believed, would in turn uplift society. For the APS the target groups were churches, colleges, and the press. In order to get its message onto pulpit and into print, the society sought the endorsement of religious, political, and literary leaders. Since peace advocates were held together by an ideal, they valued their network of convinced idealists more than large numbers of citizens. They were elated when Charles Sumner, a prominent Boston lawyer, delivered the 1845 Fourth of July address to Harvard University, "The True Grandeur of Nations." Destined for a long career in the U.S. Senate, Sumner proclaimed that "war is utterly and irreconcilably inconsistent with true greatness."[7] Although he regarded that as a practical conclusion, he was alternately praised and damned for his idealism.

Ladd and his friends further developed the biblical and economic arguments against warfare and, like Sumner, emphasized the special responsibility of the United States to lead in the cause of peace. They urged resolution of the nullification controversy with South Carolina, a conflict with France, the controversy with England over the Oregon boundary, and claims against Mexico. Moreover, they promoted practical alternatives to war, such as a congress of nations and stipulated arbitration—the inclusion in all international agreements of provisions to arbitrate disputes.

The arbitration campaign was especially strong in the decade after Ladd's death, and it was pursued vigorously on both sides of the Atlantic, notably in England, where the London Peace Society had been formed in 1816, and in France. As worked out by American jurist William Jay, the concept of stipulated arbitration became particularly attractive to Englishmen who pressed it on Parliament under the leadership of free-trade advocate Richard Cobden. Peace advocates lobbied for it with the U.S. Congress and organized a campaign of petitions and memorials from state legislators and private citizens. The accumulated pressure had its effect when resolutions were reported out of committee in the early 1850s, although they were defeated or tabled in the Senate. By that time American reformers had participated actively in a string of international conferences. [8]

As the only full-time executive of the APS, Ladd wore himself out in repeated cross-country tours, although he hired traveling agents when funds permitted. His skills as a writer, editor, and speaker enabled him to broaden the society's elite leadership. His successor, George Beckwith, was more interested in administering than proselytizing, and by the time he became corresponding secretary in 1837, the society had acquired a constituency of radical reformers whose adamant nonresistance made administration difficult.

Organizational Dilemmas   Ladd himself had gravitated toward the position of the nonresistants, biblical in orientation and absolute in their commitment. At the 1832 New Haven, Connecticut, convention of the APS, South Carolina lawyer Thomas S. Grimké drew a sharp contrast between the "law of violence" and "the law of love," condemning the violence of all warfare as "utterly irreconcilable with a Christian spirit."[9] Back home, Grimké refused conscription by his state when it threatened to secede from the Union. His address and example elicited controversy even within the APS; but it was a catalyst for the development of nonresistance, which rapidly grew in strength. Ladd himself tried to accommodate absolute nonresistants in the society.

Not even his generous spirit could bound the vigor of absolutism that flourished in that era. Radical nonresistants fed on an individualistic morality that was stimulated by both the rigorous biblicism of religion and the ethereal visions of Transcendental philosophy penned by Ralph Waldo

Emerson. Just as temperance led to total abstinence and antislavery sentiments became abolitionism, so too a disposition for peace moved some to individual nonresistance. A key role in this development was played by William Lloyd Garrison, a journalist who professed all three reforms. Garrison pressed the logic further: since force is at the heart of the "war principle," as he called it, and government is based on force, the spirit of Christian love is inconsistent with government itself. The result was a kind of Christian anarchism.

All this was in the air in 1838, as friends of peace gathered in a convention organized by the radical nonresistants. Beckwith and his supporters withdrew when the delegates voted to seat women. Amid further controversy the New England Non-Resistance Society was formed. Its declaration of principles reflected Garrison's rejection of politics along with war. Born of an insatiable thirst for personal purity that was attached to genuine social compassion, the new society had nowhere to go but inward. As historian Peter Brock observed, "an intellectual elite soon became a closed coterie."[10] It failed to grow and was defunct by 1849.

Must the absolute repudiation of war be exclusive and sectarian? Elihu Burritt thought not. Like Garrison, Burritt was reared in poverty, being apprenticed to a village blacksmith as a boy. Unlike the flaming abolitionist, he provided himself with a broad learning that included a command of modern European and Near Eastern languages, and yet he retained a modest, self-effacing demeanor. This "learned blacksmith" grounded his nonresistance and Christian faith on the brotherhood of all human beings. Both an idealist and a practical man, he refused no social reform that might extend compassion to all.

He had been dismayed by the dissention in the APS and by the fact that Beckwith retained control of it, embracing peace seekers who did not unconditionally disavow war and insisting on what a later generation would call a single-issue orientation, unconnected with other reforms. Burritt journeyed to England, where, perhaps influenced by temperance advocates, he hit upon the idea of a peace pledge. Signers would vow to sanction no war and to work for the abolition of "all institutions and customs which do not recognize the image of God and a human brother in every man of whatever clime, colour, or condition of humanity."[11] Burritt promoted his pledge wherever he could gather a few people together. Picked up by leading British friends of peace and American nonresistants, the pledge was signed by 30,000 people within a year. It led to a loose organization, which was formalized in 1846 as the League of Universal Brotherhood, with branches in England and the United States. Burritt

Elihu Burritt (1810–79), a blacksmith who educated himself as a linguist, rejected even defensive war but endorsed practical internationalism. He reached out to the working class and across the Atlantic to British and continental peace advocates. *Swarthmore College Peace Collection*

tried to promote it on the continent with limited success in France and Holland, but in his absence the movement foundered in America. A decade after its formation, the British branch merged with the London Peace Society.

Just as he crossed the Atlantic in the cause of peace, Burritt tried to bridge classes. He argued against war on economic as well as moral grounds and got signatures to his pledge from both working people and the literate middle class. He won powerful support from British advocates of free trade such as Richard Cobden, but he also formulated the notion of a general strike against war. Amid a 1845 war scare over the Oregon boundary, Burritt distributed a series of fortnightly circulars called *Olive Leaves* to some 1,500 American newspapers in order to promote the exchange of "Friendly Addresses" between English and American towns with common names or industries. The experiment in people's diplomacy mushroomed briefly. Like the nonresistant pledge, it was an attempt to enlist commitment in a period of general apathy to peace issues.

Apathy was the great challenge of the first 50 years. The organized peace movement gained only temporary focal points from crises such as the Oregon controversy. The Mexican War of 1846 was a case in point. It was widely opposed in New England and the Old Northwest, largely because it was taken to be an extension of southern and slave-owning interests.[12] The APS petitioned the government for peace and asked 1,000 newspapers to follow suit. Many did. Peace advocates suddenly found themselves in concert with an active minority of citizens. It did not last, for after the war the peace reform was again viewed with overwhelming indifference.

Worse, the APS became increasingly irrelevant as the nation polarized over slavery in the territories, an issue that had been crystallized by the Mexican War itself. Sumner, then a U.S. senator, rejected compromise with the South. Beckwith and his organization refused to confront the slavery question, although they appealed for peace until the war broke, when they supported the Union side. They had not abandoned peace, they argued; they still stood against wars among nations; but this was different, a civil war—a rebellion. Although the APS continued to exist during the Civil War, it excluded its relevance to the carnage by definition. As Peter Brock concluded, "its leaders were no longer able to discern the occurrence of war, the social evil which it was their own reason for existence to fight, when it finally came to the American nation."[13] Garrison even regarded the war as the instrument with which God would purge the Union of slavery. Most aging radical nonresistants followed his lead. A very few peace leaders took exception, like Burritt feeling that the cause of peace had been betrayed. The religious and humanitarian ideal of rejecting war, which had fueled the first 50 years of peace reform with vitality, was isolated, the movement in disarray.

It had failed to attract a constituency from the nonresistant peace churches, and it had by no means included all absolute pacifists. During the Civil War, Quakers were widely respected in the North for their earlier strong antislavery witness. Indeed, northern Friends divided over the merits of fighting for that cause. Those who could not conscientiously serve in the military were generally exempted under varying conditions, but this only drew a new line of moral choice for them. Southern Quakers suffered from persecution and deprivation. Mennonites, Brethren, and other nonresistant sects in the North and South were divided. The history of the absolute pacifist conscience during the Civil War is full of anguish, but it is a story apart from that of the antebellum peace movement.[14] The nonresistant tradition was isolated then, by contrast with its next great test, World War I, when the experience of absolute pacifists became an integral part of the twentieth-century peace movement.

In its first half century, peace reform attracted scattered adherents among the literary and professional elite, mainly from New England to Pennsylvania. It was almost wholly dependent on a few individuals for leadership. Except for Burritt's identification with working people, it appealed to the middle class, and it was dominated by Christian humanitarianism and morality.

For some the ideal of peace had the power of a commanding ideology. That loyalty was a source of both vitality and division. Early reformers differed with one another especially over two issues: (1) whether or not an absolute repudiation of war is compatible with a search for alternatives to it, and (2) whether to couple peace with other social reforms or to organize around the single issue. In the hands of the Garrisonian moralists or of a man like Beckwith, who seemed to value the APS almost for itself, doctrine divided peace reform. For leaders like Worcester, Ladd, and Burritt, a broader vision led from nonresistance to inclusive peace efforts.

Various leaders forged programs through which to apply their ideal. They petitioned and lobbied on a few foreign policy issues. They promoted international institutions for the resolution of conflict, especially a conference of nations and the practice of stipulated arbitration. They made international connections and inaugurated people's diplomacy. All of them contended with overwhelming public apathy. This largely defined their program, which was to persuade people that war was neither inevitable nor ethical. The movement itself was constrained by the political culture of the new republic. Part of that culture was a kind of moral individualism, whether expressed by Transcendentalists or by Christian evangelists, and this reinforced the tendency to treat peace as a matter of personal morality. Moreover, peace competed with other ideals in the political culture, including nationalism and social justice. In the end, it succumbed to the Civil War, which fused those values into a powerful force. The major thrust of peace reform in the first 50 years was to challenge the efficacy of war itself, and that went against the grain of prevailing assumptions. In the process, however, some of the reformers developed alternatives to war, and that was a harbinger of the second half century of the movement.

The Fulcrum of Arbitration, 1865–1899

In the half century following the Civil War, peace increasingly became identified with practical internationalism, and on this basis it became a highly organized and widely acceptable cause. Pivotal to this development was an extended campaign for the arbitration of international disputes, although in the immediate aftermath of the war, nothing appeared to have changed.

Two organizations perpetuated the nonresistant tradition. The Peace Association of Friends was organized in 1867 from an initiative by Ohio Quakers. It fielded lecturers, published large quantities of literature in addition to its own journal, and took part in the unfolding campaign for the arbitration of international conflict. The peace witness was weakened among Friends in the latter part of the century, however, as energy was expended on evangelism in the West and was dissipated over religious differences.

Meanwhile, nonresistance became identified with Alfred H. Love, who had a Quaker background, although he was not a member of the Society of Friends. A Philadelphia woolens merchant, he had refused military service during the war. In 1866 he and a remnant of Garrisonian nonresistants formed the Universal Peace Union (UPU). Love was president, and he embodied the organization, never more than a few hundred strong nor budgeted at much more than $1,000.[15] For a half century he reached out from Philadelphia to the northern seaboard states. Love kept the peace reform visible and varied its approach. To the traditional tracts, journals, lectures, petitions, letters to newspapers, and lobbying, he added peace slogans, hymns, and picnic-like celebrations, as well as exhibits on the horrors of war. At the 1893 World's Columbian Exposition in Chicago, he exhibited a peace plow forged from swords. Sometimes derided even by his supporters, he was experimenting with popular symbols that might channel the rising nationalism of the era away from its identification with patriotic war.

Although the UPU rejected warfare under any circumstances, Love broadened its agenda to include the concerns of immigrants, American Indians, and women. About a third of the UPU's membership was female, with full equality in the organization, and leading feminists were affiliated with it. In an age of labor violence, Love endorsed the rights of workers. He advocated arbitration both in labor disputes and among nations. He also strengthened connections with the European peace movement and published reprints of works by Leo Tolstoy of Russia and Bertha von Suttner of Hungary, writings that influenced leading American reformers. Thus, the tiny Universal Peace Union perpetuated nonresistance with the ecumenical breadth and practical agenda of Ladd and Burritt until Love's death in 1913, when it virtually ceased to exist.

The American Peace Society adopted arbitration as its principal focus after the Civil War. When tensions between England and America were strained by U.S. demands to be compensated for damages that had resulted from the British outfitting of the Confederate warship *Alabama,* peace advocates on both sides of the Atlantic lobbied hard for arbitration. They were elated when that was written into the 1871 Treaty of Washington.[16] With the specific issue out of the way, the general principle of arbitration emerged as the movement's cause célèbre for the balance of the century. In July 1873 Henry Richard, president of the London Peace Society and a member of Parliament, secured a House of Commons resolution for an international tribunal of arbitration, and Charles Sumner introduced a similar measure in the U.S. Senate the following December. The APA mounted a petition campaign, and its secretary, then James B. Miles, lobbied with the administration and Congress. The following June, three months after Sumner's death, the Senate and House endorsed the principle of designating third parties to arbitrate international disputes.

The North Atlantic nations were rapidly industrializing in the last quarter of the century. They developed more fully structured societies, became more interdependent, and consolidated worldwide empires. Commercial issues were the source of both cooperation and competition among them. Accordingly, peace advocates got increasing support from business and government elites for alternatives to war. The concept of arbitration was the option most vigorously pressed. It appealed not only to business interests but to reform groups such as the Women's Christian Temperance Union. Specifically, it was promoted by the National Arbitration League (1882), whose outstanding leader was Robert McMurdy, an educator and linguist with friends in the administration and legislature. Washington was the venue of the arbitration campaign and, increasingly, of the peace movement.

From 1883 on, peace advocates in Switzerland, France, and England brought pressure on their governments to negotiate arbitration treaties with the United States, while Americans lobbied for reciprocation. When arbitration was included in an 1897 treaty between the United States and Great Britain, it became a political issue, since treaties must be ratified by the Senate. Skilled lobbyists like McMurdy and Belva Lockwood, a lawyer with the UPU, worked Capitol Hill and secured support from President William McKinley, while the APA, UPU, and National Arbitration Committee (formed from a conference in Washington the previous year) mobilized public support. In a maneuver that would be repeated several times in the twentieth century, the Senate emasculated the treaty with amendments and then barely voted it down. The treaty's defeat was largely the result of a combination of many special interests, not least the Senate's jealously of its own prerogative in foreign affairs.

By that time, arbitration had been formally linked to international law. Each spring from 1895 to 1916 two Quaker brothers, Alfred and Albert Smiley, brought leaders from the ranks of business, government, religion, education, and reform to their resort at Lake Mohonk, New York, to discuss international affairs. These were practical people, and they trimmed the terms of arbitration to what they thought might be politically feasible. They also broadened the concept to include an international court. [17]

The notion of a tribunal had been advanced earlier by Worcester and Ladd, but subsequently the emphasis in international law had shifted to codification. After the Civil War, jurist David Dudley Field recommended the drafting of an international code. Rebuffed by experts, he researched and produced his own version in 1872. Early that year Elihu Burritt and James Miles thought of organizing an international association to draft a code of nations. Miles explored the idea with jurists and statesmen in Europe. International law was already being discussed there. In fact, an Institute of International Law was founded in 1873 a week before Miles, Field, and about 30 European legal experts launched their International

Law Association.[18] Neither organization made progress on an overall code in the next two decades, concentrating instead on technical questions and commercial law, but in 1895 the International Law Association drafted a plan for a permanent court of arbitration. That idea was shared with the New York Bar Association, from which a committee drafted an American version.

This considerable body of thought was unexpectedly brought into play in 1899, when Czar Nicholas II of Russia called an international conference on questions of arms limitation, the rules of war, and the peaceful settlement of disputes. Other heads of state could hardly refuse to participate in what became known as the First Hague Conference. President McKinley designated a strong delegation, but limited its scope to arbitration and mediation, sending along proposals partly modeled on the New York Bar Association plan. European delegations came with designs of their own. Since no agreement could be reached on disarmament or the rule of war, the main achievement of the Hague conference was to create a Permanent Court of Arbitration. Not really a court in a legal sense, it was essentially a panel of jurists who could be called on to arbitrate disputes under whatever conditions nations might apply. It had a permanent staff and rules of procedure, though, and it was therefore a small but potentially significant step in institutionalizing an alternative to war.[19]

What had all this to do with the peace movement? Nothing, if one refers merely to popular demonstrations, but much if one is to understand the variety of strategies and constituencies involved in efforts to redirect foreign policy. Organizations such as the APS and UPU tried to influence public opinion as of old. They harangued the newspapers, preached to the churches, challenged military drill and jingoist texts in the public schools, allied themselves with women and workers, and mobilized popular sentiment on specific issues, especially arbitration. At the same time, though, arbitration provided a fulcrum on which to align the legal experts, reformers, and business and political leaders who increasingly constituted themselves a kind of public interest lobby.

Peace advocates competed for influence within the elite group that dominated foreign policy–making in the fairly informal style of the time. In the 1880s they formed what historian Merle Curti called a "peacemakers' lobby at Washington."[20] At its core were Belva Lockwood of the UPU, Robert McMurdy of the National Arbitration Committee, and the current president of the APS. Close to them were prominent people such as David Dudley Field and Andrew Carnegie. On hand from Philadelphia at short notice would be Alfred Love. From Boston would come officers of the APA, from Europe leaders so distinguished that they could be assured of appointments with presidents and senators. In Congress itself there were a number of Quakers and other leaders who could be counted on. Sometimes the peace advocates were able to take advantage of the fact that politics was very much a matter of personal contacts and special interests, and that foreign policy was not often high on the political agenda (except for the perennial question of tariffs). On the other hand, their access to decision makers belied their lack of real influence as a public pressure group.

The Anti-Imperialist Interlude, 1898–1902

The 1898 war with Spain capped an expansive sense of national destiny that was linked to Anglo-Saxon institutions in a grand evolutionary scheme. It came to be widely assumed that the values of an open society with free access to ideals and political choices, goods, and investments were to be writ large upon the world, and never mind that at home political and economic power was being consolidated out of reach. It was argued that the ideal of Christian brotherhood was to govern all mankind, and never mind the racism of Jim Crow laws and the repression of American Indians, or sharpening class lines at home. It was generally believed that the future belonged to Anglo-Saxon institutions and that the Western Hemisphere was the special province of the United States. With rare exceptions, peace advocates shared such notions as these, coupled with a sense of the growing interdependence of the industrialized world, and this gave them a sublime confidence in the future that tended to blind them to their limitations and to contradictions between idealism and reality.

The war, which broke out in April, originated in a quarter century of Cuban resistance to arbitrary and ruthless Spanish rule. Peace advocates, although they sympathized with the Cubans and protested to Spain, resisted U.S. involvement. That they were not successful in 1898 was due in part to the force of public opinion and in part to the fact that their own formula of arbitration was adopted by President McKinley as the only alternative to war. The Spanish could not accept his terms, which amounted to Cuban independence, and the issue was decided by force.

The 100 days' war was immensely popular. The several American battle successes were relished, despite the fact that they owed much to

Spanish military weakness and revealed a good deal about U.S. Army incompetence. Numerous peace advocates accepted the Cuban campaign or even supported it. Alfred Love was an outspoken exception, and he was burned in effigy. At the Lake Mohonk Conference that year, participants were urged not to mention the war. The respected Quaker president of the APS, Benjamin Trueblood, voiced the prevailing sentiment of peace advocates. The war was an error, he said, but national responsibility would be heightened by it and the peace movement would issue in "a new tidal wave after the war closes."[21] In a sense he was right, but anti-imperialism crested first.

The issue was neither the superiority nor the expansion of American institutions but rather, whether they should be secured abroad by territorial control. There was a good deal of latent feeling that they should not, and it became political with the debate over the treaty ending the war. The peace agreement provided not only for the independence of Cuba but also for U.S. acquisition of Puerto Rico and the Philippines. The Pacific islands were the sticking point for a bipartisan group of anti-imperialists in the Senate who opposed ratification of the treaty. It barely passed on 6 February 1899, when Democratic leader William Jennings Bryan gave it his support.[22] Two days later, Filipinos led by Emilio Aquinaldo were fighting Americans. Then, with surprising speed and force, anti-imperialists generated an antiwar campaign.

Opposition to the Philippine-American War was anchored in about two dozen aged New England politicians, publicists, and intellectuals who had repeatedly demonstrated their moral independence by bolting from one party to another in search of vehicles of reform and civic leadership.[23] During the war over Cuba, they had formed the Anti-Imperialist League to challenge territorial expansion. The organization spearheaded opposition to the war for the Philippines. It attracted younger allies throughout the country, growing into a bipartisan mass movement with some 30,000 members. It sponsored speakers and flooded the country with antiwar literature. By October its campaign reached some 30 states, but it was a welter of contradictory elements. Thus, anti-imperialists in the South pleaded that their boys had not enlisted "to fight niggers,"while in Chicago the Black Man's Burden Association objected precisely to the war's racism.[24]

The league was reorganized and its headquarters moved to Chicago in an attempt to accommodate its new constituency, but momentum could not be sustained. The antiwar campaign became tied to the Democratic presidential candidacy of Bryan, who, despite his earlier support for annexation, had come to link colonialism to populist fears of the eastern and commercial establishment. Andrew Carnegie and other anti-imperialists skeptical of Bryan supported McKinley. The incumbent Republican benefited, too, from overall economic prosperity, and he won a resounding reelection.

Almost immediately, the anti-imperialist and antiwar campaign began to dissolve, even as atrocities perpetuated by American troops were fully documented and officially recognized. Between 250,000 and 600,000 Filipinos died as a result of the war, probably most of them civilians, as opposed to 7,000 American soldiers. It was no contest. Early in February 1902 Aguinaldo was captured. Within months the war was declared over by Theodore Roosevelt, who had become president after McKinley's assassination the previous year. The Philippines were constituted an unorganized territory of the United States. The Anti-Imperialist League, again based in Boston, continued to challenge American intervention abroad until 1920, but it was largely isolated from the peace movement.

The issue of colonialism divided peace advocates. It brought a few new leaders into the movement—the Boston publicist Edwin D. Mead (1849–1937), for example, and David Starr Jordan (1851–1931), president of Stanford University and a leading naturalist who began a systematic study of the impact of war on human evolution. They were exceptions, and in any case, few anti-imperialists grasped the profound economic and political redistribution of world power that was taking place (in contrast to British peace leaders who provided telling critiques of imperialism).[25] Indeed, the elderly directors of the APS had settled into a routine of genteel reform. They regarded the Philippine conflict, like all war, as an anachronism in the relations of nation-states that they proposed to refine by educating the interested public and foreign policy elite of advanced countries while uplifting backward peoples.[26] This was the sense in which, for all of his own radical opposition to war itself, Trueblood was optimistic: arbitration, mediation, international law—all grounded in goodwill and enlightened self-interest—seemed to be gaining ground.

The Established Peace Movement, 1902–1914

Trueblood found reason for optimism in the clearly defined body of internationalists emerging in the first decade of the new century. Determined to build on the precedent of the First Hague Conference, they looked to their government for encouragement. In 1902 President Roosevelt and

Secretary of State John Hay, at least partially in response to a meeting with French senator Baron Paul H. D. d'Estournelles de Constant, undertook to revive the somnolent Hague court by submitting an old dispute with Mexico to its judges and by persuading Venezuela and its creditors to do likewise. The following year the president endorsed arbitration in his annual message. Hay formulated a series of agreements that would have applied the principle widely, except that the Senate crippled them by amendment so that Roosevelt withdrew the project. Shortly afterward the president accepted a request from Japan to mediate its war with Russia. His success won him a Nobel Peace Prize and the confidence of many internationalists.

Internationalist Programs Peace advocates added a congress of nations to their agenda of arbitration and international law, largely as a result of the persuasive writings of a journalist, Raymond L. Bridgman, and a lawyer, Hayne Davis. Bridgman developed the idea in detail and promoted it with the help of Edwin Mead and Benjamin Trueblood of the APS, among others. In 1903 the Massachusetts legislature recommended a modified version to the U.S. Congress, calling for periodic meetings of "a regular international congress."[27] Well publicized in newspapers and magazines, the project won the endorsement of civic and religious groups including the Lake Mohonk Conference. It was refined by Davis, whose analysis won over Hamilton Holt, the influential editor of *The Independent,* and Richard Bartholdt, a congressman from Saint Louis. Together they formed the nucleus of a campaign to convene a second Hague conference with international organization as well as arbitration on its agenda.

Bartholdt was strategically placed, both because he was a member of Congress and because since 1899 he had been a member of the International Parliamentary Union, a mainly European association of internationalist-oriented legislators founded in 1888. At his invitation, the organization had agreed to hold its 1904 meeting in connection with the Louisiana Purchase Exposition in Saint Louis. Bartholdt enlisted well over 100 fellow U.S. representatives, who obtained a formal congressional invitation and an appropriation for costs. Moreover, they gave the Saint Louis meeting a focal point with a resolution asking the president to call a second international conference on arbitration and disarmament. A delegation reinforced that appeal by meeting with Roosevelt on its way back to Europe, while Davis and Bartholdt publicized the cause. That fall Secretary of State Hay secured the approval of the powers represented at the First Hague Conference for a second meeting; but in light of the Russo-Japanese War, it was deferred to the summer of 1907. With a year and a half to maneuver, internationalists were spurred to organize.

Peace advocacy had come to be equated with internationalism by then, and it attracted three groups: partisans of arbitration who saw their approach as a first step toward world organization; international lawyers who hoped that a new conference might create a court and code of law on which arbitral judgments could be based; and those for whom a world federation had become an end in itself. John Bassett Moore, a distinguished international lawyer, was won over, along with Andrew Carnegie, who introduced the term "League of Nations." As the concept was popularized and refined, the corollaries of an international police force and even sanctions were added. That sounded too extreme to many people, but in one form or another a congress of nations had become widely attractive.

It emerged as one emphasis in the largest peace rally in the United States until then, the National Arbitration and Peace Congress, which convened in New York City in April 1907 with the support of virtually all peace advocates. The assembly was impressive for its 1,200 delegates and for their prominence (it included cabinet officers, supreme court justices, senators, the governor of New York, and national leaders from labor and business). It was distinguished for the thoughtfulness with which a wide range of issues was addressed. Its own scrapbook, containing over 32,000 newspaper clippings, attested to the effectiveness of its publicity. The Peace Congress was the climax of a successful effort to mobilize support for action at the Second Hague Conference, which was scheduled to open in June, and its sponsors elicited resolutions of support for international cooperation from three state legislatures, the American Bar Association, and innumerable civic, religious, and business groups.

By mid-October the results were in. Treaties signed at the Hague related primarily to the rules of warfare and the rights of neutral nations and private property in wartime. There was no significant advance with respect to arbitration or a world court except that both were endorsed in principle. Instead of the proposed regular congresses of nations, the conference proposed a third international meeting. One might have thought that the results would have discouraged internationalists in the United States. Instead, the Second Hague Conference probably reinforced an old feeling that America would have to lead the way to a cooperative future beyond European politics. In any case, internationalism had become a powerful organizing idea in the mobilization of an American peace movement.

Internationalist Organizations   New associations multiplied in the decade following the Philippine-American War—by one account, 45 of them.[28] An association of Cosmopolitan Clubs (1903) brought together international friendship clubs and, with the Intercollegiate Peace Association (1904), promoted peace and international understanding in colleges. The American School Peace League (1908) directed materials to teachers, sponsored essay contests, sought to influence educational organizations, and eventually obtained an endorsement from the National Education Association and the cooperation of the U.S. Commission on Education. In addition to the arbitration groups already noted, the American Society of International Law (1906) and the World Federation League (1910) were formed. Local and state groups sprang up. The center of activity shifted away from Boston when a strong New York Peace Society (NYPS) was established in 1906, and a Chicago Peace Society (1909) heralded expansion in the West.

Substantial funding became available for specific projects and peace groups. Whole new organizations were endowed. In 1910 publisher Edwin Ginn set up the World Peace Foundation (WPF) with $50,000 a year and the promise of a million-dollar endowment upon his death, while in the same year, prodded by leading internationalists, Andrew Carnegie provided $10 million for the Carnegie Endowment for International Peace (CEIP).[29] Both of these organizations stressed education and research, and each underwrote the work of other associations.

Major Protestant church leaders understood the challenge of peace as an extension of Christian ecumenism and social concern on an international scale. Thus in 1911 the interfaith Federal Council of Churches of Christ in America formed a Commission on Peace and Arbitration. Three years later, and with $2 million from Carnegie, it blossomed into the Church Peace Union (CPU). In turn, the leaders of the CPU used their contacts abroad to convene an international religious conference at Constance, Germany. Although the meeting was interrupted by the outbreak of war, a rump committee formed the World Alliance for International Friendship through the Churches, and the next year an American branch was constituted.

In this respect, the CPU illustrated a tendency toward international association: Bartholdt promoted the IPU assiduously; Louis Lochner linked the Cosmopolitan Clubs with Corda Fratras; Carnegie's endowment provided a large portion of the budget of the International Peace Bureau, with headquarters in Geneva; and in 1906 Nicholas Murray Butler, president of Columbia University, created an American branch of the Association for International Conciliation, which had been formed to promote exchanges of lecturers across boundaries. Numerous advocates of peace and internationalism associated easily with their peers abroad, assuming that they were cutting the edge of world history.

The American Peace Society had languished at the end of the nineteenth century, but it too began to show signs of life. During Trueblood's tenure as secretary (1892 to 1913) its budget increased fourfold, its journal reached record numbers, and membership increased from 400 to 8,000. Local and state societies affiliated with the APS and able field staff members were added. In 1911 it combined with the strong New York Peace Society and moved its headquarters from Boston to Washington. The move was designed to establish the venerable peace society as a truly national organization close to the makers of foreign policy.

In truth, the peace movement had become well established. It served as a public forum for the discussion of international affairs. It gave credence to the notion that alternatives to war were desirable, and it put forward serious proposals. It even had strong connections with foreign policy decision makers. But who was in charge, and what was behind this rash of organization?

The offices and boards of the established peace movement were dominated by new leaders, an especially decisive transition since several veterans died about this time. Differences among the newcomers—and there were sharp ones—were subsumed by their similarities. They were mostly college-educated professionals drawn from the middle and upper classes, prominent in education, law, business, journalism, and religion. Many of them were strongly religious, some were church leaders, and all were Protestant. Three-fourths of them lived in Boston, New York, Philadelphia, Baltimore, Washington, or Chicago. Beyond their common background, several of them had close personal ties, and a number formed a kind of interlocking directorate among several peace societies.[30]

Relatively large financial resources became available to the new leadership, and this fact tended to create a new kind of dependency within the organized peace movement that was felt especially by the American Peace Society. For many years the APS had relied on a small endowed income to supplement its meager budget. In the first decade of the twentieth century it received major gifts from Andrew Carnegie, who became ever more committed to the cause of peace after he sold his mammoth steel empire in 1901. Carnegie built a Peace Palace at the Hague for the international court and buildings in Washington and Costa Rica for the Pan American Union and the American Court of Justice. He also supported peace societies, giving a total of $50,000 to 16 of them in 1910.[31] In that year he endowed the CEIP and turned over the subvention of peace groups to its Division of Intercourse and Education, directed by Nicholas Murray Butler. The APS and similar groups thus became dependent on the goodwill of a man who had objected even to the use of the word *peace* in the endowment's title!

For some years the American Peace Society had contemplated a move to Washington. Trueblood hoped to create a coordinated national peace organization. He appealed to the CEIP for the larger funding that would make this possible. Butler agreed to subsidize the APS, but he effectively managed its relocation and reorganization so as to deprive Trueblood of leadership, introduce new staff, and reorganize the board along acceptably conservative lines. Moreover, the CEIP made its financial support of other peace societies conditional upon their affiliating with the dependent APS.[32] Butler's attempt to consolidate and control the movement reflected pervasive changes in American society.

Rapid urbanization and industrialization were contributing to an ever more complex social structure. New opportunities and the problems associated with them led to bureaucracy, specialization, and a strong impulse for rational order. One aspect of this trend was professionalization, another was reform; but the emphasis of reform was on the improvement of the existing social order through the application of specialized knowledge and analysis. This was the Progressive Era, and its emphasis was on practical problem solving. Those who entered and led the peace movement at this time did so because they could relate it to their own primarily domestic concerns—to another reform, professional interests, or simply their civic leadership.[33] That meant that the peace reform reflected the professional interests and biases of those it attracted.

The business community formed a constituency for peace work more than it provided leadership. Although businessmen (and they *were* men) were eagerly enrolled by the New York and Chicago peace societies, served on the boards of peace organizations, and in large measure financed the work, they largely delegated executive authority to administrators from other professional fields. That was how they managed their own businesses. Increasingly aware of the economic interdependence of industrialized nations, they wanted to minimize the risks associated with it. Aspiring to national leadership, they could be persuaded to take the nation's world role seriously. Emphasizing consensus and practicality, they tended to endorse approaches that were neither controversial nor couched in moralistic terms.

Carnegie's Endowment for International Peace epitomized the professionalism of the new peace establishment. The steel magnate delegated responsibility to men whose temperament was more conservative than his. The president of the CEIP was Elihu Root, then a senator from New York and formerly secretary of war and secretary of state. He worked closely with James Scott Brown, who became director of the Endowment's Division of International Law after being chief legal officer of the State Department, where there was a virtual nest of lawyers connected with the American Society of International Law and similar groups. The programming of the CEIP profoundly reflected the technical interests and views of its constituency of lawyers.[34] It also reflected the orientation of professional educators under the leadership of Nicholas Murray Butler, who headed the Division of Intercourse and Education, and John Bates Clark, an economist who directed the Division of Economics and History. Both men eschewed controversial political issues and emphasized factual analysis.

There were, of course, differences between the managers and sponsors of internationalist groups. Edwin Ginn was inclined to use his World Peace Foundation to popularize peace, for example, whereas Edwin Mead and David Starr Jordan mainly ran it for him in the interest of professional education. Carnegie had his differences with Root and Butler. Those were matters of emphasis, though. On some things there was wide agreement among the leaders of the established peace movement.

Whatever their professions, the internationalists were confident in the efficacy of the institutions they had mastered. They measured personal and national achievement in terms of personal and national control of political, economic, and intellectual power. They wanted to build international institutions in order to bring the power of an interdependent world under control. In both domestic and world affairs, they valued rational order and systematic organization. They worked most comfortably within the relatively predictable governing elite. If in these respects they projected their own social roles, internationalists were also consciously adapting the institutions they valued to the changing conditions of an increasingly interdependent world. They were convinced that neither exclusive nationalism nor continental isolationism was tenable in the twentieth century. In sum, they regarded themselves as civic leaders, reformers who were practical, prudent, and professional.[35]

The established peace groups approached political issues cautiously. Thus, when Roosevelt proposed to add battleships to the fleet (enlisting a growing arms lobby and the newly established Navy League), the Chicago Peace Society and the APS stayed aloof. Carnegie advised the NYPS to take no stand that would put off potential recruits, despite his personal opposition to Roosevelt's plan. The American Peace and Arbitration League (1910) even promoted both naval strength and arbitration procedures.

Arbitration was not politically controversial, and it had the united support of peace advocates. It was endorsed by William Howard Taft, who succeeded Roosevelt as president in 1909. Formerly a lawyer, judge, governor general of the Philippines, and secretary of war, Taft was a member of the American Society of International Law. His administration formulated arbitration treaties with France and Great Britain that were popularized by the rapidly growing peace movement; but the Senate balked again in 1912. Still, something was salvaged from a quarter century of political effort, for as secretary of state under Woodrow Wilson, William Jennings Bryan won ratification of some 20 treaties of conciliation. The Bryan treaties required only that disputes be submitted to a joint commission during a "cooling off" period, with no provision that an arbitral decision had to be accepted.

Even the minimal step of conciliation fit into a set of assumptions that were widely shared in the established peace movement that had emerged by 1914: peace advocacy meant internationalism; the world was progressing both morally and materially, and the upward thrust of evolution was being carried by the industrialized and Christian nations (that was to say, the civilized ones); war was an anachronism in an increasingly integrated and international society, and it would be supplanted by instruments for consultation, arbitration, and adjudication; these social inventions would be created and implemented by an educated and professional elite; and therefore the real agenda of peace was to produce and convey the scientific knowledge that would develop practical alternatives to war. If such notions seem naive at the end of the twentieth century, they nonetheless generated innovations that, in retrospect, amounted to a significant reform in international relations.

There was a small minority of persons who approached peace from a different perspective. They included Jane Addams, a renowned social worker in Chicago who was active in the Chicago Peace Society, and Louis Lochner, a leader in organizing the Cosmopolitan Clubs, among others. A few of them had been aroused by the issue of imperialism in the Philippine-American War. Most of them were heavily engaged in domestic reforms, and they both identified with the needs of the disadvantaged and relied on popular support for change. Their concern for international peace was grounded in a humanitarianism that was characteristic of the older, ever less influential generation of peace advocates. In 1914 the younger idealists were not yet leaders in the peace reform. When they were thrust into it by World War I, they created alternatives to the established peace organizations and completed the outlines of the modern peace and antiwar movement.

Chapter Two

The "Protean" Peace Reform, 1914–1919

The peace movement changed rapidly during World War I. It was what historian Roland Marchand called a "protean reform"—one that took on "successively the various ideological and methodological shapes to which its new groups of adherents molded it."[1] It emerged with two wings that, with innumerable variations, continued through the rest of the century: internationalists from the peace societies established in the prewar period, and liberal pacifists who entered the movement during the war.

American internationalists had reason to congratulate themselves by 1914. In about a decade they had created a virtual peace establishment. Their organizations were widely respected, and the major ones represented a hierarchy of influence. Moreover, they were establishment-centered, in that they valued their contacts with the decision-making elite. Within months, however, they were confronted with the general European war most of them had thought to be impossible. The established peace organizations backed away from current issues, taking solace in old formulas or new proposals for the postwar era.

Frustrated with this failure to come to grips with present reality, a fresh generation of peace leaders emerged. They were decidedly political in that they sought to maintain American neutrality and opposed military spending and intervention. But they were not merely isolationists, for they urged the government to mediate an end to the war. When that failed and America intervened with force, the ranks of peace advocates contracted sharply. The word *pacifist,* coined in Europe at the turn of

The main body of the American delegation to the Women's Peace Congress at the Hague, 1915, represented a fresh, activist thrust in the peace movement. Americans (notably Jane Addams, *fourth from left*) joined women from Britain (like Emmeline Pethic-Lawrence, *extreme left*) and other countries then at war in a citizen effort to promote mediation of the conflict. *National Archives*

the century to describe all those who worked for peace, became an epithet for those who would not sanction even an apparently just war. From the new generation of peace advocates, and especially the newly baptized pacifists among them, came the second wing of the twentieth-century peace movement.

Established Peace Societies and the European War

Woodrow Wilson, pivotal at every stage of this development, won the confidence of most internationalists at the outset. He was, after all a member of the APS, and he designated as secretary of state a self-proclaimed advocate of peace, William Jennings Bryan. Wilson articulated the vision of an American mission to promote democracy and morality in international affairs. He quickly withdrew the United States from a consortium of European powers designed to exploit China, recognized the new Chinese republic, and indicated that he wanted to see a more co-operative approach to Latin America. He seemed open to proposals for arms limitation and advanced the project for a third Hague conference to the point where it was expected to take place in 1916, opening the prospect of further steps toward an international court. With this record and his reputation as a prudent reformer in domestic affairs, Wilson reinforced the optimism of internationalists.

An incident in the spring of 1914 strengthened that feeling. The president's desire for Latin American cooperation clashed with his repugnance for a revolutionary regime in Mexico, which he vowed to isolate and force out of power. By April the two countries seemed to be on the verge of war. Peace societies worked feverishly with women's groups and church leaders, generating a flood of petitions to the president and Congress. Whether or not he was influenced by public opinion, Wilson submitted the dispute to third-party mediation, and his restraint was vindicated when the Mexican regime was succeeded by one acceptable to him. The episode increased the confidence of most peace advocates in both the president's intentions and their own influence.[2] Many of them made plans to attend international conferences in Europe that summer without anticipating any serious threat of war.

It was not that they were uninformed. On the contrary, they were in close touch with Europeans and were aware of the turmoil of Balkan wars, heightened nationalism, an impetuous arms race, and alliances that could lock all Europe into catastrophe. It was, rather, that their worldview did not accommodate folly on the scale of a major war—not from the enlightened, ruling elite of civilized nations. As one after another of those countries mobilized during the summer, American peace advocates watched in disbelief, then dismay. Andrew Carnegie's whole outlook was shattered, built as it had been on sublime optimism. Grief at least aggravated the illness of Benjamin Trueblood. Many peace advocates argued that the war only confirmed the importance of their effort; but given their assumption that America had a world mission, all of them were haunted by the question: what should be the role of the United States?

That was a matter of policy, a political issue, and the major peace groups were unable to cope with it. Apolitical on principle, the Carnegie Endowment withdrew its support of European and most American peace societies. Although its directors scarcely concealed their pro-Allied sympathies, its program was officially nonpartisan. It reaffirmed the importance of international law and began a scholarly study of the economic effects of the war. Observed John Bates Clark, "The war is a terrifically costly laboratory of war, but as a rich source of data . . . it is simply incomparable."[3] In the World Peace Foundation, Edwin Mead succumbed to nervous exhaustion, leaving conservative directors almost uncontested and leadership indecisive. The foundation sharply cut its programs and promoted international-relations studies on a strictly apolitical and theoretical basis. The American Peace Society, with Trueblood ill, was led by cautious Arthur Deering Call, who had been named to his position because he was a professional administrator. James Scott Brown of the CEIP advised the society to "withdraw within itself" during the war.[4] That was essentially what the APS did, ignoring the current crisis while invoking international law for the postwar world.

"God knows what the law is! None of us know," Elihu Root remarked as European nations embarked on war.[5] Some internationalists concluded that world order had to face the reality of military power. Among them was Hamilton Holt, who in September wrote an editorial for the *Independent* distinguishing between the use of force for aggression and for police action.[6] It seemed to him that an international organization should be empowered to secure the territory and sovereignty of nations—what would come to be called collective security. Through the fall, and in consultation with British leaders who were formulating postwar plans, Holt and his friends developed the notion of a peacekeeping league of nations. In January 1915 they held the first of a series of meetings from which emerged a specific plan: member nations of a proposed federation would pledge to use collective force against any country that refused to submit conflicts to arbitration or at least informal conciliation. The proposal thus limited military enforcement to a procedural step; it did not preclude a country from subsequently going to war, and therefore it did not impinge on national sovereignty. Concluding that the new thrust needed a broader base, Holt and his colleagues in the New York Peace Society founded a separate League to Enforce Peace (LEP) in June.[7]

The new organization was supported by a wide range of peace advocates, including former president William Howard Taft. It expanded rapidly to become the preeminent sponsor of a postwar international organization. Holt wrote and spoke extensively for it, and he made especially useful converts among church leaders with whom he was associated in the Church Peace Union and the World Alliance for International Friendship through the Churches. His *Independent* became virtually an LEP journal. In January 1916 A. Lawrence Lowell, president of Harvard University, persuaded the World Peace Foundation to grant $10,000 annually to the league, and thenceforth the WPF was little more than a trustee for the new organization.

Still, the LEP encountered resistance that was an omen of future problems. The international lawyers associated with the Carnegie Endowment explicitly opposed the League of Nations idea on the grounds that it would subvert the codification of international law: there could be no true police force without prior law. The CEIP stopped funding the NYPS, whose secretary was working mainly for the League to Enforce Peace.[8] Even some LEP supporters had reservations about the provisions for the use of military force. Increasingly the organization courted the advocates of increased military spending, even printing the word *Enforce* in red letters on its stationary, thus breeding anxiety that collective security was really a way to secure American intervention in the war.

Progressive Peace Activists and the European War

New leaders moved into the peace movement in response to policy issues. Political activists who had matured early in the Progressive Era, they were mainly Protestant (a few were Jewish), and if they identified with a peace church, it was the liberal wing of Quakerism. Social workers, clergymen, educators, or publicists: they were all reformers.

In contrast to the leaders of the established peace societies, with their faith in institutions, attention to international relationships, and concern with order in a world of inherent inequality and competition, the progressive peace advocates related best to people and their communities, and they sought social harmony through justice. Movers and shakers, they preferred the public arena to the board room.[9]

They were motivated by cosmopolitan ideals. True, they opposed increased armaments and insisted that the United States maintain its neutrality, but they also envisioned an active peacemaking role for the nation. Although they were not all new to peace advocacy, they were a part of a fresh leadership that came especially from the women's rights movement, social work and civic reform, and the religious social gospel. There was at least a latent tension between the constituent interests in each of these areas and the public concerns of the small minority of peace activists in them. Nevertheless, the new leadership created a loose, shifting coalition on foreign policy that lasted until the United States entered the war.

They developed essentially two lines of action. One was to seek peace by mediating between the European alliances, and the other was to resist increases in military spending that might fit the United States for conflict and incline it to adventurism abroad. Mediation became the organizing focus of a coalition of peace advocates in 1915, antipreparedness in the following year.

Women acted first. Hardly a month after European nations began to mobilize in 1914, hundreds of women demonstrated their sorrow in a solemn walk down New York's Fifth Avenue. The committee that organized the parade would provide much of the initiative for the organization of the Woman's Peace Party (WPP) early in 1915. It was led by feminists, including Fanny Garrison Villard, who perpetuated the legacy of her nonresistant father. Like her friends, Villard complained that the older, male-dominated peace societies were enmeshed in the very institutions that had locked the world into war. "The fear of being called peace-at-any-price men makes cowards of them all," she said.[10] Women needed to organize courageously and in their own right.

Peace-minded feminists prevailed upon Carrie Chapman Catt, the main strategist and leader of the women's suffrage movement, to break with her avowed policy of not linking women's rights to any other reform movement. In turn, Catt appealed to Jane Addams, the founder of Hull House and the most respected woman in the United States. Other women also urged her to assume leadership, and not only Americans. Militant English suffragist Emmeline Pethik-Lawrence and her Hungarian counterpart, Rosika Schwimmer, toured the country in the fall of 1914, in their lectures linking peace with suffrage as distinctly women's issues. In Chicago both of them met with Addams, who agreed to call for a conference in Washington on 10 January 1915. Careful organizing preceded the founding of the Woman's Peace Party, but the planning revealed significant internal differences related to feminist politics. Catt was put off by the initiative taken by the New York group, whose militant strategy she regarded as impolitic and whose social philosophy she thought radical. Even though she lent her name to peace activism, she began to edge away from it, apprehensive that it would compromise the cause of universal suffrage.

Ironically, perhaps, the very eclecticism of the WPP attracted numerous women to it. Peace suffragists held that society had evolved from structures of control to processes of consent and participation, so that war and hierarchical government had become anachronistic. Their argument was rooted in sophisticated social analysis that was especially accessible to radical feminists in America and England. It led them toward the conclusion that there were fundamental problems in the international system, faults related to gender injustice. Suffragists also held that women were distinctly suited to supplant the masculine resort to force and domination with the feminine virtues of nurturing and cooperation, and that view reinforced conventional attitudes about the special, apolitical role of women.[11] Accordingly, and as Catt feared, peace action threatened to eclipse the single-minded emphasis on suffrage, since some women identified feminism with a broad challenge to social injustice while others tended to miss altogether the connection between their own rights and world peace.

Although that relationship was implicit in the WPP platform, its suffrage plank was ignored or rejected by some local branches—an example of the decentralization characteristic of all the new peace organizations. Just as they called for a democratic foreign policy, in contrast to the elitism implicit in both force and law, so too the founders of the Women's Peace Party intended their group to be more participatory than the older peace societies. The WPP initially attracted women from many organizations besides those devoted to women's suffrage, and its leaders disagreed over the politics of obtaining women's rights. Differences were mitigated for about a year by the fact that the women were not explicitly confronting the Wilson administration and by the élan of an international movement of women for peace.

Neutral Mediation   The WPP platform called for "a convention of neutral nations in the interest of an early peace."[12] This had already become a serious policy proposal. In December 1914 Julia G. Wales, an instructor in English at the University of Wisconsin, circulated a detailed plan for "continuous mediation" by an international commission of experts who would make proposals for peace terms. That idea was the basis not only of the WPP plank but also of other organizing efforts. While Jane Addams worked on the women's convention, she and Louis Lochner used the Chicago Peace Society to create an Emergency Peace Federation of Peace Forces. In turn, the federation and the Women's Peace Party assembled a large conference in Chicago, from which a National Peace Federation emerged by March 1915. Its chief officers were Hamilton Holt, Addams, and Lochner; its program was the idea of continuous mediation by a conference of neutral nations. The proposal was sent to President Wilson, attracted national attention, and was even commended to Congress by the Wisconsin legislature.

At the end of April, Dutch suffragists convened an International Congress of Women at the Hague.[13] Addams led a large delegation to the congress, over which she presided. Discussions there related the immediate war crisis to secret treaties, munitions and other economic interests, and the need for popular representation in policymaking. The congress created an ongoing committee and called for a conference of neutral nations that would stay in continuous session to clarify war aims and negotiate peace terms as opportunities opened. Small delegations of women presented the plan to statesmen in belligerent and neutral capitals. The Americans among them became convinced that neutral mediation was feasible if only the United States would take the lead, and upon their return home they tried to convince Wilson of their view. The president was polite, but he clearly preferred unofficial and unilateral diplomacy, which he had, in fact, explored.

By this time the Germans had sunk the British passenger ship *Lusitania* with the loss of American lives. Clearly, U.S. neutrality itself was at stake. The future hinged on the definition of *neutrality*—whether it referred to the commercial rights of a nonbelligerent, as established in international law, or to the position of not taking sides at all. The Wilson administration gravitated to the former interpretation. Increasingly it became clear to the president that the protection of the neutral right to trade was edging the country toward the Allied side, and that only a European peace would keep the nation from involvement. But it was not all clear that Germany and England were ready to compromise. Under these circumstances, Wilson sought to keep his options open and played his diplomatic cards secretly. There was, therefore, a measure of truth in his repeated assurance to peace advocates that he was waiting until the time was ripe to offer mediation. There was some deception, too, in that he avoided outright rejection of the multinational initiatives recommended by peace progressives whose political support he valued.

A coalition of new national and local peace groups tried to force the president's hand on mediation through a public campaign that peaked in November 1915. Demonstrations arranged by Louis Lochner and other peace workers, notably from the WPP, elicited a flood of petitions to the White House. The program even attracted some leaders in the older peace societies who sought an alternative to inaction. Thus, Hamilton Holt enlisted several of them to form the American Neutral Conference Committee. Founded in June 1916, it was intended to be the agency of a national campaign that never materialized. An August meeting with Wilson proved discouraging, military spending had emerged as a current issue, and in any case mediation had been given a different twist.

Lochner and his colleagues had learned from the 1915 mediation campaign that public demonstrations require money. In search of funds, the zealous Rosika Schwimmer wrangled an appointment with Henry Ford in November. The wealthy auto manufacturer warmed to his own sense of the drama of prominent Americans sailing abroad to create an international citizens' conference for mediation. This represented a significant change from the idea of an official commission of neutral nations, but Ford swept up Schwimmer and Lochner with his money and energy. Within weeks he chartered space on the *Oscar II,* visited the president, and put to sea. The press had a field day, generally ridiculing the expedition and Ford's promise to "get the boys in the trenches home by Christmas."[14] Except for Addams, no leading peace activist accepted an invitation to make the trip, not even the executive committee of the WPP, which was sponsoring it. Partly there was widespread apprehension among activists of Ford's style of publicity and Schwimmer's domineering, if wholly sincere, form of leadership. Partly the venture deviated sharply from the original mediation plan and, in any case, lines were being drawn on military spending. Even Addams canceled at the last moment because of illness. The somewhat ad hoc "official" party of 55 persons represented an "illustrious unknown," as they called themselves.[15]

After stops in Scandinavia, the Americans settled at the Hague, where they and the few Europeans who joined them constituted the Neutral Conference for Continuous Mediation. Crises over program and leadership resulted in Schwimmer's resignation in the spring. A reorganization resulted in the formulation of serious peace proposals, but the experiment in citizen diplomacy was under enormous handicaps, not the least being its isolation in Europe. Mediation itself became isolated during the year as the alternatives narrowed to either intervention or isolationism and peace advocates found themselves resisting preparations for war.

Antipreparedness   Indeed, the new leadership was galvanized as it sensed that militarism threatened democratic reform in America by making government less accountable and diverting resources from social needs. Toward the end of 1914 that apprehension had led to the formation of the American League to Limit Armaments by Oswald Garrison Villard, the editor of the *Nation,* and Quaker lawyer Hollingsworth Wood, with financial support from the Church Peace Union. Early the next year the same anxiety was expressed in the platform of the Women's Peace Party. Most important, it surfaced in the conversations of about two dozen reformers—editors, social workers, and religious leaders—who began meeting at Lillian Wald's Henry Street Settlement in New York City.[16]

These people had previously worked together on campaigns against child labor and other domestic injustices, and now they met in search of a handle on the war question. In the summer of 1915 they aligned briefly with Addams and the WPP to promote neutral mediation, but they found a focus for activism only in November, when Wilson came out for a new army reserve and significant increases in the navy. In response, the Henry Street group organized the Anti-Preparedness Committee, designating as its secretary Crystal Eastman, who had graduated from Columbia University Law School, was an authority on industrial-accident law, and had managed the suffrage campaign in Wisconsin. She had been pressing the WPP to challenge preparedness.[17]

To a later generation it might seem strange to oppose "preparedness," but the progressives of the early twentieth century inherited a long national tradition of minimal military capacity. In opposing the president's appeal for arms increases, they felt that they were defending democratic institutions, the more so since they explained the European war as a result of an arms race and related authoritarianism. What they objected to was the preparation of offensive military capacity that could stifle political and social reform and lead to active belligerency.

The anxiety of the Henry Street group struck so responsive a chord that in the course of a year the Anti-Preparedness Committee grew from about 15 to 15,000 members, distributed over half a million pieces of literature, and spent $35,000. It lined up support from social agencies, unions, farmers' organizations, and civic groups. It built a mailing list of anyone with a known interest in peace. Its leaders lobbied in Congress and used their ready access to national journals such as the *Nation* and the *Survey*. In the process, the committee was transformed into the American Union against Militarism (AUAM, 1916), which Senator William E. Borah aptly called the "brains" of the peace movement.[18] Indeed, the AUAM was the core of an antipreparedness coalition that included nominally separate groups formed by its own members, as well as the Women's Peace Party, and received substantial funds from the Church Peace Union.

While mounting its antipreparedness program, the AUAM responded to another crisis over Mexico. In March 1916 Wilson sent a force of 15,000 soldiers in pursuit of a band led by Mexican revolutionary Francisco Villa that had killed 16 Americans in a raid on Columbus, New Mexico. There was a clash at Carrizal, south of the border, and war seemed

This 1916 parade in New York City was part of a mobilization against military preparedness that engaged the new elements of the peace movement in a popular debate over American policy prior to intervention in World War I. *Swarthmore College Peace Collection*

altogether possible. Prompted by Crystal Eastman, the AUAM placed a firsthand account of the incident and American responsibility for it with major newspapers. The organization also convened a joint commission of American and Mexican citizens, chaired by David Starr Jordan, to explore ways of reconciling national interests. In this context, and with public opinion overwhelmingly for peace, the administration opened negotiations with Mexico that averted war. The incident led Eastman to conclude that "the people acting directly . . . can stop all wars."[19]

Accordingly, when in April President Wilson challenged opponents of increased military spending to hire halls and go to the people, the AUAM replied with a mass meeting at Carnegie Hall, where Lillian Wald was flanked by representatives of labor, social workers, the National Grange, and church groups. From the platform the Reverend John Haynes Holmes conceded the point that "peace at any price is damnable," but asked, "what about . . . security at any price?"[20] The New York rally was followed by others in over half a dozen other large cities. The significance of the campaign lay in its political style and organization rather than its result, for in August Congress authorized a large preparedness program. The issue faded as election day approached.

The president's domestic record in 1916 had encouraged partisans of progressive reform, and the Democrats' fall campaign was waged in part under the slogan that Wilson had kept the nation out of war. Despite some qualms, most of the new peace activists stood by him in the election. They seemed to have no other choice. The Women's Peace Party was dissipated by a renewed campaign for suffrage; conservatives took the Church Peace Union out of politics; and the AUAM itself became less active, its members pinning their hopes on the government.

Activists were heartened, despite American occupation of the Dominican Republic in November, by peace initiatives that the administration negotiated with the British and Germans during the fall. When Wilson spoke out for "peace without victory" on 22 January 1917, many peace workers felt that their confidence in him had been vindicated. The feeling was premature. On the last day of the month Germany announced that it would resume unrestricted submarine warfare. Wilson answered, as he had threatened he would do, by severing diplomatic relations. All hopes of a mediated peace were dashed, and the nation faced the issue: it could affirm its neutral rights to trade freely with the Allies or it could stand clear of the European war. It could no longer do both.

By this time, a small number of people who repudiated war altogether had become organized in the Fellowship of Reconciliation (FOR), as women had associated in the WPP, and social workers and reformers had come together in the AUAM. The catalyst for the formation of the FOR was an American tour by Henry T. Hodgkin, a leading English Quaker and chairman of the British Fellowship of Reconciliation, which had been formed in the last days of 1914 to provide a supportive fellowship for those persons who chose to go against the strong current of militant patriotism. The American counterpart was formed at Garden City, New York, in November 1915, its members including especially Quakers, leaders in the Young Men's Christian Association (YMCA), and social-gospel clergymen. [21]

The social gospel is the name given to an emphasis in religion that extended the ideas of sin and salvation from the individual to society, and that stressed the responsibility of churches for the quality of community. It was manifested in the increasingly active role of church leaders in social issues early in the century, and in ecumenical cooperation. The Church Peace Union had put social gospel–oriented Americans in touch with like-minded Christians abroad. Its secretary, Frederick Lynch, participated in the Garden City conference, but he could not bring himself to join those who rejected war totally, which was the basis on which the Fellowship of Reconciliation was formed. The FOR was not intended to be highly organized or action-oriented. Nonetheless, some of its officers worked in the 1916 antipreparedness campaign, and early in 1917 the fellowship became fully integrated in the campaign against intervention in the European war.

Anti-intervention   The United States continued to trade with the Allies after diplomatic relations with Germany were severed. American ships were sunk. The German government assumed that this would incur an American declaration of war, but it calculated that Great Britain would be decisively weakened before the United States could weigh seriously in the military balance. Well into March the toll of American ships rose while a small group of senators blocked the administration's attempt to arm U.S. merchantmen. In those hectic weeks, progressive peace groups waged a desperate campaign against intervention, and their constituency shifted toward the political left.

Many small peace groups were dormant by mid-February. There were resignations in the WPP, and most executive committee members of the American Neutral Conference Committee resigned. The American Union against Militarism lost a few key leaders, too, but the core of social workers and reformers remained. In fact, the crisis brought to it New York clergyman Norman Thomas and Saint Louis social worker Roger Baldwin, both destined to play key roles in the movement. Moreover, the AUAM drew fresh support from socialists and from members of New York's cultural avant-garde (such as journalist John Reed, artists John Sloan and Art Young, and authors Max Eastman and Randolph Bourne).

The AUAM expanded its staff and reached out to the public. It circulated a plebiscite to 100,000 people who voted decisively against war. It filled Madison Square Garden in a mass protest meeting and sponsored rallies across the country. Lochner and others lobbied in the capital. The Emergency Peace Federation, which he directed, created an informal commission of citizens for alternatives to war, working from the precedent of the Carrizal incident. David Starr Jordan chaired the commission and spoke at numerous meetings. This was not Carrizal, though: the national mood was running for intervention. On Palm Sunday, after escaping a mob that broke into a Baltimore rally where he was speaking, Jordan wrote to William Jennings Bryan, "It seems to me that exactly the same thing is going on here as in Germany in 1914. The fair weather pacifists make the same excuses for sliding into the abyss, and the faithful stand out without flinching as they did in Germany."[22] On Good Friday, Congress opted for war. Jordan concluded that since the country was at war, "the only way out is forward."[23]

That was the rationale of the established peace societies, which had followed the administration's lead all along. The CEIP offered its Washington office to the Creel Committee, the official propaganda arm of the government, and its Division of International Law to the State Department. On its own stationery it placed the slogan "Peace through Victory." Encouraged by the Creel Committee, the Church Peace Union joined with the World Alliance for Friendship through the Churches and the League to Enforce Peace to create a National Committee on the Churches and the Moral Aims of the War. The American School Peace League became the American School Citizenship League. The American Peace Society proclaimed, "We must help in the bayoneting of a normally decent German soldier in order to free him from a tyranny which he at present accepts. . . . We must aid in the starvation of a German baby in order that he, or at least his more sturdy little playmate, may grow up to inherit a different sort of government from that for which his father died."[24]

The People's Council   By "going forward," David Starr Jordan had something else in mind than prosecuting the war. He was thinking of the postwar settlement and, more immediately, the protection of civil liberties during wartime. Those concerns prompted Roger Baldwin, Louis Lochner, Emily Balch, Rebecca Shelley, and a small remnant of the antiwar coalition to form the People's Council of America for Peace and Democracy at the end of May. They moved further leftward, aligning with antiwar factions in the Socialist party and organized labor.

The national convention of the then eclectic and vigorous Socialist party was convened in Saint Louis on the day after war was declared. Although socialists had not participated in the U.S. peace movement before 1917, they had criticized their European comrades for rallying behind their governments despite their long-held position that national wars subvert the true interests of working people. Would American socialists also forsake that principle? After a turbulent debate, the party adopted a provocatively antiwar resolution. Several socialist intellectuals resigned, but others joined AUAM activists in the People's Council of America.[25]

What was left for peace workers to do? They demanded a quick and liberal peace, respect for the civil liberties of dissenters and conscientious objectors, an equitable distribution of war costs, and a more representative form of political organization. To this end, the AUAM and its socialist allies launched the People's Council of America with a large Madison Square Garden rally at the end of May.

Threaded through the People's Council program was the effect of revolution in Russia. The overthrow of the czar in March furthered the war effort by removing the main totalitarian regime among the Allies and thus isolating Germany and Austria-Hungary as authoritarian powers. This meant that the war could plausibly be prosecuted to destroy autocracy itself, which presumably was the barrier to peace. Paradoxically, however, the Russian revolution also gave impetus to the opponents of the war who took the name People's Council. It approximated the Russian word *soviet*, which identified the groups of workers and soldiers who overthrew an unrepresentative government with whose war they did not identify. That was the point for the leaders of the People's Council of America. The western governments were not truly representative either, they thought, and militarism threatened to undermine such democracy as had been attained. Working people should be loyal to one another across national boundaries—that was the thrust of socialist internationalism—rather than to nation-states and their ruling elites. The People's Council was intended to be a grass-roots coalition that would enjoin the government to make a quick and liberal peace and protect dissent, if it did not indeed restructure political power.

In a move that would be replicated during the Vietnam War, the leaders of the People's Council attempted to align disaffected minorities in a constituent assembly, which they called for 1 September. They organized their would-be radical coalition during the summer, holding large meetings in New York, Chicago, and Los Angeles. The radical-culture community of New York was engaged. Local councils were formed among radical farmers' groups. Early endorsement came from labor leaders who were challenging the conservative American Federation of Labor. Support came from Jewish leaders opposed to czarism and suspicious of capitalism. By the time of the scheduled constituent assembly, however, the coalition was falling apart and was feeling the effect of wartime repression. Prevented by local authorities from meeting in Minnesota, delegates to the assembly met hastily, almost covertly, in Chicago. By that time, conservative labor leaders and prowar socialists had launched a formal attack on the council with financial backing from the Creel Com-

mittee. Workers were responding to wartime prosperity; Jews were encouraged by Great Britain's promise of a postwar homeland; and
radicalism was branded as subversive.

The People's Council was never as radical as the image it projected,
but the image itself was a problem for progressives who, like Lillian
Wald, were still with the AUAM. She and several others resigned when
it voted to send delegates to the People's Council assembly. It was not
only the council issue that was divisive, however, but also the work of
Roger Baldwin, Norman Thomas, Crystal Eastman, and others on behalf
of conscientious objectors and, increasingly, other dissenters. After the
declaration of war they had formed a Civil Liberties Bureau within the
AUAM,[26] anticipating that a "Union Against Militarism becomes, during
war time, inevitably a Union for the Defense of Civil Liberty."[27] Lillian
Wald and Paul Kellogg, among others, felt that association with absolute
pacifists would render the group unacceptable to internationalists who
sought to direct the war toward a constructive peace. Even though the
National Civil Liberties Bureau became an independent organization in
October, the AUAM dissolved into a paper organization.

The progressive peace advocates of 1914–17 identified war as yet another issue of social injustice to which they felt a moral obligation to
respond. The turn of the century was a period of sweeping reforms designed to adapt American society to industrialism, urban concentration,
and ethnic diversity. Connecting all reforms and underlying each of them
was an attempt to vest government with more responsibility for social
welfare and to make politics more accountable to the public. Accordingly,
reformers were activists in the sense that they readily took their demands for social and political change into the public arena. At the same
time, however, they valued their contacts with progressive political leaders like Wilson and were loathe to cut their ties to decision makers. As
long as there seemed to be any flexibility in national policy, they tried to
marshal public opinion in order to influence the administration. They
were in this sense liberals, out to reform the social system but confident
of the political process, in contrast both to conservative internationalists
who relied on the decision-making elite and to the more radical activists
who entered the movement in the spring of 1917 altogether skeptical of
the political system.

As the nation moved to war, inexorably it seemed, most progressive
peace advocates left the organized movement and tried to imbue the war
with their peace aims. The legacy of their activism and their view that
war was part of a faulty social system endured to shape the wing of peace

advocacy they had inaugurated. Those progressive peace advocates who could not sanction the war or the military system of conscription provided the connecting link between the peace societies of 1914–16 and the movement that was reorganized after the war.

The Progressive Era was also a period of growing professionalism, in which constituencies for reform were increasingly formalized by businessmen, lawyers, educators, women, clergy, members of the cultural avant-garde, and labor leaders, among others. The professions were served by organizations with paid staff and by specialized journals. Freelance reformers, often writers or organizers, found employment in public service related to professional goals. As national policy impinged on them, lawyers, social workers, clergy, and labor leaders adapted their positions—accepting or opposing intervention, supporting or challenging the war effort, and seeking to influence the postwar settlement. "Men and women joined the peace movement," as historian Roland Marchand demonstrated, "when it expressed conceptions of world politics and the social order that coincided with their most immediate social and professional biases, their political prejudices, and their conceptions of appropriate means."[28]

Peace advocates were a minority in each constituency, generally more likely than their colleagues to be from the East Coast, more active in the national affairs of their professions, and more cosmopolitan in outlook. A still smaller minority were pacifists after the spring of 1917, when that meant opposing war policy. For this antiwar core, social and professional concerns were subordinated to the concept of peace because it had come to embrace the values of social justice that primarily motivated them.

Wartime Peace Advocates

Liberal Pacifism   Like nonresistants, many liberal pacifists abjured warfare on moral or religious grounds, but in a fresh way they also subjected World War I to the kind of social and political analysis they had brought to domestic issues. In particular, they rejected the "devil" theory, which converted that war into a crusade—the notion that Germany alone was to blame for it and that Allied victory alone would usher in peace. Following the lead of British pacifists like philosopher and mathematician Bertrand Russell, they distributed responsibility for the war and its atrocity among all belligerents. And they distinguished between the motives of the warring governments and the ideals of people on both sides of no-man's-land.

Their analysis led pacifists to a skeptical neutralism: they stood aside from the war effort, although they did not actively obstruct it. Given the prevailing mood, however, neutrality was itself a crime. Socialist presidential candidate Eugene Debs was imprisoned for it. Others were indicted under the Espionage Act. Some pacifist clergy lost their churches. Socialists and pacifists were harassed by vigilante groups, their meetings broken up, their headquarters raided, and their publications sometimes withheld from the mail.

Under these circumstances, the Fellowship of Reconciliation became a refuge for its members—established leaders like Jane Addams and younger people like John Nevin Sayre, A. J. Muste, and Kirby Page.[29] The war both confirmed their pacifism and expanded their social concern. "We are no mere anti-war society," its exclusive committee wrote, "but a fellowship of those who by the method of love, seek the triumph of justice and the establishment of a social order based upon the will of God revealed in Christ Jesus . . . Our great task is preparation for a worthy peace."[30] Isolated from most of their countrymen, these cause-oriented pacifists prepared themselves by probing the nature of war and the relationship between peace and social justice.

Unlike internationalists, who sought order among nations, the liberal pacifists responded to a *transnational* allegiance, arraying themselves in a struggle for human dignity and decency that they found *within* all nations. Their own experiences seemed to confirm their belief that militarism exacerbated the gulf between social ideals and reality. Kirby Page, who had been trained in the emerging field of sociology before serving the YMCA in its work with Allied troops and German prisoners of war, insisted that "war is always and everywhere a *method,* and it is as a method that it must be discussed."[31] With other pacifists, he believed that violence and authoritarianism in the social order were precisely what threatened his liberal values. Conversely, the struggle for human dignity must be carried on by some other method than violent force. This led directly to the premise that absolute pacifism is socially relevant, and to the search for effective forms of nonviolent action in the struggle for social justice.

These ideas were not given systematic form during the war, but they were so pervasive that they defined the thrust of the FOR. The fellowship became more organized. In its annual conferences as many as 200 people weighed the implications of their ideals for social action. Most important, it began to publish *The World Tomorrow* in January 1918. Initially edited by Norman Thomas, the magazine became the leading journal of liberal Christianity until it was discontinued in 1934. On three occasions during the war the Post Office Department withheld it from the mail on the ground that its message of love beyond political boundaries violated the Espionage Act. This further convinced liberal pacifists of the importance of defending civil liberties. In particular, the FOR worked with the peace churches and the National Civil Liberties Bureau on behalf of conscientious objectors (C.O.'s) to military service.

The 4,000 C.O.'s were a tiny fraction of the nearly 3 million men inducted during World War I, but they created a disproportionate problem for the government because of the way they were handled. For President Wilson and the War Department, the treatment of conscientious objectors was an irritating detail in the vast work of mobilizing the country and assembling an army. Legislation for the military draft allowed the exemption only of members of a "well-recognized sect or organization whose creed or principles" forbade participation in "war in any form," and of men who sincerely accepted that principle. Furthermore, draftees in either category were still required to perform noncombatant military service. This formula created four difficulties. First, it was restricted to the historic peace churches and excluded men who were from the major denominations or objected to military service on secular grounds, as Socialists did. Second, it excluded men who objected to this particular war but not necessarily to the principle of defense. Third, it assumed that sincerity could be ascertained. And fourth, it made soldiers even of those men exempted from combat, which contradicted the tenets of the peace churches.

None of those difficulties was satisfactorily resolved. Administrative regulations and practice allowed the FOR to represent C.O.'s who were not affiliated with peace churches; but neither secular nor selective objection was accommodated. Eventually a civilian Court of Inquiry was established to test the sincerity of objectors, and the War Department was allowed to furlough men to nonmilitary service, although it retained legal jurisdiction over them. Even those adjustments came late in the war. By its end, about a third of the C.O.'s had been accepted for noncombatant service; another third had been furloughed for civilian service of national importance; and the rest had been court-martialed and imprisoned (450), had been released upon review (54), or had remained in camps segregated from the regular army (940).[32] However much the government adjusted to conscientious objection, C.O.'s suffered physical and psychological abuse from lower-echelon officers who derisively labeled them "yellowbacks." Even before conscription was legislated, leaders in the AUAM and the Civil Liberties Bureau urged that alternative civilian service become available to all C.O.'s. After the draft went into effect in June, peace church leaders lobbied the War Department for modifications of its provisions.

Meanwhile, in April 1917 several Quakers formed the American Friends Service Committee (AFSC) in order to create a unit of C.O.'s that would undertake reconstruction projects in devastated France. A precedent for this kind of service had been set by English Quakers. The American Friends expected that their young men would be completely exempted from military service, but they felt an obligation to "express their positive faith and devotion in the great human crisis."[33] By the time it was clear that Quakers would not be exempted for voluntary service, a reconstruction unit had been trained. Several of its members became leaders in the postwar peace movement, notably Frederick Libby and William I. Hull. While the AFSC continued to negotiate with the administration, the group sailed for France. They were the first of 340 Americans that came to be engaged in a million-dollar project as the Friends Service Committee expanded its program in devastated Europe and Russia after the war.[34] Mennonites formed their own relief committee, and other nonresistants worked through similar agencies or the AFSC. Persistent lobbying by the peace churches also resulted in the limited furlough of C.O.'s for public service.

Their wartime effort strengthened the organization of liberal pacifists. It also reflected a view growing among C.O.'s themselves that conscription epitomized the principle of authoritarianism, violating not only religious but also social ideals. In this respect, the evolution of conscientious objection, like organizational and relief work, reflected the social activism of liberal pacifists who located the seeds of war in the social order.

Internationalism   By contrast, most of the prewar internationalists identified the cause of war in the relations of nations. They supported American intervention in World War I in the hope that it would lead to an enduring world order. That was "the challenge of the present crisis," as theologian Harry Emerson Fosdick called it. The challenge was epitomized in the League of Nations.

In the spring of 1918, a League to Enforce Peace study committee prepared its own version of a League of Nations in an attempt to reconcile differences among the established peace organizations. Collective force would be used only to enforce the submission of disputes to conciliatory procedures. Sovereignty, including the right to wage war, would not be affected. Even that limited use of force was opposed by the lawyers associated with the CEIP, and it probably represented the outer limit of acceptable internationalism in America.

It did not satisfy the most liberal internationalists, including AUAM founders Lillian Wald and Paul Kellogg, journalist Herbert Croly, historian Charles Beard, and not even James T. Shotwell, who was working with a committee on peace plans that was established by the president. Meeting occasionally from the summer of 1917, these people and others organized themselves as the League of Free Nations Association in the fall of 1918. Although they accepted the use of collective force, they wanted an international organization that, representing the people of the world, would replace the exclusive sovereign claims that led to violence with an equitable international order. It was, as Charles DeBenedetti has observed, "a systematic effort to institutionalize managerial controls over the fragile interdependence of modern industrial civilization."[35] Vigorously, they took their program to the public.

By this time, however, Wilson had gone beyond what was politically possible. In early drafts of the League of Nations, he included the collective use of force to guarantee the territorial integrity and independence of nations (this became article 10 of the league's Covenant) and to respond to the threat of war (article 11).[36] Those provisions were construed as compromising national sovereignty when, a year later, the president submitted to Congress the peace treaty and League of Nations Covenant. Intense political opposition and attempts to amend the Covenant were fed by many sources of personal and political dissatisfaction, but in large measure they revolved around the impression that the obligation to use collective force would curtail the nation's ability to choose its own policy. Wilson denied that implication, but he also rejected qualifying amendments. The Covenant was defeated, and the United States did not join the League of Nations, which owed so much to its president and, before him, its peace movement.

The established peace organizations were ambivalent during the intense contest over the League of Nations in 1919 and 1920. The Carnegie Endowment opposed it. The League of Free Nations Association endorsed both the league and its modifications. Increasingly it subsumed the issue in public discussions of the whole range of international affairs, emerging as the Foreign Policy Association (FPA). The League to Enforce Peace initially launched a strong campaign for ratification, but as the issue became increasingly partisan during 1919, its Republican-dominated leadership was torn between those who favored congressional amendments and those who endorsed the Wilson version. Even so ardent a supporter of the league as Hamilton Holt complained of both the "uncompromising President and obdurate Senate."[37] Holt and a core of LEP leaders would eventually form the League of Nations Non-Partisan Association (1922). Most important, the controversy helped to distinguish conservative from liberal internationalists. The former would rely on international law and arbitration to secure order among sovereign nations, whereas liberals would modify the state system with a collective security organization.

Internationalism was taken a step further with the formation of the Women's International League for Peace and Freedom (WILPF), an outgrowth of the 1915 International Congress of Women that met at the Hague.[38] Since delegates from the Central European powers were not allowed to travel to Paris, where the peace settlement was fashioned, the women met in Zurich, Switzerland, in May 1919. Sixteen countries were represented. The WILPF was organized on a permanent basis, with Jane Addams as president, Helena M. Swanwick of Great Britain and Lida Gustava Heyman of Germany as vice presidents, and Emily Balch as international secretary.[39] National sections were established, and shortly afterward an international office was located in Geneva.

The women knew the terms of the peace treaty by the time they met in Zurich, and they denounced the "victor's" peace for departing radically from the ideals enunciated by Wilson during the war. They also criticized the League of Nations for not being sufficiently strong and universal. It should be open to all states that wanted membership, they said; it should guarantee the self-determination of nations and equal access to raw materials, promote disarmament, and do away with regional arrangements (such as the United States' special role in Latin America). Thereafter, the WILPF promoted every practical modification of the system of sovereign states, and not merely for the sake of international order. Its view was implicitly transnational—beyond the nation system—and it was interested in both "peace and freedom."

The women in Zurich were acutely aware that demands for political and social justice threatened several European countries with revolutionary violence. They barely passed a resolution that limited WILPF endorsement for only peaceful methods of change. The issue of violence in the struggle for justice came up again and again in the interwar period, and although the organization repeatedly condemned all organized violence, it did not make that principle binding on its national sections. Differences of perspective were too sharp, and in any case, it seemed inappropriate to prescribe ethical behavior to the victims of injustice. Nonetheless, within the Women's International League (especially in its British and American sections) a strong strain of absolute pacifism accompanied practical transnationalism.

That combination also characterized the Fellowship of Reconciliation and the American Friends Service Committee. Both of them had overseas connections, the FOR with the International Fellowship of Reconciliation (1919), and the AFSC with a similar Friends committee in England and with Quakers the world over. The transnationalism of liberal pacifists was based on a worldview quite different from that of even the most liberal internationalists in the established peace societies. It was a view with varied sources, including Quaker tradition, universal religion like that of Elihu Burritt, the evolutionary and social-systems approach of progressive thinkers, and the Socialist sense of class lines cutting across national boundaries. Whatever their roots, liberal pacifists tended to think in terms of the needs of a human community that pervaded the atomistic world of sovereign states.

Thus, by the end of World War I the American peace movement had two fairly well-defined wings. Internationalists had organized established societies before the war in a search for order in the midst of a rapidly changing and industrializing world. They had identified constituencies of educators, businessmen, and politicals who shared their concerns, and their program of arbitration and international law was designed to secure international order with minimal change in the state system. Their preferred strategy was to work with the policy-shaping elite. They followed the lead of the government into and though the war, sharpening their sense of Anglo-American world mission but dividing over the terms of the postwar settlement, especially the League of Nations. A core of them emerged as liberal internationalists committed to a strong international organization, one that might even adapt the state system in the interest of world order. The League of Nations Non-Partisan Association became the principal agent of liberal internationalism.

A second wing was formed by progressive reformers who responded to the outbreak of war in Europe by organizing within constituencies including women, social workers and publicists, and social-gospel clergy. They were habitual activists whose preferred strategy was to mobilize public opinion for change, although they valued the political system and their contacts in it. They challenged the government on the questions of neutral mediation, military preparedness, and intervention, although most of them supported the war when it seemed to be unavoidable. Then a minority of them organized to defend civil liberties, especially those of conscientious objectors to military service, and also sought ways to pursue peace without endorsing the war, often in concert with the traditional peace churches. In their isolation from the public, they also probed the implications of their dual commitment to peace and social justice and deepened their transnational view of a world community. They developed enduring organizations—the Fellowship of Reconciliation, the American Friends Service Committee, and the Women's International League for Peace and Freedom—each of which had strong ties abroad. This core emerged from the war as liberal pacifists committed to any form of nonviolent change, from the personal level to international organization, that would contribute to peace with social justice.

Each wing evolved as various groups tried to adapt to the rapidly changing world of the half decade following 1914. Neither was static or fully formed at any time. Nor were they mutually exclusive, because people could be attracted to various positions in each. The peace movement as a whole was shaped and reshaped by the combination of elements within it. Constituencies and leaders constantly shifted, coalitions dissolving almost by the time they were recognizable. Taken together, peace advocates offered the full panoply of foreign policies from which the United States then had to choose, and they anticipated the alternative approaches to peace during the balance of the century.

Chapter Three

Peace and Neutrality Campaigns, 1921–1941

The war that was supposed "to end war" and "to save democracy" was succeeded by domestic and international instability. Disillusionment with the so-called Great War was reinforced by a spate of memoirs, war stories and poems, films, historical analyses, and revelations of how public opinion had been managed by propaganda techniques. Capitalizing on antiwar sentiment throughout the 1920s, liberal pacifists made inroads in churches, women's groups, and colleges. They learned to lobby and mobilize public pressure. They cooperated with other internationalists, although efforts to build effective coalitions were repeatedly frustrated by the maneuvers of politicians and by differences among peace advocates themselves.

Early in the 1930s the fragile system established with the Treaty of Versailles came apart with the rise of aggressive dictatorships and military oligarchies: the Japanese army rolled into Manchuria and on to China; the Nazis took power in Germany and constructed a powerful *Wehrmacht;* Mussolini's Italian troops invaded Ethiopia; and a socialist republic went down in a Spanish civil war that involved the great powers. In 1936, in response to unfolding crises, pacifists aligned with other internationalists in a national Emergency Peace Campaign (EPC). Designed to promote peaceful solutions to world conflict and to keep the United States out of war, this campaign was the most impressive coalition in the history of the American peace movement before the Vietnam War. It was as brief as it was dramatic. Cooperation was undermined by an unstable mixture of isolationist and internationalist sentiment in the nation. It was fractured by differences among peace groups. When war ripped through Europe again in 1939, many internationalists promoted

Dorothy Detzer (1893–1981) was the national secretary of the U.S. section of the Women's International League for Peace and Freedom and represented the political activism that crested in the 1930s peace movement. She was an effective lobbyist who coordinated political campaigns with other peace and civic groups. *Swarthmore College Peace Collection*

American intervention, while absolute pacifists shored up their community against the prospect of involvement.[1]

It was necessary to adapt to new conditions following World War I. In the first place, the widespread prewar assumption of inevitable progress gave way to the haunting memory of catastrophe. The challenge now was not only to advocate peace but to avoid being drawn into another horrendous conflict. And almost nothing had been done to deal with the causes of war itself. Second, the League of Nations existed. No longer a mere dream, international organization was a part of international reality. As yet it was very tenuous and satisfied no one. For some peace workers that underscored the need for the United States to give form and substance to the league by participating in it. For others, the league's inadequacy was an excuse to pursue other approaches. In either case, its existence was a fact with which to reckon. Third, American society was increasingly responsive to mass communication and was organized along ever more specialized lines. Peace organizations themselves were heterogeneous and highly specialized. The challenge of mobilizing influence on foreign policy issues became correspondingly broader and more complex.

Internationalist societies that predated World War I had lost much of their initiative. The American Peace Society continued from inertia, apparently wedded to its wartime identification of world peace with American predominance. The World Peace Foundation regained vitality, still with an emphasis on public education. The Carnegie Endowment for International Peace remained a source of scholarly studies and the bastion of international lawyers. Its influence derived from its affluence rather than from innovation or initiative, except for the work of James T. Shotwell, who directed its Division of Economics and History after 1923. The Foreign Policy Association (formerly League of Free Nations Association) promoted public understanding of foreign policy issues without taking a stand on them. Some members of the League to Enforce Peace worked for a world organization through the major parties until 1922. Abandoning that futile tactic, they formed the League of Nations Non-Partisan Association (LNNPA; after 1929 simply the League of Nations Association [LNA]). Only toward the end of the 1920s did it become at all strong. The Church Peace Union and the World Alliance for International Friendship were connected to the denominational structures of American churches through the Commission for International Justice and Goodwill of the Federal Council of Churches. This gave them a measure of independence from their original patron, the CEIP, and helped to align them with liberal pacifist groups.

Transnational it its outlook, the U.S. section of the Women's International League for Peace and Freedom included a core of liberal pacifists. It began to organize only after the war. It had but 20 members at the end of 1920, compared with the 40,000 members of the Women's Peace Party in 1916, but it had determined leaders. In April 1921 they set up a national office, and two years later claimed 5,000 members.[2] The WILPF leadership had strong ties to the women's movement which, having won the vote during the war, was looking for new issues. Early in the 1920s, though, the WILPF was smeared as being radical, even communist, so that for a time it was alienated from national women's groups. Quite possibly, this impelled Carrie Chapman Catt to form the National Conference on the Cause and Cure of War (1924) as an umbrella group for several women's associations. Its annual meetings defined war and peace issues for women to study, but it did not engage in political action.[3]

On the other side, a few absolute pacifists around Fanny Garrison Villard were dissatisfied with the very breadth of of the WILPF program, and they organized the Women's Peace Society. In 1921 these women divided over the merit of personal or political action respectively. Some of them formed the Women's Peace Union, which promoted a constitutional amendment to prohibit the United States from engaging in war.[4] Pacifist organization was completed in 1923 and 1924 with the creation of the small War Resisters League (WRL), a branch of the War Resisters International, which hoped to thwart war by enlisting people in all nations who would pledge to resist it.

The core organizations of liberal pacifism were the American Friends Service Committee and the Fellowship of Reconciliation. The AFSC expanded as it engaged in reconstruction abroad and social work at home. By 1924 it had a staff of administrators and fund-raisers and was organized in four sections: foreign service, home service, interracial work, and peace action. It was a project-oriented service agency rather than a membership organization. The FOR entered the decade with a tightly knit leadership and a journal, *The World Tomorrow,* that was ever more widely read outside pacifist circles. Its strong orientation to social reform was formalized with the creation of a Fellowship for a Christian Social Order (1921) through which liberal pacifists and other progressives cooperated on political goals. Pacifists associated with the FOR made converts among leaders in churches and women's organizations, gained access to youth groups, and produced a large antiwar literature. Their Committee on Militarism in Education (1925) challenged the introduction of Reserve Officers Training Corps programs in high schools and colleges.

Thus, in different ways, both the Friends Service Committee and the Fellowship of Reconciliation reached out beyond their own constituencies of absolute pacifists. The AFSC did this by operating diversified service programs, which increasingly required a supporting staff for administration, public relations, and fund-raising. Leaders from its peace section and the FOR also worked within other groups—the churches, the YMCA, the Intercollegiate Socialist Society, the American Civil Liberties Union, and the Socialist party—or formed new organizations with nonpacifists. The organizational style of the AFSC and the FOR reflected the fact that their leaders identified peace with social justice as well as conflict resolution, and were willing to support a variety of programs for domestic and international reform.

Peace groups during the interwar period also reached out across international boundaries. The CEIP helped to finance a research center working with the League of Nations Secretariate, and the League of Nations Association was linked to support groups in other nations, as well as to the league itself. Shotwell's work on the history of World War I and his activity on behalf of the league and the International Labor Organization established wide-ranging, if informal, contacts abroad. The AFSC was part of a worldwide network of Quakers. The U.S. section of the WILPF was part of an international organization with a headquarters in Geneva that monitored and lobbied the League of Nations. National delegates to its conferences kept one another well informed throughout the interwar period. The FOR was in active contact with the International Fellowship of Reconciliation (IFOR, 1919), which organized relief work in Germany and France after the war, sponsored tours of goodwill among former belligerents, and developed exchange programs and summer camps for young people and an early version of the Peace Corps (Service Civil International) for relief work. Through the IFOR, pacifists had close ties to European church leaders, contacts that were supplemented through the Church Peace Union. The WRL maintained contact with secular and socialist war resisters through the War Resisters International (WRI). Although small, the American branch shared information from abroad with the FOR, Indeed, in 1933 Devere Allen used his contacts with the WRI, IFOR, and socialist friends to launch an independent news service, No-Frontier-News, through which information about peace advocates abroad—and their plight—was distributed well beyond the pacifist constituency.

Peace societies were more highly organized than ever before. They had definable constituencies, and they tried to influence specific publics. They had reasonably coherent ideologies—concepts and values that affected their judgments on various proposals for peace and internationalism. With the exception of the smallest groups, such as the WPS, WPU, and WRL, peace groups were becoming professionalized. Increasingly they relied on paid staff, often with experience in public relations, lobbying, administration, or fund-raising. They depended on contributions from major donors or institutions such as foundations and churches for specific projects, if not for operating expenses. They communicated with one another and the public through speaking tours, press releases, direct mailings, newsletters, and professional journals. During the interwar period peace groups completed the process of professionalization. Repeatedly, they also attempted to coordinate their efforts in order to create a national peace movement with professional leadership and public influence.

Competing Peace Campaigns in the 1920s

An important step toward cooperation was prompted by the issue of military spending.[5] In mid-August 1919 the dormant AUAM was awakened by a War Department bill that included compulsory military training in peacetime. Hastily, it set up a lobby in Washington. When the navy proposed a major expansion the following year, the public was ripe for a proposal sponsored in the Senate by William E. Borah for the United States to sponsor an international conference on arms limitation. Early in 1921 leaders from the National Women's Party formed a committee on disarmament. Women from several organizations sponsored mass meetings, distributed literature, scheduled speaking tours, and lobbied at the White House and on Capitol Hill. Secretary of State Charles Evans Hughes capitalized on the resulting base in public opinion to persuade President Warren G. Harding to call a conference on limitation and reduction of armaments for November.

That stimulated further organization by peace advocates. A group of Quakers prompted Christina Merriman, the executive secretary of the Foreign Policy Association and a regional representative for the League of Women Voters, to call together representatives of several civic organizations in September. From this meeting emerged a national clearinghouse for disarmament efforts. By the time the Washington conference convened two months later, the coalition had set up an office two blocks away and across the street from the State, War, and Navy departments.

The National Council on Limitation of Armaments, as the clearinghouse was called, was run by Frederick Libby, one of the Friends who originally had promoted the idea. Libby had only recently become a Quaker. He had been a teacher, school administrator, and Congregational pastor. During the war he worked with the Friends' reconstruction unit in France. He returned to work on publicity for the AFSC, which loaned him on salary to the clearinghouse. Libby was assisted by an experienced staff of four, including Laura Puffer Morgan, officer and legislative representative of the American Association of University Women. The National Council was the legislative clearinghouse for a wide range of civic organizations. A few of them were peace groups, to be sure— the AUAM, FOR, WILPF, FPA, and CPU, for example—but most represented quite different constituencies, such as the American Association of University Women and the National League of Women Voters, for example, the Farmers' National Council and the National Women's Trade Union League, the Federal Council of Churches and the Central Conference of American Rabbis, the National Education Association and the National Consumers League, and even the Veterans of Foreign Wars. It was the leaders rather than the rank and file of these organizations who had foreign policy concerns, and they relied on the council to direct such political influence as they could elicit from their memberships. Accordingly, policy was largely made in-house. Years later, Libby recalled that the basic goals of progressive world organization, international disarmament, and education for peace were never formally voted on, but rather "evolved."[6]

The council made itself the source of information and analysis on the proceedings of the arms limitation conference, where most sessions were closed. Laura Puffer Morgan arranged frequent public forums with international delegates to the conference. The council issued posters, letters, press releases, pamphlets, and a biweekly *Bulletin* with a circulation of 5,000. It operated a speakers' bureau and sponsored essay contests. The clearinghouse continued to be the source of information and the foreign policy agent of its participating organizations after the Washington conference achieved a treaty limiting the naval powers to a prescribed ratio in battleships. It was renamed the National Council for Prevention of War (NCPW) and absorbed what was left of the AUAM.

The peace lobby in Washington was reinforced in 1923 by the arrival of Dorothy Detzer, national secretary of the Women's International League for Peace and Freedom. Detzer had worked with Jane Addams and, like Libby, had joined the Friends' reconstruction unit. She became the capital's foremost "lady lobbyist," with access to presidents, secretaries of state, and congressional leaders.[7] Detzer coordinated the American side of a campaign for universal disarmament under League of Nations auspices which also engaged the WILPF in Europe.

The decade-long drive peaked in 1931 and 1932 in connection with a World Disarmament Conference called by the League of Nations. The U.S. WILPF allocated $50,000 for the campaign. It generated a flood of petitions from its members and sponsored a Peace Caravan from the West Coast to Washington that brought to President Herbert Hoover a petition for disarmament with 150,000 signatures. When Franklin Roosevelt assumed the presidency in 1932, the WILPF directed its petitions to him, broadening its network of local and state chapters and working with the FOR and the NCPW. The National Council had over 50 workers on its payroll by that time, and it was sending literature to 125,000 individual contacts and 2,500 newspaper editors. Moreover, the AFSC, FOR, WILPF, WRL, and a committee of the Brethren coordinated their efforts through a Pacifist Action Committee (1930). This was supplemented by an Interorganization Council on Disarmament (1931) of 28 peace groups. Before the would-be coalition could become effective, however, the international campaign for disarmament foundered.

Thus, in the first decade of the interwar years, peace advocates— especially those with a progressive and pacifist orientation—created agencies through which to mobilize public influence. They even tried to create an encompassing peace movement. But they could not set the foreign policy agenda, even for themselves. This was well illustrated by campaigns to secure American participation in the World Court and to outlaw war.

The Permanent Court of International Justice, or World Court as it was popularly known, emerged from the general settlement of World War I. American lawyers Elihu Root and James Scott Brown had worked with the advisory committee that shaped the court, but they were dissatisfied with what they regarded as its too-close ties to the League of Nations. Implicit in their reaction was a line of division that fragmented peace advocacy throughout the 1920s between those who hoped that agencies like the League might resolve political conflict and those who sought a rule of law altogether bereft of politics. The issue of American accession to the World Court was ambiguous. For some it signaled a step toward U.S. participation in the international political order, whereas for others it was a way to keep the United States isolated from European politics while promoting peace. Root and Scott belonged to the latter camp. A World Court made sense to them only if, on the model of the U.S. Supreme Court, it would subordinate political conflicts of interest to an international code of law.

During World War I it became clear to Chicago lawyer Samuel Levinson that the status of warfare itself was a critical gap in international law. As long as war was regarded as a legitimate solution to conflict, he reasoned, there was no real prospect of peace: war must be outlawed by treaty. Questions of defensive and aggressive force aside, there was something so obvious about Levinson's proposition that it formed the basis for an American Committee for the Outlawry of War (1921). And yet, like the World Court, the proposal to make war illegal masked contradictory approaches to foreign policy. If it was coupled with sanctions against nations engaging in warfare, outlawry of war could lead the United States to closer cooperation with the League of Nations system. If on the other hand it was regarded only as a moral or legal principle, then it could be offered as an alternative to collective security, precluding U.S. intervention abroad. It was the latter view that appealed to William Borah and brought the doctrine of outlawry of war into national politics.

Borah was a shrewd and irascible senator from Idaho with ambitions of national influence if not the presidency itself. He had led the fight to defeat Wilson's League of Nations legislation in the Senate on the grounds that it could obligate the United States to fight for the collective security of European powers. He had proposed what became the Washington disarmament conference, and in 1922 he recommended an international economic conference. With this record, he appealed to a peace constituency that included international lawyers like his friend James Scott Brown and also the growing outlawry movement. Indeed, its proponents came to view Borah's support as essential to their political success. For his part, Borah found the concept of outlawry of war useful as a way of derailing other plans that threatened to entangle the nation in collective obligations.

Early in 1923 he introduced a Senate resolution that he hoped would head off President Harding's support of membership in the World Court. Borah would make war a crime, incorporate that principle in a code of international law, and create an international court whose decisions would have only a moral sanction. If this would build a "judicial substitute for war," as Borah claimed, it would also preempt involvement in collective politics that might lead to war. As always, the Idahoan acted independently and in his own interest, but the outlawry advocates were thrilled.

Support for the World Court was growing by this time. Women's groups led the campaign and formed a Woman's World Court Conference on the model of the NCPW. The Foreign Policy Association and League of Women Voters were active. The prospects seemed bright. Suddenly, in June, President Harding reversed himself and attached new conditions to American membership that sharply restricted the court and explicitly cut it away from the League of Nations. Harding died soon afterward, and the World Court issue was inherited by the new president, Calvin Coolidge, who also had to establish his authority within the Republican party, where Borah had great influence. Moreover, the modifications of the court legislation separated league supporters from pro–World Court advocates.

That was the situation for the following year. Liberal pacifists and their allies in the churches tried hard to frame a compromise that could align all the peace groups. In the summer they managed to get outlawry, World Court, and League of Nations advocates to draft a Harmony Plan under which everyone would work for membership in the World Court on the condition that the court itself would outlaw war. Borah would have none of it, and only his political weight could have provided the necessary leverage for an acceptable compromise. The Harmony Plan became but one more competing proposal.

Still, peace advocates organized considerable support for the court when the administration's bill came to the floor of the Senate in December 1925. There it was snarled in debate until yet another condition for U.S. membership was added: the court was prohibited from offering an advisory opinion on any matter that the United States reserved to its exclusive jurisdiction. On that basis the bill passed. In response, the members of the World Court arranged a special meeting and tried to meet the conditions established by the U.S. Congress. The Coolidge administration refused to either interpret or negotiate the congressional position, and the whole effort died by default.

Peace advocates were left with the alternatives that divided them. The LNNPA renewed its commitment to U.S. participation in the League of Nations, but failed to mount a significant public initiative. The WILPF put its energies into disarmament. Pacifists educated people to see war as impractical and immoral. Outlawry activists tried to rebuild their lines. Legalists like James B. Scott continued to argue that international law had to be codified before it could be safely institutionalized. Even the old program of arbitration was revived, partly in response to U.S. military intervention in Nicaragua. And then, in 1927, the decade of peace advocacy took an unexpected twist.

The initiative came from James T. Shotwell, a distinguished professor of history at Columbia University who had been a member of Wilson's wartime committee to study the issues that would surface in the peace settlement.[8] As an advisor to the American peace commission at Paris he had helped to construct the International Labor Organization, and afterward he had campaigned for the League of Nations and other forms of international cooperation. In Europe during the spring of 1927, he suggested to French foreign minister Aristide Briand that European efforts for collective security and disarmament might be facilitated by a bilateral treaty outlawing war, coupled with a revision of U.S. neutrality policy. In April Briand called for a U.S.-French treaty that would outlaw war and pledge arbitration of disputes between them, although he diplomatically refrained from mentioning U.S. neutrality.

The French appeal stimulated alternative responses from peace advocates, politicians, and the State Department. Borah was suspicious of the French offer from the beginning, and as chairman of the Senate Foreign Relations Committee, he was able to enlist Secretary of State Frank B. Kellogg to negotiate with Briand on the basis that the "American government would renounce all war or no war at all."[9] Borah portrayed himself as all dove, opposing a naval expansion program and introducing a resolution on maritime law. In the process he divided peace advocates while Kellogg maneuvered with the French. In March 1928 Briand agreed to a multilateral treaty against all war. Known as the Pact of Paris, or Kellogg-Briand Pact for the Renunciation of War, it was soon signed by most of world's great powers. War was illegal—except that a memorandum attached to the treaty exempted wars of self-defense. Assistant Secretary of State William R. Castle insisted that the pact was no more than "a declaration of principle" and did not bind the nation to any course of action. It promised "co-operation without commitment, independence without isolation," Castle said.[10]

In that respect, it symbolized the mood of a generation that wanted to get beyond war but could not agree on what specific policies that might entail. The felt need of peace advocates for some accomplishment impelled them to compromise and to dilute debate on political issues, which were largely subordinated to the symbolic treaty. The disintegration of the Wilsonian progressive coalition in national politics gave special leverage to politicians like Borah who were willing to exploit both the peace advocates' differences and their desire for at least a repudiation of war. Although peace activists had acquired a new level of public influence, they could neither set the foreign policy agenda nor determine its outcome. The Pact of Paris articulated the minimal common denominator of peace advocacy in the 1920s, but it obscured the issues that would have to be faced in the following decade.

The Emergency Peace Campaign of the 1930s

The Japanese army invaded Manchuria in September 1931. Suddenly peace advocates were presented with an issue more immediate than their long-range designs for the general repudiation of war, a World Court, a League of Nations, disarmament, and international economic relations. What could be done about real aggression? This question was raised in the Interorganization Council on Disarmament when it was formed in April 1932 to coordinate work on behalf of the Geneva conference on disarmament.

Some members of the council, notably liberal pacifists, pressed for a policy of cooperating with the League of Nations to apply economic and diplomatic sanctions against Japan. When the league deferred action, they even promoted a popular boycott of Japanese goods and urged the administration to formalize it. Instead, the government responded with the Stimson Doctrine: the United States would not recognize any territorial changes resulting from aggressive war. That made sense in the light of the Kellogg-Briand declaration, but it did not solve the problem in the Far East. The League of Nations was indecisive with respect to Japan, while its disarmament conference foundered in Geneva. By the of 1933 Japan had consolidated its control of Manchuria, which it organized as a puppet state, while Adolf Hitler had consolidated his control over Germany, which he withdrew from the league. All this profoundly affected American peace advocates.

Throughout the 1920s a core of liberal pacifists had not only campaigned for a popular repudiation of war but had also convinced themselves that there were feasible nonviolent alternatives to warfare. They argued that aggressive force could be constrained by nonmilitary sanctions if applied early and collectively. They also insisted that the nations should address the underlying causes of war, notably economic disparities between nations, which, they felt, exacerbated internal instability and turned it outward in the form of aggression.

The liberal pacifist analysis of international conflict was articulated especially by author and speaker Kirby Page and by socialist leader Norman Thomas. Page had worked with the YMCA's overseas ministry to German prisoners of war. Then, after a brief stint as a pastor, he struck out as a free-lance evangelist for social reform. He was a popular speaker, an editor of *The World Tomorrow,* and the author of numerous books with a large circulation. Many of them popularized the social gospel, but some were serious treatments of war, which was condemned on both moral and pragmatic grounds. Page was a close associate of Norman Thomas, the original editor of *The World Tomorrow* and also a popular speaker. In the 1920s Thomas emerged as the leader of the Socialist party, and he was its perennial presidential candidate after 1928. Both men used revisionist history to discredit World War I and rejected warfare as a method because of its consequences. For each of them the roots of war were the domination of economic power by competitive, oppressive classes and the division of political power among sovereign and ambitious governments. For both of them the alternative to war was social change leading to greater equity, democracy, and stability within and among nations.

This view was pervasive among liberal pacifists. Through their church, socialist, and peace movement contacts abroad, they were acutely conscious of the internal and international threat posed by the growth of nationalistic totalitarianism in Germany, Japan, and the Soviet Union. That threat was magnified, they thought, by the inflexibility of the international economic and political order. Even democratic nations would fight to retain their colonial possessions and privilege, after all. In the absence of international institutions that could accommodate change, collective security had the effect of freezing the status quo. The answer was not to appease aggressors in piecemeal fashion, but rather to create an equitable international order that would reinforce the peaceful resolution of conflict within as well as between nations. This analysis coincided with the thinking of leading internationalists, who like Shotwell, had vested their hope for peace in international organization.

As the League of Nations increasingly appeared incapable of addressing aggression after 1931, either with constraints or with change, pacifists and other internationalists became disillusioned with it. Many of them concluded that the great powers would act together only in their own interests, and that collective security had become little more than a form of military alliance. It seemed to follow that the United States should exercise its influence to reform the international order but, failing that, the nation should not allow itself to be drawn into another war.

There was strong, if inchoate, popular sentiment along these lines. Liberal pacifists helped to catalyze it by raising the issue of revising American neutrality policy—jettisoning the traditional neutral right to trade with belligerents, and adopting *strict* neutrality. In 1934 Dorothy Detzer and the WILPF were instrumental in getting Senator Gerald P. Nye to set up an investigation of the role of the munitions industry in World War I. Frederick Libby, Nevin Sayre, and other pacifists helped to provide material for the investigation and publicized its findings. The

Nye committee concluded that private weapons makers had violated neutrality policy and received excess profits from sales of arms to both sides,
if they had not indeed helped to involve the nation in the war. Accompanied by several sensational books, the Nye disclosures fueled public
interest in legislation for strict neutrality, which was introduced the following spring.[11]

The NCPW staff largely planned the campaign for neutrality revision
that year, carefully coordinating congressional maneuvers with the mobilization of public opinion. They wrote speeches and sponsored radio
talks by members of Congress. They largely arranged a congressional
hearing on neutrality legislation and lobbied intensely. With the WILPF
and FOR they distributed propaganda and solicited pressure from labor
and civic groups. The campaign crested in August and led to the Neutrality Act of 1935. That act abandoned the traditional right of a neutral
to trade with impunity during wartime and instead required an impartial
embargo of all belligerents. It also provided for regulation of the munitions trade. Pacifists were pleased with the legislation, although they
were dissatisfied with the amount of discretion it reserved for the president, who could determine when an embargo should be applied and on
what terms.

Internationalists associated with the Foreign Policy Association and
the League of Nations Association could agree with much of the pacifist
analysis of war, but they had developed no clear position on neutrality.
In part this was because they were still in pursuit of traditional objectives, such as U.S. participation in the World Court, which again reached
the Senate floor in 1934. In part, too, internationalists were divided
among themselves between those who favored cooperation with the
League and those legalists who opposed any entanglement in European
politics. Even internationalists like Shotwell had concluded that strict
American neutrality could facilitate international collective security arrangements, however. That is to say, if the United States relinquished
the right to trade with any belligerent, other powers would be free to act
in concert against an aggressor nation in the knowledge that it would be
cut off from American supplies. Accordingly, neutrality was not a critical
issue for internationalists early in 1935.

They were aroused at the end of January, though, when the Senate
voted down participation in the World Court. Complained Raymond Rich,
the general secretary of the World Peace Foundation, "The peace forces,
having for the most part disregarded the popular, are losing the popu-
lace."[12] With that observation, the stage was set for the Emergency

Peace Campaign. Rich expressed a view prevalent among his colleagues: the public needed to be mobilized for a comprehensive program of internationalism.

A series of meetings among liberal internationalists led to such a program. Popular issues such as the control of arms traffic, restriction of war profits, and disarmament would be coupled with the objectives of world economic cooperation and association with the League of Nations. Internationalists would create a coalition that would include the pacifists, with their political experience and access to civic organizations, but pacifists would not be allowed to dominate the coalition. The coordinating agency would be the National Peace Conference (NPC, 1932), which had been constructed out of the ephemeral Interorganization Council. The nonpacifists expected to dominate the NPC by providing its funds and designating its leadership.

Almost immediately, however, they were outflanked by the pacifists from the FOR, AFSC, NCPW, and WILPF. Leaders in these organizations wanted to create a base in the political center of the country that could resist the threat of totalitarianism and war. Like liberal internationalists, whose legitimacy and elite contacts they valued, the pacifists designed a broad coalition. Like them, they offered a comprehensive program of internationalism. They too hoped to associate America with a League of Nations that would be stronger and more independent, and to stimulate economic cooperation. They too intended to restrict trade and profits in arms. But first and foremost, they wanted to further tighten neutrality in order to "keep the United States from going to war."[13]

The pacifist campaign was initiated by Ray Newton of the AFSC. During World War I Newton had lost his position as instructor at Phillips Exeter Academy and subsequently had worked with Quaker relief in Europe. Later he joined the staff of the Peace Section of the AFSC. In November 1935 the Friends Service Committee approved his plan for a broad peace coalition, agreed to sponsor it, and helped to contact donors. Early the next month over 100 pacifists met at Buck Hills Falls, Pennsylvania, where they outlined the Emergency Peace Campaign. It was agreed that the campaign would be run by a council composed of pacifists acting as individuals rather than as organizational representatives, in order to simplify decision making. The council in turn would select an executive committee to fill in the details of the campaign and appoint staff. The key staff members were Newton, who was executive director, and Kirby Page, who chaired the speaker's bureau, but Frederick Libby of the NCPW and Nevin Sayre of the FOR were also critical to the success of the campaign—Libby because of his contacts on Capitol Hill, Sayre because he had the respect of nonpacifist internationalists, and both of them because, with Page and Newton, they were effective fund-raisers.

Indeed, by the time the National Peace Conference met later in the month, the pacifists had pledges of over $100,000, whereas the liberal internationalists had not even secured the $50,000 they had counted on getting from the Carnegie Endowment. Moreover, although the internationalists named Walter Van Kirk as chair, the well-organized pacifists obtained numerical balance on the steering committee, which was chaired by Nevin Sayre, who also served as president. Finally, the Emergency Peace Campaign was already so comprehensive and specific that the NPC was quickly subordinated to it. On the surface, the campaign offered something to each wing of the coalition: it met the internationalist priority for changes in the international economic and political order; it responded to the pacifist priority of keeping the United States out of war; and it reflected their mutual desire to build a unified public peace movement. In operation, however, the initiative quickly passed to the pacifists.

The EPC was organized through a number of semi-autonomous departments for specific constituencies such as farmers, workers, churches, college youth, and blacks, most them run by experienced pacifists. Pacifist organizations cooperated closely with the campaign, in several cases releasing staff on salary to work with it. Some aspects of the campaign were coordinated directly from the AFSC office in Philadelphia, and lobbying was handled by the Washington staff members of the NCPW and WILPF—notably Libby and Detzer. While the national staff worked through constituent organizations, it also reached the public through public meetings. That is why Kirby Page's position as head of the speakers' bureau was so strategic: he played a key role in the selection of speakers, themes, and material.

The campaign officially opened in April 1936 with a nationwide radio announcement featuring a short message from Eleanor Roosevelt, which was timed to coincide with an already-planned student strike. Some half million high school and college students left their classrooms and demonstrated against war. Annual antiwar student strikes had been held since 1934. They were initiated by groups with socialist or communist leadership, but had acquired a broader base. They were the counterpart to the celebrated "Oxford Pledge" of undergraduates at the University of Oxford to "not fight for King and country in any war." American student antiwar sentiment was folded into the EPC.

The campaign rapidly expanded. Spring meetings and study conferences were held in 278 cities. About 3,500 ministers promised to give five talks on peace over two months. The campaign's labor department developed a labor press service and sent troupes of players through 24 states to present antiwar skits. During the summer the labor and farm departments conducted institutes on foreign affairs, while teams of young people canvassed rural communities regarded as critical in the forthcoming elections and legislative contests. From April on, the focus was the November election. Speakers were sent to over 1,000 events in nearly every state. The legislative department compiled and distributed congressional voting records, targeting specific legislation for public consideration. The national conventions of both major parties were lobbied, and Detzer persuaded Senator Borah to include a strong proneutrality plank in the Republican foreign policy report.

Although the campaign's literature, public meetings, and institutes covered many aspects of international relations, its political objective was to maintain the degree of strict neutrality already achieved and to tighten it still further. The embargo feature of the 1935 Neutrality Act extended only to 29 February 1936, but when the administration and Congress failed to agree on definitive legislation, the original act was extended to 1 May 1937. Moreover, the issue of presidential discretionary authority was raised by Roosevelt's decision not to invoke full economic sanctions against Italy after the invasion of Ethiopia and not to embargo arms to Germany and Italy in connection with the Spanish Civil War. Accordingly, the EPC agenda came to include the goal of making strict neutrality permanent and mandatory.

The campaign burgeoned in January 1937 when 20 area offices were opened and the national staff was expanded to include 150 members. During the winter it promoted a "Neutrality Campaign," with businessman Charles P. Taft II as titular chair. In the spring this phased into a "No-Foreign-War Crusade," inaugurated by another national radio program, this time featuring Admiral Richard E. Byrd as well as Eleanor Roosevelt. By this time, local peace committees (often quite small) had been formed in 2,000 cities, on 500 campuses, and in farm and labor groups. Many civic meetings passed resolutions in favor of neutrality legislation and international economic reform. These were funneled to Congress by the campaign's legislative department, which also lobbied assiduously, distributed press releases, obtained airtime for congressional doves, and circulated its views through Devere Allen's No-Frontier-News Service.

Following the 1937 No-Foreign-War Campaign, the EPC was sharply cut back. Under financial pressure, area offices were closed and most of the 91 members of the field staff were released. After a desultory summer and fall, the National Peace Conference took over the last part of the Emergency Peace Campaign, an attempt to generate support for an international economic conference. Beneath its financial problems, and partly responsible for them, were widening fissures in the coalition. These became painfully clear in the autumn.

In October President Roosevelt called for a "quarantine" of aggression without spelling out the implication for policy. Pacifists worried that he might be headed toward collective military security. They resumed their challenge to his discretionary authority by campaigning for a proposed constitutional amendment that required the passage of a national referendum before Congress could declare war, except in the case of invasion. This amendment had been urged by the Women's Peace Union and had been sponsored by Representative Louis Ludlow of Indiana since 1935, but it had not attracted much attention. The NCPW mobilized its constituencies, helped to organize a hearing on Ludlow's bill, and lobbied hard with legislators. A Gallup poll suggested that 73 percent of the population endorsed the amendment. Even with the utmost effort, the administration prevented the amendment from coming to a floor vote in the House by only 21 votes.

The Ludlow amendment polarized the peace coalition. Pacifists found themselves uncomfortably aligned with conservative isolationists, while nonpacifist internationalists worked for discretionary embargoes against aggressor states. In order to challenge the Ludlow amendment, Clark Eichelberger and his League of Nations Association staff organized a Committee for Concerted Peace Efforts. This grew into a national pressure group endorsed by over 1,000 prominent figures as well as by peace societies such as the LNA and the National Committee on the Cause and Cure of War. Libby's National Council for Prevention of War could no longer presume to speak for a broad coalition. Along with its supporting pacifist groups, it was isolated from the rest of the peace movement.

For a few months the Emergency Peace Campaign played itself out under the auspices of the NPC. The last event was a Conference on World Economic Cooperation at the end of March 1938. Eichelberger directed the program, and establishment internationalists dominated the assembly. Although they could agree with the pacifists on economic issues, they disagreed over neutrality legislation, arguing that it should be flexible enough to distinguish between aggressors and victims. That fixed the split among internationalists between those who supported collective action against aggression and those who opposed America's contributing to the further alignment of the world into armed camps.

Shortly after the March conference Eichelberger organized a coalition of internationalists with which to assault strict neutrality.[14] In the summer of 1940, with Europe again at war, this coalition emerged as the Committee to Defend America by Aiding the Allies. From then until 7 December 1941 Eichelberger's group worked to revise neutrality legislation and build public support for intervention "short of war," while President Roosevelt used his discretionary authority to funnel economic and even military support to Great Britain, then under siege. Well before Pearl Harbor, the opponents of intervention had suffered political defeat.

In the wake of the EPC, liberal pacifists joined socialists led by Norman Thomas to form the Keep America Out of War Congress (6 March 1938). It was a tenuous coalition. The Socialist party was sharply divided over foreign and domestic issues, and was trying to ward off the disruptive influence of infiltrating communists. Outside the party, Thomas faced another communist challenge. Taking their cue from Moscow, the Communist party had set up an American League against War and Fascism (1933) around a Soviet proposal for total disarmament. Some liberal pacifists were attracted until they became convinced that the organization was merely a party front, when they withdrew. Activists in the EPC found themselves competing with communists in the field, especially for youth constituencies. Thomas's Keep America Out of War Congress also competed with the communist front, but by April 1939 his group was virtually "moribund" anyway.[15]

Reluctantly, Thomas associated his group with the right-wing, isolationist America First Committee, which was formed in the summer of 1940, largely in reaction to Eichelberger's Committee to Defend America by Aiding the Allies. That connection only hastened the withdrawal of liberal pacifists, whose organizations, especially the FOR and AFSC, were working with the peace churches and the War Resisters League for the defense of conscientious objectors in the event of war. By the fall of 1941, the Keep America Out of War Congress was a paper organization. Whatever organized opposition to intervention remained did not have the internationalist vision that characterized the Emergency Peace Campaign or the decade and a half of effort that preceded it.

How shall we assess the Emergency Peace Campaign? Certainly, it must be understood in the light of the world's headlong plunge toward war at the time. At the heart of the campaign was a fundamental contra-

Some 15,000 people rallied in Chicago Stadium on 4 December 1940 against adopting military conscription and sending destroyers to Britain. Sponsored by the Committee to Defend America by Keeping Out of War, this demonstration was part of a nationwide debate on neutrality that split the peace movement. *Swarthmore College Peace Collection*

diction. It was a desperate attempt to both foster international coopera-tion and avoid war, but events abroad made those two objectives look like mutually exclusive alternatives. The 1932 disarmament conference failed; collective sanctions could not be applied to check Japanese ag-gression in Manchuria and China, or Italy's invasion of Ethiopia: Germany and Italy could not even be prevented from intervening in the Spanish Civil War; an initiative by President Roosevelt for world economic co-operation failed in 1938; the Nazis dominated Austria with impunity; and Japan, like Germany earlier, withdrew from the League of Nations. As the world became more sharply divided, the American public and the interwar peace movement were ever more polarized. International co-operation came to be identified with collective resistance to aggression, while avoiding war seemed to imply isolation from a world in conflict. In the process, pacifist internationalism lost its political relevance long be-fore the nation went to war.

What is impressive, therefore, is not that the Emergency Peace Campaign failed in its objectives, but rather that it was undertaken on so large a scale. What is instructive is the particular form of the organized peace movement that marshaled the campaign. The leaders of the EPC came into the movement after World War I and became professional staff members. They found careers in the peace reform. Each of them had an established set of contacts. Some of them, like Frederick Libby and Kirby Page, were movement entrepreneurs; that is, they developed programs for which they organized support and raised funds. Most of them exercised great discretion in forming policy for their organizations.

The EPC itself reflected those leadership characteristics. Its staff people were mainly loaned on salary by its constituent groups. Its departments were semi-autonomous, and leaders like Dorothy Detzer and Kirby Page were often chosen for the experience and contacts they already enjoyed (as Clark Eichelberger was chosen to direct the world economic conference program). Accordingly, the individual members of the leadership team exercised considerable independence. Their work for the EPC did not diminish their loyalty to the organizations and goals with which they were affiliated. Accordingly, the leadership structure of the campaign neither mitigated the conflicts of ideals and interest among its constituent groups nor cultivated cohesiveness among its leaders.

On the other hand, the structure of the EPC did facilitate specialization and outreach through its highly differentiated member groups. There were liberal internationalists with access to the intellectual and policy-making elite and also pacifists with access to labor and the Socialist party, leaders from the major Protestant churches as well as a strong core of Quakers. There were groups with small staffs and no memberships that specialized in media—Devere Allen's No-Frontier-News Service, for example, and World Peaceways (which solicited $800,000 of free print space between 1931 and 1937 and circulated ads to 25 million Americans in 1938). There were also membership groups such as the WILPF (which peaked at 14,000 members in 1938), and the LNA (about 10,000 members). Some groups served limited constituencies, others cultivated civic and economic associations outside the peace movement. Like the Foreign Policy Association, some specialized in research and education; like the National Council for Prevention of War, others engaged in political pressure and lobbying. The EPC's loose alignment of leaders gave it broad access to the public, but its message was diluted alternately by the particular goals of its member groups and by compromise among them.

Accordingly, public opinion could be turned into political pressure only on a few issues such as neutrality legislation, and then only as long as compromise could be sustained.

The EPC was not designed to be a membership organization, and it explicitly refrained from developing its own activist cadre. It was intended to work through existing groups and to supplement them with public appeals that would activate supporters of the movement's goals. It appears the campaign did significantly increase public pressure on Congress, and it collected some 23,000 names on pacifist enrollment cards, but it did not significantly increase the membership of its member organizations. In fact, it was sometimes perceived by member groups as an organizational threat. Mildred Scott Olmsted of the WILPF vigorously objected to the setting up of regional EPC offices, for example, as violating the principle of working through the constituent groups. To Frederick Libby, among others, the campaign seemed to divert money from traditional donors while draining its sponsors. Thus, the very leverage that liberal pacifists achieved by assuming financial responsibility proved to be a source of tension between them and the EPC itself. In sum, with respect to its leadership, constituency, and funding, the campaign could not develop its own exclusive base of support, and yet the demands of its program strained its relationship with the peace groups on which it relied.

It was, after all, an *emergency* peace campaign. It articulated a powerful current of public opposition to involvement in war. It translated that sentiment into political pressure, significantly contributing to the revision of neutrality policy and probably delaying American involvement in the European war. Despite a heroic attempt, however, it did not imbue the popular desire to avoid war with an international vision. Peace advocacy was both raised to a high level of political involvement and polarized by the political issues in which it engaged.

The result was ironic. As internationalism became identified with collective security from 1938 to 1941, its liberal values were unconditionally committed to one side in a polarized world. As pacifism was increasingly associated with moralism and isolationism during the same period, it was interpreted as being irrelevant to political reality. The basis was laid then for the myth that the desire to avoid war had led only to inaction and appeasement in the face of militant totalitarianism. Conveniently forgotten were the hardheaded analyses of the international system by Kirby Page, Norman Thomas, and others, their early warnings about authoritarian governments, and the fact that liberal pacifists, along with other internationalists, had sought American leadership in reforming international relations.

Many of the approaches they had proposed were institutionalized during and after World War II: international organization, including collective security, negotiated international monetary and economic relationships, an end to colonies, cooperation for social and cultural progress, the formal recognition of nongovernmental organizations, and even the extension of international law in the form of the Nuremburg trials and declarations of universal human rights. All of these achievements were rightly identified with victory over the Axis powers. Wrongly, however, they were identified exclusively with those internationalists who had early supported American intervention in the war and who emerged dominant from it. The polarization of the Emergency Peace Campaign reinforced the impression that it had been the work of moralists and isolationists. Otherwise, it might have been remembered as an eclectic coalition of peace advocates who desperately attempted to forge a common political force—a campaign that epitomized an interwar peace movement of breadth and specialization, vision and professionalism, international contacts and national organization, common values and sharply divergent priorities.

Chapter Four

New Reference Points, 1941–1955

Once more the United States mobilized for war, this time on a world scale. Men and munitions flowed to debarkation ports on both the East and West coasts, then abroad to engage the Germans in North Africa and the Japanese in the Pacific. Agencies forged to deal with the Great Depression were converted to war use. Many others were added. The nation was driven by a unity of purpose rare in American history. The Asian and European fronts were linked in a common threat to national security that was understood to be not only military but also ideological: this was a war of democracy against dictatorship.

Differences between the United States and the Soviet Union were subsumed in their common struggle for survival, until toward the end of the war Americans perceived a new threat from Stalinist Russia that rapidly acquired global dimensions. Within half a decade of victory over the Nazis and Japanese, the superpowers found themselves locked in a Cold War. A historic isolation from world affairs was left behind, although there remained a pervasive mistrust of foreign influence. Internationalism dominated American foreign policy. It was a Cold War version, though, in which responsibility in world affairs was associated with national security and the defense of a free world where the extent of America's power meant that its leadership was not seriously challenged.

Nazi aggression and Soviet expansion accented divisions between liberal internationalists and liberal pacifists for two decades after 1935. Developments within each wing of the peace movement in that period created new reference points for peace advocates when, in the mid-

In a direct, nonviolent challenge to segregation, George Houser (*front*), Bayard Rustin (*back, center*), and an integrated team from the Congress of Racial Equality boarded busses for the Journey of Reconciliation into the South in April 1947. Actions such as this were forerunners of the radical pacifism of the 1960s. *Swarthmore College Peace Collection*

1950s, atmospheric nuclear testing offered them an issue on which to build a new coalition and challenge the Cold War arms race.

Pacifist Wartime Witness

During World War II absolute pacifists were reduced to a small, isolated minority—hardly 0.5 percent of the population.[1] Very few of them actively challenged the war effort, although they maintained their witness against war itself. The Fellowship of Reconciliation protested saturation bombing of German cities, for example, and secured the endorsement of 28 religious leaders to an exposé of it called *Massacre by Bombing*. The FOR also rallied opposition to the forced relocation of thousands of Japanese Americans from their West Coast homes and jobs and, with the AFSC, tried to mitigate the hardships of displacement. Beyond this, the experience of pacifists in World War I prepared them for World War II in at least three respects: their isolation, their opportunities for humanitarian service, and the challenge to their civil liberties, especially the right of conscientious objection.

The Isolated Pacifist Community   Absolute pacifists anticipated that they would be repudiated again by the public and that their civil liberties would be curtailed. There was indeed repression, but it was much less severe than earlier. In some measure this may have been because after Pearl Harbor the nation swung so fully behind the war effort that it was not necessary to mobilize opinion with the belligerence of World War I. In part, disillusionment with the earlier experience made belligerency itself suspect. The nation's churches overwhelmingly endorsed the new war effort, for example, but by and large support was subdued by a sense of tragedy. Some prominent Protestants remained faithful to the absolute pacifism they had espoused in the interwar period.

The FOR formulated a plan for wartime as early as 1935, and it was applied in 1940 with the development of small, mutually reinforcing groups of pacifists.[2] The strategy appeared to meet the need for solidarity in crisis, as the organization's membership grew from 4,271 to 12,526 between 1935 and 1941, and to nearly 15,000 by 1944. Its budget increased by two-fifths during the war, and by 1944 it had 20 paid staff members and 400 local chapters as well as groups in most of the C.O. camps. The War Resisters League also grew during the war. Its membership rose from 900 in 1939 to over 2,300 in 1945, while its budget quadrupled.[3] Meanwhile, the historic peace churches held relatively steadfast and, indeed, the proportion of C.O.'s to the total number of inductees was three times that of World War I.

On the other hand, groups that had enlisted nonpacifists in peace efforts declined sharply. The WILPF was reduced by two-thirds between 1939 and 1946, presumably down to its absolute pacifist core. The pacifist Catholic Worker Movement, formed in 1933 by French-born Peter Maurin and American Dorothy Day, lost the support of numerous people who had been attracted to its humanitarian programs for the poor.[4] Antiwar coalitions like the Keep America Out of War Congress and the National Peace Conference disintegrated, and the NCPW was reduced to the person of Fred Libby, nominally continuing until his death in 1953. Isolated, liberal pacifists and peace churches put their energy into refugee work and the administration of C.O. services.

Humanitarian Service   With their many contacts abroad, leaders in the AFSC and FOR had been acutely aware of rising Nazi repression early in the 1930s. International centers established in several European cities by American and British Quakers became havens for persecuted people. It was the flood of refugees from the Spanish Civil War of 1936, though, that convinced the AFSC that, as its executive secretary, Clarence Pickett, recalled, "the days of war relief were not over."[5] The Service Committee plunged into the work of assisting Spanish children, in which it cooperated with British Friends and international agencies. Their relief programs followed civilian refugees and the remnants of the Republican army into southern France.

Within two years there were refugees from Nazi persecution all over Europe. Relocation services were added to relief, often in cooperation with Jewish organizations (a third of the people fleeing Germany in 1938 were Christians). Along with other agencies, the AFSC lobbied in vain for modifications of U.S. immigration restrictions on refugees. Pickett played a leading role in organizing relief work, and he served on the executive committees of Jewish and Protestant refugee agencies. Within half a year of the outbreak of war in September 1939, a British blockade left innumerable Europeans facing starvation. Pickett and his colleagues mounted a large relief program for children in southern France, at one point securing the intervention of President Roosevelt to facilitate it. By that time, the AFSC had gone far beyond the precedents with which it began in 1917.

Famine relief and refugee work under the Quaker red and black eight-pointed star continued throughout the war.[6] It greatly expanded afterward, when there were some 40 million displaced persons in Europe. The AFSC and peace churches joined with the United Nations Relief and Rehabilitation Administration and numerous voluntary associations that were sustaining and relocating refugees. In recognition of the Quaker record, the 1947 Nobel Peace Prize was awarded jointly to the AFSC and the Friends Service Council (of Great Britain, 1927). Refugee work was not unique to pacifists, of course, but the Nobel committee explicitly recognized the pacifist principles that led to what its chairman called "the silent help from the nameless to the nameless."[7]

In the following years the AFSC and the other peace churches extended their relief and reconciliation services throughout the world. Indeed, the AFSC used its share of the Nobel Peace Prize to promote peace between the United States and the Soviet Union.[8] Citizen service abroad increasingly became an integral part of the broad American peace movement and linked it to international nongovernmental organizations.

Conscientious Objectors   Anticipating war, the three major peace churches—Friends, Mennonites, and Brethren—formed committees in 1939 and 1940 to protect the interests of conscientious objectors. The most important of these committees was the War Problems Committee, created by Quakers. The Roosevelt administration avoided a peacetime draft until a well-financed campaign by the Military Training Camps Association got conscription legislation before Congress in 1940.[9] At that point the peace churches coalesced behind Paul Comly French, a Quaker who had directed the Federal Writers Project, and E. Raymond Wilson, associate secretary of the AFSC Peace Section. After intensive lobbying, they secured exemption from military service for individuals whose objection was based on religious training and belief, provided that they were assigned to work of national importance under civilian administration. There were difficulties: "work of national importance" was not defined, nonreligious objectors were not provided for, and the whole process was placed in the Selective Service Administration, which was headed by military officers.

French and Wilson pressed on, encouraged by director Colonel Lewis Hershey of the Selective Service to believe they might be given responsibility for administering programs of alternative service for C.O.'s. A National Service Board for Religious Objectors (NSBRO) was formed to represent all interested parties to the Selective Service.[10] On 6 February 1941, after the peace churches agreed to take on the burden of funding service programs, President Roosevelt authorized the Selective Service director to create what became the Civilian Public Service (CPS).

Under the plan, conscientious objectors in CPS were to be assigned primarily to soil conservation and reforestation projects. The government was to provide sites, transportation, technical supervision, and equipment; but the peace churches were responsible for onsite administration and subsistence costs. By the time CPS ended in 1947, it had established 67 camps and more than 130 detached service units for over 11,000 C.O.'s from some 200 sects and denominations or with no religious affiliation at all.[11] Most of the men worked on conservation projects—dull, unproductive work for the high level of education often characteristic of them. Some were furloughed to farms, and about 2,000 were employed in mental hospitals and training schools. About 500 were used as guinea pigs in medical and scientific research.

Although at the outset the role of the churches and the NSBRO was ambiguous, the Selective Service soon clarified it: "the draft is under United States government operation. Conscientious objectors are draftees just as soldiers are. . . . The peace churches are only camp managers."[12] Not only were CPS men essentially under military jurisdiction, but their work was far from the "moral equivalent of war," which they had been led to expect.[13] Increasingly, objectors criticized the church leaders who, they felt, had led them into a surrogate conscription. Some expressed their frustration by work slowdowns and strikes. Others walked out of CPS camps and courted imprisonment, concluding that conscription itself and not military service was the essence of militarism. That belief was not unique to radical C.O.'s. It was the springboard of postwar efforts to end Selective Service and to preclude peacetime conscription.

The campaign was led by the Friends Committee on National Legislation (FCNL, 1943), which was set up when pacifists encountered legislative roadblocks in relation to conscription, relief and reconstruction, international organization, and civil liberties.[14] The FCNL was a lobby— the first lobby of a Protestant church, observed its first executive secretary, E. Raymond Wilson. It was organized to keep Friends informed about pending legislation, to generate public pressure on selected issues, and to work on Capitol Hill. The FCNL quickly challenged a rider to a defense appropriation act that prohibited the use of military funds for overseas work by C.O.'s. Similarly, it tried to get Congress to allocate for humanitarian purposes money collected as wages for C.O. services to civilians. Neither campaign was successful. Nor was the FCNL able to end peacetime conscription, which continued until 1972. It was successful, however, in defeating universal military training in the United States.

Proposals for that program were formulated in 1944, and they were pushed by the military and the Truman administration after the war. In response, peace and other civic groups formed a coalition agency, the National Council against Conscription. The FCNL mainly coordinated legislative strategy, while the AFSC, FOR, and WILPF committed personnel and special funds. The pacifists enlisted major educational, religious, farm, and labor associations. Given this widespread opposition, universal military training did not come to a vote in the House of Representatives until 1952, when it was turned down. In the legislative fight liberal pacifists effectively returned to the kind of political action devised by the NCPW in the disarmament campaigns of the 1920s. That their victory was so singular suggested the new circumstances facing them: the increasingly entrenched institutions of military security, a Cold War that was used to justify those institutions, and a form of internationalism that was conditioned by the Cold War perspective. Moreover, although little noticed at the time, to the political left of liberal pacifists there had developed a modern form of radical pacifism.

Radical Pacifists and Nonviolent Direct Action

The word *radical* is difficult. Often it is used to imply "extreme." Perhaps it is best approached in the sense of "root"—seeking the basic cause of injustice or war, for example, or refusing to compromise on fundamental principle. With respect to the tactics of social movements, it implies confrontation rather than political compromise. Absolute pacifists became radical insofar as they elected to confront war and injustice and identified those conditions as the result of social systems rather than of specific events or decisions. The word is also a term of opprobrium. It is used to stereotype and dismiss all manner of movements, and therefore it is very often ambiguous. To characterize an individual or organization as radical can be very misleading, so that with respect to pacifism the term radical is useful only in a relative sense to suggest a particular trend of thought and action.

That line of thought was anticipated in some respects by the Garrisonian nonresistants of the early nineteenth century. Christians are obligated to work for justice, they believed, but they are prohibited from using the instruments of war. They reasoned further that since governments are based on the rule of military force, Christians should not cooperate with them. The Garrisonian formula broke apart when it was faced by an apparently just war against slavery, but a half century later the liberal pacifists of World War I felt both impelled to engage in social action and prohibited from using violence. Implicitly, they introduced a distinction the Garrisonians had not made: they distinguished between force and violence in the struggle for justice. The quandary they faced, then, was to identify effective forms of nonviolent force. The problem was put in this way by several liberal pacifists, notably by a distinguished Unitarian minister and reformer, John Haynes Holmes.

In his influential book, *New Wars for Old* (1916), Holmes asserted that there was power in nonviolence, that it could be an effective force. He was not really able demonstrate that point, however, and so when he first heard of Mohandas K. Gandhi, Holmes seized upon the Indian's example and popularized it. Throughout the 1920s Gandhi developed political initiatives for independence in India which he interpreted as *satyagraha,* or truth-force. His American devotees then understood him only in the familiar terms of Jesus' self-sacrificing love. In Europe, where various socialist groups sought to restructure society during the decade, Gandhi's thought was introduced by French novelist and biographer Romain Rolland in the hope that the Mahatma's example might generate a revolutionary ethos uncorrupted by violence. It did not. In the 1930s, with apparently no other alternative than violence, totalitarianism gripped Central Europe and raised the specter of war. By that time, some American pacifists were taking a deeper look at Gandhi's movement. [15]

For a brief time in the mid-1930s factional conflicts in both the Socialist party and the FOR revolved around the abstract issue of whether violence should be endorsed if it seemed necessary to obtain social justice. The socialists never recovered from the bitter divisiveness that swirled around that question. The FOR emerged all the stronger for dealing with it. Its council adopted the principle that staff members could endorse nonviolent coercion but not more extreme methods. Distinguishing between coercion and violence, it assumed that nonviolence involved social as well as spiritual power.

Its judgment was influenced by the writing of Richard B. Gregg. Trained in law and active in the labor movement, Gregg worked in the Gandhian movement for over three years. From his experience in India he produced *The Power of Non-Violence* (1934), a book that transformed Gandhi from a saint into a practical leader, and *satyagraha* from sacrificial love to a form of nonviolent coercion. It could now be understood as a process of redistributing power to reach an approximation of justice. That approach was explored by theologian Reinhold Niebuhr and by liberal pacifists Devere Allen and Kirby Page. All three were involved in the Socialist party and the FOR when those were disrupted over the issue of violence in the cause of justice. Each of them valued the political realism implied in Gregg's analysis because it implied a form of social struggle in which nonviolent means were consonant with the ideal of justice. This idea was developed in the light of western sociology by Krishnalal Shridharani, an Indian who had participated in the Gandhian movement. Shridharani frankly acknowledged that *satyagraha* included an element of compulsion, but he interpreted it as a method of action that was also open to self-criticism and social cooperation. The concept of nonviolence thus developed was given organizational form by A. J. Muste and a group of young people in Chicago.

An absolute pacifist during World War I, Muste afterward entered the labor movement, where he employed nonviolent techniques in a 1919 textile strike. In the 1920s he experienced the outright oppression of workers. He became enmeshed in labor agitation and the factional politics of the left as the Great Depression deepened in the early 1930s. He increasingly qualified his pacifism. Counting himself a revolutionary Marxist, he began to interpret social conflict as virtual civil war, and he defended the use of violence in it. Then, on a trip to Europe in 1936, Muste found himself suddenly restored to his Christian and pacifist roots. Still a revolutionary, he rejected the violence and manipulation of political radicals. He was committed to fundamental but nonviolent social change. Returning to the United States, he rejoined the FOR, becoming its executive secretary in 1940. By that time he had helped to get Shridharani's *War without Violence* published and had written his own *Nonviolence in an Aggressive World.*

Muste brought onto the FOR staff young pacifists interested in Gandhian nonviolence, notably George Houser and Bayard Rustin, who had been imprisoned for draft resistance, and James Farmer. In 1942 he supported their proposal to build a group in Chicago that would experiment with nonviolent direct action for civil rights. They formed a Committee of Racial Equality, whose acronym, CORE, conveyed their intention "to get at the roots of the problem of discrimination."[16] As the Chicago experiments were picked up in other cities, the committee evolved into the national Congress of Racial Equality (CORE, 1943).[17] Muste retained Rustin, Houser, and Farmer on the FOR staff and provided other assistance to the civil rights organization. Although CORE maintained its own autonomy, its local chapters often included FOR members who challenged segregation in specific situations, drawing explicitly on Gandhian techniques of nonviolent direct action for demonstrations and sit-ins.

Meanwhile, pacifism was being radicalized in the CPS camps. In 1940 Muste aligned the FOR with the peace churches in the administration of CPS until, disillusioned, he led the organization out of the NSBRO four years later. Beyond his frustration with the bureaucracy, he was responsive to a number of C.O.'s who were employing noncooperation for the redress of unacceptable prison conditions, including racial segregation. These were often men from nonpacifist churches or without any religious affiliation, and they were by and large well educated. Their most dramatic resistance came in prisons, where they staged hunger strikes to protest racial segregation and constraints on civil liberties. A group of 18 integrated the dining hall at the Danbury Correctional Institution after 135 days of noncooperation.

As historian Lawrence Wittner has shown, the CPS experience had a radicalizing effect on a significant minority of C.O.'s.[18] From witnessing to their individual beliefs, these men began to act for social justice; they tried radical noncooperation and they survived. Exhilarated by the success of their nonviolent confrontation, some of them even talked seriously about revolutionary pacifism: "a resistance that will renounce . . . essentially violent acts . . . is equally unyielding to tyranny, but at the same time is humble, straightforward, and loving."[19] After the war, the existence of this minority of radical pacifists posed a challenge for the Fellowship of Reconciliation and the War Resisters League. The FOR maintained its traditional emphasis that the application of nonviolence was a personal decision, but the WRL shifted leftward under the impact of CPS veterans and other advocates of radical pacifism. Increasingly, the confrontational experience of CPS was extended to a radical critique of society.

The few radical pacifists in 1945 and 1946 associated loosely in a Committee for Non-Violent Revolution. Although its name was an important clue to their long-term goals, the committee itself was absorbed by the more enduring Peacemakers (1948). "More Gandhian and less Marxist" than the ephemeral committee, Peacemakers was a loose network of absolute pacifist groups whose most striking contribution was the tactic of refusing to pay federal taxes on the ground that they subsidized the military.[20] The small minority of pacifists were all but lost in the population. As the Cold War chilled the 1940s, some of them joined pacifist cooperatives, where they could pursue their ideals in common isolation. If they could not inaugurate a social revolution, they reasoned, they could at least "begin to live as free men."[21]

Some radical pacifists moved into CORE and similar endeavors, which "constituted our attempts to apply effectively on the outside the nonviolent methods of protest which we had used in prison," as Jim Peck recalled. "Somehow it seemed a continuation of the same struggle."[22] For two decades after its formation, CORE was largely funded by the FOR, which also experimented with direct nonviolent action on its own. CORE sponsored annual workshops on nonviolent direct action, and in 1947 it challenged segregation in interstate transportation by sponsoring an interracial trip into the South on a commercial bus. All 16 of the "freedom riders" were arrested and sentenced by southern courts. CORE's membership declined significantly by 1956; but when Martin Luther King, Jr., emerged as a proponent of nonviolent direct action in the Montgomery bus boycott that year, he had the help of experienced FOR-CORE staff members. Gandhi had become Americanized.

Thus, within liberal pacifism and as an extension of it there grew a form of pacifism that was radical in the sense that it confronted injustice directly with nonviolent action. Rooted in American labor history and in Gandhianism, radical pacifism was sharpened in opposition to CPS during World War II and was attached to the civil rights movement during and after the war. Hardly noticed outside pacifist circles before the mid-1950s radical pacifism in this sense acquired a solid if small coterie of adherents. It offered a new reference point to the peace movement.

Internationalists during and after World War II

World War II gave internationalists a "second chance," an opportunity to redeem the defeat of the League of Nations 20 years before.[23] This time they did not fail. They contributed to the design of a United Nations, worked closely with the State Department to popularize the new organization, and helped to create a consensus for American participation in it. In the process, they anticipated issues that modified internationalism after the military and diplomatic victories of 1945.

A universal federation or a great-power consortium: these alternative visions of a postwar order were veiled in the common cause to secure a national consensus for the United Nations and the compromises that defined it. The promise of that victory was clouded, however, by the advent of nuclear weapons. Perceiving a new threat to peace, some scientists and other intellectuals stressed the importance of constructing a stronger, even transnational world government. By 1948 they generated a substantial public movement behind that idea. In the meantime, though, the wartime alliance of great powers became polarized between communist and noncommunist blocs. The attraction of world government evaporated. Real warfare in Korea sealed a broad consensus for employing national force in the pursuit of international peace and order. A kind of Cold War internationalism pervaded the nation's intellectual and political elite.

The U.N. Campaign Internationalists began to think about the postwar order soon after the outbreak of war in Europe in 1939. Using the League of Nations Association as a base, James T. Shotwell assembled a Commission to Study the Organization of Peace with Clark Eichelberger as director. Organizations such as the Association of University Women, the Church Peace Union, and the National Board of the YWCA cooperated. The commission enrolled experts to prepare a series of reports on postwar organization, sponsored a radio series, and encouraged the formation of public study groups. Meanwhile, the Council on Foreign Relations stimulated Secretary of State Cordell Hull to initiate studies on postwar issues within the State Department.[24] Preoccupied with the European war and a mounting crisis in Asia through 1941, the government let its planning lapse. The LNA faltered with the demise of the League of Nations. The Commission to Study the Organization of Peace continued, but internationalists invested most of their resources to secure aid for beleaguered Great Britain. When the United States entered World War II, the construction of a postwar world order had become fully identified with the war effort itself.

By then, other internationalist groups had entered the field of postwar planning. One of them was Federal Union, Inc. (1939), which capitalized on a revival of journalist Clarence Streit's 1935 book *Union Now.*[25] Streit argued for an Anglo-American federation of democratic nations, an idea that had a wartime appeal. In effect, it would be a collective security organization purged of totalitarian states such as Germany and the Soviet Union. A second group was the Commission on a Just and Durable Peace, established by the Federal Council of Churches early in 1940.[26] To a large extent, it was the project of John Foster Dulles, a prominent Presbyterian international lawyer and future secretary of state. Internationalists were poised to promote some form of international organization.

The form was largely determined for them by the exigencies of war. The very term "United Nations" was originally applied to the 26 countries allied against the Axis powers in January 1942. The United Nations Organization, chartered at San Francisco in 1945, was a product of that wartime alliance, and its structure reflected the relationships among the Allies, especially the United States, Great Britain, and the Soviet Union. Since unconditional surrender was demanded of the Axis after January 1943, the main role of diplomacy was to coordinate the war effort. Postwar planning was not allowed to disrupt that unity. That was one reason for the caution and secrecy with which the Roosevelt administration developed its plans for an international organization.

There were at least two other reasons. For one thing, there was the painful memory of the U.S. rejection of the League of Nations. Roosevelt had campaigned for the League as a 1920 vice presidential candidate, and Secretary of State Cordell Hull had been a Democratic congressman from Tennessee then. Both of them took pains to avoid repeating Wilson's mistakes. In particular, they cultivated a bipartisan consensus and avoided controversy that might disrupt it. In addition, Hull jealously guarded his own policy-making role in the State Department, which, however, he did not administer very efficiently (he was 70 and often ill when the nation went to war). The greatest stimulus for postwar thinking in the department came from Undersecretary of State Sumner Welles, an experienced diplomat and confidant of the president, but Hull found ways to keep the work under his own control, even forcing Welles's retirement in 1943.[27]

By that time, leading internationalists from the the private sector were involved in State Department planning. They included Norman H. Davis of the Council on Foreign Relations; Hamilton Fish Armstrong, editor of *Foreign Affairs*; James T. Shotwell; and Clark Eichelberger. While they fed ideas into the secretive labyrinth of the government, these leaders also broadened public discussion of the postwar world order.

Their campaign surged once America was at war and the neutrality issue was settled. Eichelberger stepped up the work of the Commission to Study the Organization of Peace. With a half million dollars from the Carnegie Endowment, he and Shotwell set up regional centers across the country to coordinate the efforts of local groups and national organizations such as the Commission to Study, LNA, Foreign Policy Association, and Woodrow Wilson Foundation. Streit's Federal Union endorsed a world organization that would include the Soviet Union, China, and other countries with which the United States shared national interests, while Dulles's Commission on a Just and Durable Peace enlisted church leaders for a strong world government that would considerably restrict national sovereignty. Several state legislatures endorsed some form of world government.

The idea of U.S. participation in a world organization drew support from 73 percent of people polled in mid-1942, compared to 50 percent in 1941 and 33 percent in 1937.[28] This enthusiasm reflected a generalized desire to give point to the war effort. It was accompanied by a revival of interest in Woodrow Wilson. Books, articles, and even a Broadway play adulated the former president and popularized the view that World War II resulted from the rejection of his vision for peace. In 1942 that vision was undefined and relatively untroubled by political choices. Although isolationism was giving way to the ideal of active American leadership in the world, the terms of that role were as yet unclear.

Already in that year, the issue was taken up by leaders beyond the peace societies. Former president Herbert Hoover, writing with career diplomat Hugh Gibson, injected a note of cautious realism in a best-seller, *The Problems of Lasting Peace*. Wendell Willkie, the 1940 Republican presidential candidate, moved well beyond Hoover to lobby for internationalism in the party. On the Democratic side, Vice President Henry Wallace made a dramatic appeal to turn from national wars to a "people's peace," from power politics to a "century of the common man." Sumner Welles and Minnesota governor Harold Stassen supplemented Wallace's rhetoric with concrete proposals for a strong world federation with police power. In the State Department, Hull tried to retain the initiative, but his effort was hampered by his policy of shrouding postwar planning in secrecy. That was something of a pattern. When, toward the end of 1942, Roosevelt encouraged Clark Eichelberger to rally support for international organization through the LNA, the president cautioned that the effort should not be seen as an extension of administration policy; he wanted bipartisan public pressure.

Eichelberger aligned several groups in a Citizens Council for the United Nations, a coalition that might transform the anti-Axis alliance into "the nucleus of the final United Nations of the world," and persuade America "to take its rightful place in the organization of nations."[29] About the same time, John Foster Dulles's Commission on a Just and Durable Peace got prestigious endorsements for its widely distributed statement of "Six Pillars of Peace" (all of them internationalist). By 1943 over a dozen regional commissions were bringing together business, labor, and community leaders, distributing literature to hundreds of local groups and training people for a sustained campaign on behalf of international organization.

As the war ground on with little indication of the administration's postwar plans, a bipartisan core of congressional internationalists became involved. Those in the Senate were especially important because of the upper chamber's power to ratify treaties. Recalling the debacle of 1918–19, they wanted to commit the country in advance to participate in a collective security association, and they were not about to be reigned in by the president. In March 1943 Republican senators Joseph Ball and Harold Burton and Democrats Lister Hill and Carl Hatch introduced a resolution endorsing a postwar international organization. Popularly dubbed the B_2H_2 resolution, it crystallized administration and public debate.

Internationalist groups rallied behind the B_2H_2 resolution. Eichelberger converted the Citizens Council into a new United Nations Association for the explicit purpose of supporting the legislation. Funded by individual patrons and by the Carnegie Endowment, the UNA did not enroll individual members. It coordinated the work of local committees, many of

them former LNA branches, and it established a congressional committee for electoral action. The UNA was hardly underway when journalist
and editor W. W. Waymack persuaded several peace organizations to
cooperate on B_2H_2 through a Non-Partisan Council to Win the Peace.[30]
About the same time, a Women's Action Committee for Victory and Lasting Peace was formed to coordinate the work of women's organizations.
Thus, liberal internationalists had coalesced around a common campaign
by mid-1943. Although still heavily dependent on funding from a few
wealthy patrons and the generous Carnegie Endowment, they were organized for political action along lines that had been learned in the interwar period.

The campaign grew to massive proportions by the end of the summer.
Senators reported a heavy flow of mail during the spring, overwhelmingly
in support of an association of nations. By May nearly three-fourths of
the people polled favored American participation in an international police
force.[31] Nonetheless, chairman Tom Connally followed Hull's cautious
line and kept the B_2H_2 resolution on hold in the Senate Foreign Relations
Committee. In July the internationalist senators threatened to force a
floor vote when the chamber reconvened in the fall. Internationalist
groups stepped up their efforts. With funding from CEIP and help from
the Women's Action Committee, the UNA fielded eight bipartisan teams
of legislators on intensive tours throughout the nation. Liberal pacifists
in the AFSC and WILPF became involved. Labor unions and the National
Association of Manufacturers went on record for postwar collective security, as did the American Legion and the Veterans of Foreign Wars.
Teams of ministers preached internationalism at church and civic meetings in over a hundred cities. Isolationism was neutralized even in the
Republican party.

Threaded through the campaign was the veneration of Wilson's earlier
vision and Wendell Willkie's new one. The Republican had made a round-
the-world trip in the fall of 1942. The following spring he shared his journey in *One World,* concluding with an appeal for American leadership in
the creation of global peace and freedom. For readers hungry to know
better the world into which they had been plunged, the book was a mental journey from which there was no turning back. By June it had sold a
million copies. It was also widely distributed in a cheap paper edition, and
in magazines and newspapers. *One World* was an important part of the
B_2H_2 equation.

When Congress reconvened, initiative passed to the House of Representatives, where J. William Fulbright had introduced a resolution for

Women discussed proposals for a United Nations Organization in 1945 as part of a broadly based mobilization to form a public consensus behind liberal internationalism during World War II. *Swarthmore College Peace Collection*

U.S. participation in a collective security organization. The legislation was quite general, and it passed overwhelmingly. With the president's encouragement, Connally's committee proposed a similarly vague resolution in the Senate, but the internationalist core there held out for stronger language. In the midst of Senate debate, the foreign ministers of the four major allies—the United States, Great Britain, the Soviet Union, and China—signed an agreement in Moscow that included a pledge to create a collective security organization based on the sovereign equality of states. That pledge was incorporated into the Senate resolution, which passed with only five dissenting votes. Roosevelt and Hull had their bipartisan base of support in the public and the Congress for an international postwar policy. The battle was half won.

The other half of the task was to define and ratify an association of nations. At this point the internationalist groups became the captives of the very consensus they had achieved. Whatever their reservations about the administration's plan, they felt obligated to sell it to the public.

The momentum of their crusade continued. In 1944 the UNA absorbed much of the League of Nations Association's membership, and in February 1945 the LNA was renamed the American Association for the United Nations. Yet another coalition agency was set up, the United Nations Educational Campaign Committee, which developed a strong working relationship with the State Department. But the broad consensus on internationalism was fragile. It could not bear the weight of disagreement over specific issues. The formulation of policy was reserved to administration as it negotiated with its wartime allies and with a bipartisan committee of Senate leaders.

Negotiations got underway seriously after Roosevelt met with Winston Churchill and Joseph Stalin at Tehran in November 1943. By the following April the State Department had worked out its proposals. The administration's plan was approved by a bipartisan committee of Senate leaders that Hull had convened, and it became the basis of a four-power conference at Dumbarton Oaks from August to October 1944. There the basic structure of the United Nations organization was agreed upon, although the key question of veto power was deferred. Roosevelt resolved that issue in negotiations with Stalin at the Yalta conference of February 1945. The resulting arrangement was approved by the American delegation to the international conference at San Francisco (25 April to 26 June 1945), where the United Nations' Charter was framed. There was much drama and uncertainty throughout this negotiating process, but the critical issues were largely hidden from public view until they were resolved. The combination of public campaigning by internationalists and astute negotiating by the administration assured relatively easy ratification by the Senate on 28 July 1945.

Two issues were most troublesome during this period. One was the question of whether the Senate, in ratifying U.S. participation in the United Nations, would be authorizing a president to commit American troops to any future collective action without legislative approval. To do so, some argued, would violate the Senate's constitutional prerogative to declare war. Compromise language enabled the United States to commit itself to the principle of collective security while assuring the Senate of its right to review and sanction the use of force on the magnitude of war. The other difficult issue was the veto—the unilateral right of each permanent member of the Security Council (the United States, Great Britain, the Soviet Union, France, and China) to reject collective security measures that threatened its national interest. Eventually, it was agreed that any one of these major powers might veto the collective use of military or economic sanctions, but not the consideration of disputes.

The very fact that five seats on the Security Council were to be allocated to major powers on a permanent basis, while seven were to be rotated among all other states, suggested broader questions: was the United Nations organization to be an extension of great-power influence or a truly universal organization of equally sovereign nations? Was peace and security to be based on a great-power consortium or on a worldwide confederation? Was the future to be secured by an enforced world order of large powers or did it point toward a cooperative world government? Although the San Francisco charter pointed in both directions, it was weighted to a great-power order. Voting in the General Assembly was based on the sovereign equality of all nations, but real decision making on security matters was reserved to the Security Council, where power was weighted.[32] Security would be assured, in fact, by Four Policemen— the four major allies in the war. In this measure, the United Nations extended the U.N. alliance and the balance of force in 1945.

Pacifist groups criticized the postwar design. The WILPF regarded it as "the domination of the world by the five most heavily armed powers."[33] A. J. Muste and the FOR agreed that it merely ratified the existing power structure. The WRL objected that it made no attempt to deal with the causes of war. Certainly, the UN did not embody the transnational outlook of liberal pacifists. Some internationalist groups also expressed reservations to the big-power peace (notably Americans United, the Catholic Association for International Peace, and Dulles's Commission on a Just and Durable Peace), but they minimized them in the interest of public consensus.

Other internationalists endorsed the new world order with a logic they heralded as "realistic." This point of view was privately anticipated by Roosevelt. It was developed in public by historians such as Charles Beard and Carl Becker, political scientists such as Nicholas J. Spykman and William T. Fox, commentator Walter Lippmann, and theologian Reinhold Niebuhr. The war itself demonstrated the primacy of force in international affairs, they reasoned, and the nation-state was the true basis of power. Nations necessarily pursue their self-interest with whatever power they have, and the realistic objective of collective security is to restrain national interest, not to ignore it.[34] Reinhold Niebuhr pressed that point in his influential 1944 book *Children of Light and Children of Darkness*. Walter Lippmann elaborated on it in his *United States Foreign Policy* (1944). The only realistic guarantee of world order is the collective interest of sovereign nations, Lippmann insisted, especially those whose economic power enlarged their geopolitical interests. It was no doubt true, as Robert Divine observed, that public support for the United Nations rested on a common desire to "make the world safe for the United States."[35] For the self-proclaimed realists of internationalism, that was not an ignoble viewpoint: another world catastrophe could be avoided only insofar as the sovereign national interests of America and the other major powers were secure. The structure of the United Nations represented that version of international reality.

World Federalism   Seven weeks after the United Nations was chartered in San Francisco, the world encountered the reality of atomic destruction at Hiroshima and Nagasaki. There were outcries against the annihilation of those cities from liberal pacifists and some religious leaders, but Americans overwhelmingly supported the bombing. As the atom's destructive power became apparent, public opinion followed intellectual leadership in concluding that, as President Harry Truman bluntly put it, "we can't stand another global war," but atomic weapons were nonetheless developed and incorporated into the nation's security planning.[36] Those who believed that atomic weapons precluded war as a rational instrument of security were called "nuclear pacifists."

Even before the bombs were dropped, scientists in the Manhattan Project had voiced apprehensions about their military use. A number of them tried to influence government policy. In their "Franck Report," a group in Chicago warned against the unilateral and surprise use of the atomic bomb on the grounds that it would aggravate mistrust of American intentions and trigger a nuclear arms race.[37] The Franck committee went unheeded and, in any case, the larger community of atomic scientists was divided. The bombs were exploded without warning.

In the aftermath of Hiroshima, the Franck committee became the nucleus of a larger organization of scientists, the Federation of Atomic Scientists (November 1945), which was closely associated with the *Bulletin of the Atomic Scientists* (December 1945). In less than a year, the group expanded to the 2,000-member Federation of American Scientists. An Emergency Committee of Atomic Scientists was set up to raise funds, and a National Committee on Atomic Information linked the scientists to some 60 civic and professional groups.

The federation was designed to confront the scientific community with ethical responsibility for the results of research, specifically the international control of atomic energy. Scientists mobilized fully when they learned that the administration was pushing legislation that would neglect international control, stress weapons development over peaceful applications, and wrap the field in tight military security. They lobbied the Congress and campaigned to educate and enlist public opinion. They denied that the technology of atomic bombs could be kept secret and argued for international control, but they gave their highest priority to the development of atomic energy and to civilian jurisdiction over it. They were only partially successful. The Atomic Energy Act of 1946 did provide for civilian control of atomic energy, but it included a liaison between the Atomic Energy Commission and the military, while the issue of international control was negotiated in the United Nations, to which the scientists had little access. The political campaign exhausted the federation. What remained was mainly the *Bulletin,* and that was primarily the work of Chicago biologist Eugene Rabinowitch. It provided a platform for those few scientists, such as Leo Szilard and Linus Pauling, who crusaded for international control during the Cold War.

They argued that, in Albert Einstein's words, "a world authority and an eventual world state are not just *desirable* in the name of brotherhood, they are *necessary* for survival."[38] That view was the essence of nuclear pacifism. It led scientists like mathematician and missile expert Norbert Wiener to refuse to cooperate in military research. It linked other atomic scientists with world federalism.

The "major testament of the world government movement" appeared in June 1945, as the campaign for the United Nations reached its climax.[39] The book was *The Anatomy of Peace,* the author an immigrant publisher named Emery Reeves. A world of sovereign nations was a form of anarchy that offered only insecurity in the face of economic integration and military technology, Reeves argued; the logic of history led to a federated world government. His book became a best-seller when, within two months of its publication, the United Nations was established, and then, in the view of many it was rendered obsolete by the advent of an atomic age. At that point the coalition promoting the United Nations disintegrated, leaving mainly the United Nations Association, and the momentum for internationalism fed enthusiasts into world government organizations.

A plethora of them emerged. Ulric Bell's Americans United for World Organization (1944) was converted to Americans United for World Government (1946), acquiring a prestigious board of directors led by radio commentator Raymond Swing and the editor of the *Saturday Review of Literature,* Norman Cousins. World Federalists, U.S.A., was organized in Cleveland in the fall of 1945. Led by German émigré Otto Griessemer, it attracted mainly intellectual leaders, including Reeves. Americans United and World Federalists (about 5,000 members each) attempted to educate the public and lobby the Congress for their cause, although the latter was better organized on a state and local level. In addition, there were two important student groups. Student Federalists, organized by Harris Wofford, Jr., spun off Streit's Federal Union as its members moved closer to the program of World Federalists, U.S.A.; it had a membership of some 3,500 high school and college students by early 1947. A smaller group, World Republic, organized youthful activists for war relief and world government. To these groups were added smaller national and local ones with a combined membership of perhaps 17,000 by the end of 1946.[40]

At Asheville, North Carolina, early the next year most of them merged into the United World Federalists (UWF). World Republic remained aloof, regarding the new organization as too gradualist in its approach, and there were two other independent groups: University of Chicago president Robert Hutchins formed a committee to draft a constitution for world government, and contract bridge expert Ely Culbertson parleyed his version of federated collective security into a Citizens Committee for the United Nations Reform.

The UWF carried the world government movement. Its president was Cord Meyer, a vigorous, 27-year-old Yale graduate whose war experience as a marine had converted him to a peace advocate. His postwar hopes dashed by the weakness of the United Nations, as he saw it, the articulate Meyer welcomed the opportunity to promote a stronger world government. The UWF established headquarters in New York and Washington and organized on state and local levels. It acquired the support of leading atomic scientists, as its growth accelerated through the winter of 1949. Paid membership rose to 40,000, the number of local chapters to over 700, and its budget to $550,000.[41]

The movement was grounded in an East Coast, urban, and Protestant elite. It enlisted prominent political and intellectual leaders and a few businessmen. Ideas generated by this elite were publicized through the media and through the hierarchies of a large number of cooperating civic and interest groups—from the American Legion to farmers' and workers' unions, from the Young Republicans to women's clubs. The UWF spread its message through speakers, radio addresses, and newspaper articles, and capped its public-relations blitz with petitions and letter-writing campaigns. In the election of 1948 world government was endorsed by the Progressive party, which ran Henry Wallace for president. The Republican and Democratic platforms advocated merely a stronger United Nations.

Indeed, the vision of a sovereign world government was indiscriminately mixed with a pervasive desire to strengthen the United Nations (although the UNA felt that the federalists actually undermined confidence in the United Nations itself). Attempting to assemble the broadest possible support, most world federalists advocated only a world government with enough power to prevent war. They criticized both U.S. and Soviet policy makers for pursuing their national interests at the expense of the security and welfare of the rest of the world, but in the absence of an alternative form of security, they did not challenge U.S. defense policy.

By the fall of 1949 UWF membership reached its peak of nearly 50,000. It had support from government leaders abroad, where a World Movement for World Federal Government had been formed by delegates from 18 nations and had set up headquarters in Paris. In America 20 state legislatures had petitioned Congress to initiate plans to transform the United Nations into a more truly world government, and others had resolved in support of the idea.[42] Building on the experience of the wartime campaign for a United Nations, world federalists arranged for bipartisan resolutions to be introduced in the House and Senate. Hearings on those resolutions were held by the House in 1948 and 1949. They revealed much about the movement, including its division over specific plans for world government. Most important, testimony from Cord Meyer and others suggested that the UWF was becoming "more gradualist and more willing to adapt to the increasing American nationalism generated by the cold war." The legislators conducting the hearings themselves seemed disposed to view a stronger United Nations as a bulwark against the Soviet bloc.[43]

Cold War Internationalism   As a matter of fact, the world government movement coincided with the sharpening Cold War, and it succumbed to the very polarization of the world that it tried to avert. No sooner had the UWF been organized early in 1947 than the Truman administration made the containment of Soviet expansion a cornerstone of U.S. foreign policy. The following year, the Soviet Union added Czechoslovakia to the bloc of states under its control and sealed off West Berlin from land traffic. Truman responded with a dramatic airlift of the beleaguered city that lasted nearly a year. In 1949 communist forces of Mao Tse-tung won control of China, and the Soviet Union tested an atomic bomb. Anxiety over atomic war became associated with the Soviet adversary, and in January 1950 Truman authorized the development of a hydrogen bomb. In June communist North Korean forces invaded the South. The United States mobilized and secured U.N. endorsement of a military response to that aggression. While containment turned into war abroad, at home anticommunism grew into a political force known as McCarthyism (after Wisconsin senator Joseph McCarthy, who exploited it most blatantly).

As a movement, world government collapsed. In the year after the invasion of Korea, UWF membership plummeted to 22,000, most students splintered away, and the organization was in financial trouble. The other world government organizations failed too, and the *Bulletin of the Atomic Scientists* avoided policy questions. The World Movement for World Federal Government was crippled by the loss of American financing. Numerous states rescinded their world government resolutions, and congressional resolutions were forgotten. Worse still, world federalists became the targets of charges of communist collusion.

That was ironic, because they grounded their internationalism ever more clearly in a nationalist perspective and interpreted their ideals in a "realistic" assessment of power. Cord Meyer had already resigned as president of the UWF when the Korean War began. Then he left the movement and returned to Harvard University, where intensive study convinced him that Soviet expansion was the root of the Cold War. Obtaining a position with the Central Intelligence Agency (CIA), Meyer joined what he called "the worldwide effort to contain the outward thrust of Soviet power." As historian Wesley T. Wooley observed, he took "a political realist's logical step once it became clear that traditional politics among nations were not being fundamentally reformed."[44]

World federalists were only the slowest internationalists to reach that conclusion. Clarence Streit had argued throughout World War II that only a federation of the North Atlantic governments would be realistic: democratic union had to stand up against totalitarianism. His Federal Union had been sapped by wartime enthusiasm for the United Nations and then by the world government movement, but it was revived as the Atlantic Union Committee (1949). This group included prestigious leaders, but it had no popular base at all, nor any attraction for other civic and interest groups. Although it excited some interest in 1950 and 1951, especially in *Fortune, Time,* and *Life* magazines, it quickly declined, lingering on until about 1962. Part of its problem was its "narrowly elitist" base, but the larger difficulty was, as Wooley observed, that it couched Atlantic

Union as a solution to the Soviet threat when there were other responses at hand: "military rearmament, a new intelligence agency, the Marshall Plan, NATO, and foreign aid."[45]

All of those measures could be and were taken unilaterally. That is to say, they represented independent initiatives by the United States, acting in concert with other powers but not bound by them. On the other hand, they also reflected the internationalists' long-standing goal of an American foreign policy that would accept responsibility for maintaining international order. Given a world of superpower adversaries, the government and the people of the United States were inclined to keep a lot of powder dry and act independently.

Self-proclaimed realism became the hallmark of internationalist thought. Disenchanted with ideals that had twice eluded the world in the wake of two wars, people asked, why? Reinhold Niebuhr had already offered an explanation in 1944. The "children of light" had neglected the fact of darkness, he had said. The goal of a harmonious world order was worthy enough, but its pursuit had to be chastened by the reality of conflict. That point of view came to pervade the writings of commentator Walter Lippmann, state department analyst George Kennan, political scientist Hans Morgenthau, and many others who regarded themselves as realists.

A kind of Cold War internationalism emerged as a consensus among the foreign policy elite—government officials, major foundations, prestigious university faculties and institutes, and nonacademic intellectuals.[46] In their view, American responsibility to model and insure world order was challenged by the expansionist bloc of China and the Soviet Union, both dominated by an alien, totalitarian ideology and amassing huge military force. Under the circumstances, the application of internationalist ideals was couched in the calculation of national power, especially military and economic power, while the domestic test of realism was resistance to communist blandishments.

This view affected the scientific community. The *Bulletin of the Atomic Scientists* narrowed its attention to technical questions, and most scientists who expressed their views were committed to military security. Ever-larger numbers of scientists entered the service of governmental defense agencies as researchers and advisors. Although they differed over the best strategic use of nuclear technology, they agreed that a nuclear arsenal was realistic.[47]

The major foundations, such as Ford, Rockefeller, and Carnegie, applied the theme of American responsibility for world order to the developing world. A kind of "club" of business and professional leaders with innumerable direct connections to foreign policy-makers, the foundations also worked with internationalist and educational agencies in order to educate public opinion and mobilize it in support of their preferred programs. The foundations had become a "microcosm" of the decision-making establishment in the United States.[48] By the mid-1950s they were concentrating their efforts on third-world development, where they made significant contributions. However much that investment was altruistic or reflected capitalist expansion, it was rationalized—justified— in terms of American national interest. Specifically, it was interpreted as an alternative to Soviet influence and to communist forms of development through revolution and socialism.

But was this internationalism at all? In the view of the small circle of decision makers that designed postwar foreign policy, it was. Virtually insulating themselves from dissent, high-level presidential advisors around Secretary of State Dean Acheson not only framed policy but vigorously promoted it in an effort to forestall a return to isolationism.[49] As much as they wanted to retain freedom of action for the United States, they wanted to extend the American order—with its open access to ideas, power, and goods—throughout the world. They wanted to secure an international order commensurate with the national ideals. If this was a Pax Americana, it seemed to them like a realistic alternative to the kind of compromising idealism they associated with Munich and appeasement. Whereas Franklin Roosevelt had urged a "quarantine" of aggression, they framed the "containment" of communism; their Stalin was his Hitler. In a sense, their Korea was his Pearl Harbor, for they seized the wartime opportunity to implement a grand design for international leadership, in this case to isolate the Soviet bloc through cultural, political, economic, and increasingly military power.

That design was pursued vigorously in the 1950s, notably by John Foster Dulles. As a leader in the wartime campaign for a United Nations, Dulles had expressed serious reservations to a postwar order dominated by the big powers, but by 1948 he was convinced that force had to be mobilized to check the expansion of Stalinist Russia. In the election of 1952, Dulles went beyond containment to espouse "liberation" from communist rule. If, as secretary of state under Dwight Eisenhower, he proved to be more flexible and pragmatic than his rhetoric implied, he remained an implacable cold warrior. In particular, he defined a new line of defense policy. In place of large military forces, the administration would rely on the threat of "massive retaliation" by atomic weapons to check even limited aggression. Moreover, third-world neutralism would not be countenanced in the struggle to align the world against communism. John Foster Dulles epitomized cold-war internationalism.

Thus, from 1939 to 1954 peace advocacy underwent profound changes. Its pacifist wing endured, and its humanitarianism expanded into large-scale service programs, but liberal pacifists were forced to defend their own conscientious principles during World War II. With the sole exception of the universal military training issue, and although they participated in the U.N. campaign, liberal pacifists did not exercise political leadership within the peace movement. Meanwhile, a form of radical pacifism found expression in Civilian Public Service camps and in the civil rights movement.

Internationalists, on the other hand, mounted a massive, successful campaign for the United Nations. In the process, they left obscure the distinction between a world order based on universal principles and one based on spheres of power. After a brief but well-organized flirtation with world government early in the nuclear age, most internationalists adapted to the exigencies of a Cold War, identifying peace with the military and economic power of the noncommunist industrialized world and particularly the United States.

By the mid-1950s the peace movement seemed as irrevocably shattered as the world it had meant to save. In the intense light cast by Cold War realism on apparently obsolescent ideals of peace, it was but a faint shadow. What issue could realign the various pacifists and internationalists? On what basis could they possibly mobilize sufficient resources to be counted as a social movement? The answers to those questions came unexpectedly and from the east, first from radiation-laden winds and then from an undeclared war.

Chapter Five

The First Campaign Against Nuclear Arms, 1955–1963

World power was thoroughly polarized between the Soviet Union and the United States by 1954. Containment policy had become militarized, Americans had learned to live with the bomb, and the various wings of the peace movement were dormant. History is filled with unexpected turns, though, and this was illustrated when the United States tested a hydrogen bomb in the South Pacific that spring. As the bomb was detonated everything seemed to be under control, but a change in wind patterns carried radioactive debris to the Marshall Islands, where islanders were contaminated. A Japanese fishing trawler, ironically named *Lucky Dragon*, sailed near the test zone and was exposed. The ship returned to port with sick crew members. Fear of radioactive fish swept Japan, and increased radiation levels were measured over the American mainland. The fallout from the BRAVO test was not only physical. It was political, and it led to a revival of the peace movement in a coalition against the testing of nuclear weapons.

The issue of nuclear arms sharpened in the next two years. The Soviet Union and Great Britain tested hydrogen bombs, while the United States maintained its nuclear advantage by developing an array of new weapons systems. Meanwhile, atomic scientists began to challenge claims by the Atomic Energy Commission that minimized the hazards of atomic fallout, and there were several appeals from scientists to stop testing, one from Bertrand Russell and Albert Einstein, another from the Federation of American Scientists. Peace groups such as the WILPF called for the

Led by Scott Herrick, pacifists completed their journey from California (December 1960) to Moscow (October 1961) in the San Francisco to Moscow Walk for Peace, coordinated by the Committee for Non-Violent Action, to protest nuclear weapons. Sign on left gives name of march; sign on right reads "We call upon all nations to unilaterally disarm." *War Resisters League*

cancellation of scheduled atomic tests, and presidential candidate Governor Adlai Stevenson of Illinois introduced the idea of an international test ban into the 1956 campaign. Stevenson persisted despite the Eisenhower administration's insistence that any treaty to limit testing must follow agreement on verification procedures. Although the Democratic candidate lost the election decisively, he raised the salience of the issue.[1]

That fact was not lost on peace advocates. Some of them objected to atmospheric testing itself. This was the case for Norman Cousins, world federalist and editor of the *Saturday Review of Literature,* who had been instrumental in persuading Stevenson to address the problem openly. Others, including pacifists like A. J. Muste, viewed a test ban as a first step toward the reevaluation of military containment and cold-war policy. In this vein, Robert Pickus, a regional peace secretary for the AFSC, created Acts for Peace in order to stimulate discussion of peace issues on a local level, starting in San Francisco. One of his colleagues was Lawrence Scott, who had become frustrated in his work as director of peace education for the AFSC in Chicago. At Scott's instigation, some 20 liberal peace advocates and absolute pacifists met in Philadelphia on 22 April 1957, where they agreed that the time was ripe for a major campaign to get a comprehensive test ban treaty.

Two of the people at the Philadelphia meeting, Norman Thomas and A. J. Muste, epitomized the campaign's loose alignment of liberal peace advocates with radical pacifists and its dual approach: traditional public information to generate political pressure and the newer technique of direct action. Each thrust was to be developed separately, but the established peace organizations agreed to support both of them. At the outset each form of action was undertaken on an ad hoc basis. Within a few months, however, two new peace groups were created: the Committee for a Sane Nuclear Policy (SANE) and the Committee for Non-Violent Action (CNVA).[2]

CNVA

The CNVA took form first. Its Gandhian style of direct action and civil disobedience under law was particularly attractive at the time, because it had been employed dramatically on behalf of black civil rights in the 1956 Montgomery Alabama bus boycott. Before that, of course, nonviolent action had been developed during World War II in civil rights and CPS, and even earlier in the labor movement.

Radical pacifists of the WRL and Catholic Worker Movement had committed civil disobedience under law when they refused to comply with annual civil defense drills starting in 1955, but they became determined "to go beyond words" and to challenge not only atmospheric testing but also the expanding arms race.[3] On the twelfth anniversary of the Hiroshima bombing, 12 August 1957, CNVA activists held vigils at the office of the Atomic Energy Commission in Las Vegas, Nevada. Then they sought to get through the gates of the Camp Mercury atomic test site 70 miles to the northwest. They were arrested, tried, and convicted of trespassing. Released with suspended sentences, they returned to the test site, where their prayer vigil was illuminated by the white light of the first explosion in the series.

The Nevada action established the form and thrust of the CNVA. Initially, it was not so much an organization as a network of radical pacifists who periodically trained and planned together for specific direct actions, which increasingly involved some form of civil disobedience. Formal organization was minimal and functional. In the Nevada action, for example, Lawrence Scott was designated project director and Robert Pickus was detailed to handle public relations, including the press. The CNVA was essentially the volunteers at Camp Mercury and other direct actions. Even though a national committee spoke for the decentralized network, it had leadership status by virtue of the fact that its members were particularly active in CNVA projects or articulated the radical pacifist philosophy at the heart of them.

In the spring of 1958, CNVA member Albert Bigelow and four Quaker pacifists sailed their ketch, the *Golden Rule,* to Hawaii with the intention of entering the Pacific zone around Eniwetok atoll, where H-bomb tests were scheduled. Twice they were arrested under sail for defying a court injunction and were sentenced to jail. Earle Reynolds was not a member of CNVA, but he was in Hawaii at the time, on the final leg of a round-the-world cruise with his family. Aroused by the trial of the *Golden Rule* crew, Reynolds sailed his yacht, the *Phoenix,* into the testing zone, where it was overtaken by a U.S. destroyer. Reynolds was arrested, taken back to Hawaii, and sentenced to two years in jail. His conviction eventually was overturned, but in the meantime he made an extensive tour and, like the *Golden Rule* crew, received a good deal of favorable publicity. During the summer, CNVA activists conducted nonviolent civil disobedience at Wyoming and Nebraska missile sites.

A year later CNVA members conducted a summer-long program of local organizing in Omaha and undertook civil disobedience at a nearby Strategic Air Command base. Some activists initiated a vigil against germ warfare at Fort Detrick, Maryland, and others picketed the missile-launching Polaris submarine facility in Connecticut. Between December 1960 and October 1961 activists organized by CNVA dramatized their protest against the arms race in a walk from San Francisco to the East Coast and through Europe to Moscow. By this time, leadership had passed to organizer Bradford Lyttle, and the group had become somewhat more centralized in New York. Increasingly the radical activists in CNVA expressed concern not only about nuclear testing but also about the arms race, and they advocated unilateral disarmament.

They also developed a multi-issue agenda that included a wide range of social ills. In the area of civil rights, nonviolent direct action was applied in the early 1960s by the Student Nonviolent Coordinating Committee (SNCC) and Martin Luther King, Jr.'s Southern Christian Leadership Conference. Those organizations integrated civil disobedience into a comprehensive social strategy with specific goals. They attempted to extend and enforce laws, and they related direct action to politics. They had an indigenous base of leaders and activists. Some of the CNVA founders pulled away from the organization as they concluded that, by contrast, CNVA activists were increasingly fascinated with direct action for its own sake. The pullout left the organization more closely associated with political radicalism and correspondingly more distanced from SANE and the mainstream test ban campaign. In any case, the direct actions of radical pacifists were not well coordinated with the political objectives of the peace activists. Tensions among them were minimized by organizing on dual lines, but differences were not managed within the framework of a coherent strategy.[4]

SANE, 1957–1960

Although it was slower to get started, SANE became the core of the test ban campaign. Through the summer of 1957 it was limited to a small organizing committee, which enlisted prominent supporters, notably Norman Cousins and Clarence Pickett, and designated Unitarian minister and peace activist Homer Jack as secretary and coordinator. In September the small group adopted a name suggested by psychologist Erich Fromm, the National Committee for a Sane Nuclear Policy, with the acronym SANE. It agreed to expand its efforts to stimulate public discussion, focusing on the single goal of a multilateral ban on atomic testing.[5]

The arms race was accelerating rapidly. Two months after its Nevada series, the United States conducted an underground atomic test and brought into service a fleet of B-52 superbombers, while the Soviets tested an intercontinental ballistic missile. On 4 October they placed the satellite Sputnik in orbit around the earth. The little SANE committee met with a new sense of urgency later that month, and it decided to place a full-page ad in the *New York Times,* appealing for an end to testing. Written largely by Cousins over the signature of prominent public figures, the advertisement began, "We are facing a danger unlike any danger that has ever existed." The text emphasized not only the danger of atomic weapons but the importance of internationalism. The ad brought a wave of enthusiastic letters and financial contributions. People around the country ran it in local papers and distributed it as reprints—25,000 of them. Local committees were started, some building on existing groups that were "looking for national leadership," and others bringing in new constituencies.[6]

SANE's basic goal was a comprehensive ban on the testing of nuclear weapons, in the hope that this would be a step toward a broader settlement of Cold War issues. Disarmament and the peaceful resolution of conflicts were woven into SANE's test ban agenda. Although the leadership frequently debated what positions the organization should take, essentially it conducted a single-issue campaign through 1963. More divisive than overall goals was the issue of strategy. A minority of leaders wanted to conduct a quiet program of lobbying at the level of elite decision makers. Some of them left the group when it chose also to conduct a campaign of public information and to act as a clearinghouse for emerging local committees.

The response to its first *New York Times* ad changed SANE from a small committee to a membership organization. An executive secretary was acquired on leave from the Friends Committee on National Legislation of Northern California, and the AFSC provided a base of support. An executive committee was formed that included Norman Cousins, Clarence Pickett, Homer Jack, Norman Thomas, Robert Gilmore, a few business and educational figures, and leaders in peace groups such as the AFSC, WILPF, and American Association for the United Nations. Even though Norman Cousins borrowed against his *Saturday Review* stock for the organization and wealthy New Yorker Leonore Marshall made substantial donations, SANE, unlike the Emergency Peace Campaign of the 1930s, did not have access to large funding sources. As the national office expanded, therefore, it depended on contributions from individuals and affiliating locals, so that grass-roots support became critical.

In April 1958 representatives from local chapters met with national leaders, who agreed to reorganize the organization along more representative lines in the fall.[7] By the summer SANE claimed about 130 chapters with a combined membership of some 25,000. Most of them were in New York, New Jersey, Connecticut, Pennsylvania, California, and Illinois.[8] A Student SANE was formed, too. In its September conference SANE was converted from a committee into a federation of locals with a council of local SANE committees for coordination and fund-raising. In turn, the council elected five representatives to a 15-member executive committee of national SANE.[9] The locals retained substantial autonomy. They agreed to follow the national's lead on policy positions and to raise funds for it (although they never provided as much as they pledged).[10] On the strength of this relationship, SANE replaced its temporary secretary with an executive director, Donald Keys, who previously had worked for United World Federalists. It became less of an ad hoc coalition and more of an independent, long-range organization.

The test ban campaign expanded through 1958. Large newspaper ads were run in March, April, and October. There were fresh appeals from scientists. The New York City SANE organized a petition campaign and sponsored 19 days of public meetings and a demonstration at the United Nations. Peace advocates lobbied in Washington. The Eisenhower administration came under pressure from both those appealing for an end to atmospheric testing and those demanding a further arms buildup. After a flurry of atmospheric tests in October, the United States and the Soviet Union each initiated a moratorium, pending negotiations on a permanent ban, although the administration encountered continued pressure to resume testing.

The moratorium and negotiations somewhat removed the issue from the public area, but nonetheless the campaign continued to grow. It was reported in the spring of 1959 that radioactive strontium 90 released into the atmosphere from atomic tests the previous fall was getting into the food and milk supply, from which it was absorbed in children's bones and teeth. SANE publicized the hazards of fallout and, with other test ban proponents, challenged government reports that minimized the danger. The widely publicized controversy deepened popular anxiety and generated a consensus that atmospheric testing was unacceptable.[11]

Even so, peace advocates conceded that the issue had lost a measure of political force in view of the protracted negotiations.[12] In an attempt to get beyond a vague, generalized fear, they sponsored public petitions and appeals from international leaders for a comprehensive agreement in Geneva. In April SANE and the AFSC sponsored Easter demonstrations in several cities that were modeled on the disarmament marches of the Campaign for Nuclear Disarmament (CND) in Great Britain. Founded early in 1958 to protest England's testing of a hydrogen bomb, CND had grown rapidly. In the spring of 1959 it assembled 10,000 people in a walk to London from a nuclear weapons facility at Aldermaston. The American demonstrations for disarmament began on a much smaller scale, but like the British one they became ever-larger annual affairs (in April 1961 they involved an estimated 25,000 people). To some extent the April mobilizations were measures of SANE's endurance.

By autumn it had seven full-time and five support staff, 150 local chapters, and some 25 student ones, and its annual conference authorized an expanded program. Responding to an appeal by founder Robert Gilmore, it moved into electoral politics. In February 1960 it opened a Washington office under political-action director Sanford Gottlieb.[13] With the coalition of peace and religious groups he organized, called the 1960 Campaign for Disarmament, the peace movement returned to politics after a generation of estrangement. Some local committees endorsed congressional candidates, while the coalition publicized the disarmament issue and prepared testimony for party platforms. On 19 May some 20,000 people filled Madison Square Garden for a SANE rally.

By this time, civil rights action was spilling over into disarmament efforts. Student sit-ins to protest racial discrimination started in North California in February and spread rapidly throughout the South. Experienced activists from CORE and the FOR provided support to the black students who organized as the Student Nonviolent Coordinating Committee. Numerous northern college students, electrified by the moral example of the sit-ins, felt challenged to emulate their social action. For many of them, the Student Peace Union (SPU) provided a ready vehicle of organization. It had grown out of a University of Chicago–based group started in April 1959 by activists Kenneth and Ele Calkins. An AFSC worker and FOR member, Kenneth had participated in a CNVA action at a missile base near Cheyenne, Wyoming. With help from the FOR, the Calkinses expanded their group into a Midwest and then a national organization. It was through the Student Peace Union that the CND logo—the semaphore signs for *N* and *D* within a circle (hence Nuclear Disarmament)—was introduced in the United States, gradually to become the widely recognized "peace symbol." By August 1960 the SPU membership had grown to 5,000, with more than twice that number subscribing to its newsletter, and it had gathered 10,000 signatures to a peace petition in May.

Abruptly, movement was arrested for SANE, at least. Democratic senator Thomas Dodd, a former world federalist and a Connecticut neighbor of Norman Cousins, launched an attack on the organization through the Senate Internal Security Subcommittee, of which he was temporary chair. When SANE organizer Henry Abrams was subpoenaed on the allegation that he was a communist, he took the Fifth Amendment and refused to testify. Cousins was among several national leaders who had feared that SANE was vulnerable to just such charges. Their memories of communist disruption of peace and social justice groups in the 1930s vied with their more recent experience of anti-communist attacks. Unsatisfied after a conversation with Abrams, Cousins dismissed him and tried to reassure Dodd. The senator returned to the attack later that month, claiming that the test ban campaign had been infiltrated by communists. Cousins denied it, but the affair had already created a rift in SANE.

The majority on the board rejected the pleas of several pacifist members to resist Dodd's pressure on the grounds of civil liberties. On the contrary, they tightened control over local chapters by requiring them to take out charters with the national. Locals would have to certify that their members were not tainted by association with communist "or other totalitarian doctrine."[14] About half of all local chapters were in the greater New York area, and half of those refused to take out charters and were expelled. The controversy within SANE continued into the fall, as Dodd subpoenaed other leaders in the test ban campaign, notably chemist Linus Pauling, who had been active in securing antinuclear petitions from scientists. The whole affair was debilitating. The fact that the national board seemed to have succumbed to intimidation led to the resignation of key leaders and prominent sponsors. When the national conference barely endorsed the board's policy of excluding communists, a large number of members left Student SANE for the SPU or the newly formed Students for a Democratic Society (SDS). The CNVA became still further distanced from the liberal test ban campaign. The damaging effect of the controversy over principle was aggravated by financial problems. A great deal of momentum was lost, just as the presidential election approached.

One effect of the Dodd controversy and an endemic lack of funds was to further centralize national SANE and to strengthen its political orientation. The executive staff was consolidated, pledging to make greater contact with the field.[15] A national membership program was discussed. The annual conference reaffirmed the goal of a test ban as a first step toward disarmament and economic conversion and endorsed the strategy of education, lobbying, and electoral work. Many agreed with Gottlieb that a political strategy required a coalition with religious, labor, student, and business groups, and a strong presence in one major party.[16]

Neither that coalition nor that presence existed in the fall of 1960. SANE had access to Hubert Humphrey, a strong supporter of a test ban; but he lost the Democratic presidential nomination to John F. Kennedy. The Republicans nominated Richard Nixon. Both candidates opposed resumption of atmospheric testing, but each campaigned within the framework of Cold War containment. SANE found Kennedy only a slightly better candidate than Nixon, and in any case the election was set against the background of a vastly expanded arms race. That autumn submarines carrying Polaris missiles roamed the Atlantic, and the United States conducted new series of underground atomic tests, having already accumulated an arsenal of about 18,000 nuclear weapons. The Democratic victory in November did not promise a reversal of that trend.

Toward a Partial Test Ban Treaty, 1961–1963

Throughout his short presidency, Kennedy was regarded with ambivalence by peace advocates. He conveyed an idealism that was clearer and more visionary than the policies he could apply. Early in 1961 Homer Jack tried to assess the new administration on the basis of conversations he and Gottlieb had held with some of its key members. He advised SANE that the president would evaluate his options with deliberation. Probably Kennedy would not adopt a thorough disarmament program, he said, but he could be influenced on the test ban issue by organized peace action.[17] Jack's evaluation of the administration implied something about the peace movement itself: a fresh coalition of peace advocates had in fact been formed. Amid the frustration of advocating a test ban, it was easy to lose sight of the achievement of creating a campaign at all, and one with a grass-roots base at that. Some latent sense of accomplishment impelled its leaders to engage the new administration, although for the next three years they would find themselves more reacting to events than shaping policy.

SANE was the coherent center, but not the whole, of the peace movement. It had been created by established peace organizations that sustained its test ban campaign, notably the AFSC but also the WILPF, FCNL, and FOR. The CNVA was still a viable, if small and loosely organized group aligned with the WRL. The United World Federalists held back from any issue-oriented program, although numerous world federalists individually supported the test ban campaign (indeed, the fact that Cousins and other SANE leaders were active in both organizations led to suggestions that they should merge). Traditional internationalist groups such as the Carnegie Endowment and the Council on Foreign Relations had become part of the containment-oriented establishment of foreign policy "realists," but important liberals were coming to conclude that an open-ended arms race was not realistic.

In an attempt to make inroads among liberal intellectuals, AFSC chairman Stephen Carey had convened about two dozen of them at Bear Mountain, New York, early in 1960. The conferees included several pacifists as well as nonpacifists like linguist S. I. Hayakawa, historian H. Stuart Hughes, and sociologists David Riesman and Lewis Coser. They discussed a wide range of foreign policy issues, deploring the logic of deterrence for security as "a deep malaise from which . . . both the Western and Communist blocs suffer."[18] The single most important recruit for their position was perhaps Reinhold Niebuhr, precisely because he had established himself as a trenchant critic of pacifist idealism and a proponent of ethical realism. Niebuhr became very critical of deterrence, and he endorsed a comprehensive test ban treaty. The attempt to reach a "realistic" constituency on a broader basis continued. Late in 1961 a number of peace groups sponsored Turn Toward Peace, headed by Sanford Gottlieb and Robert Pickus and based in San Francisco. They hoped to promote mutual goals through national and local clearinghouses that could also relate to other groups such as religious, veteran, and political associations. There were political and personality differences in Turn Toward Peace, which some perceived as developing into a competitive membership organization, and it dissolved two years later.

In the meantime, other constituencies were organized for disarmament. A study group of doctors in Cambridge, Massachusetts, formed Physicians for Social Responsibility and publicized the medical implications of atomic war. Nuclear scientist Leo Szilard organized scientists and other professionals in a Council for a Livable World.[19] Television personality Steve Allen and other entertainers (including folksingers like Pete Seeger and Peter, Paul, and Mary) had been involved from 1959 or before, and Hollywood became ever more supportive. Most impressive of all was the growth of Women Strike for Peace (WSP), started by children's book illustrator Dagmar Wilson and coordinated through SANE and WILPF networks. WSP attracted perhaps 25,000 women to demonstrate against the arms race in the fall of 1961. Like SANE five years earlier, WSP became an organization in the wake of a grass-roots apprehension of atmospheric testing.

There was reason for anxiety. Cold War confrontation accelerated, even as the Kennedy team studied its options. In April 1962 an American attempt to invade Cuba at the Bay of Pigs failed miserably. In June Soviet premier Nikita Khrushchev demanded that American soldiers leave Berlin. Kennedy responded by calling up National Guard troops and increasing defense spending, but in August the Soviets sealed off their zone behind a monstrous wall. An autumn series of Soviet atmospheric tests shattered the three-year moratorium. The United States detonated blasts underground and prepared to resume atmospheric testing in the spring. All this worried Dagmar Wilson and WSP.

Peace advocates responded at each stage of gathering crisis. In the spring they demonstrated against Kennedy's Cuba policy and organized large demonstrations against the arms race. SANE gave wide distribution to Norman Thomas's analysis urging that Berlin issues be addressed in a multinational framework. The wall went up anyway. Thousands of peace advocates in New York and Washington protested the Soviet resumption of testing. SANE again placed ads in American newspapers, bringing to bear an important new resource—Dr. Benjamin Spock. The author of the most widely used book on child care in the United States, Spock had immediate name recognition. His association with the test ban campaign gave it a concrete, human focus. A full-page ad was dominated by a picture of the baby doctor looking down on a child over the caption, "Dr. Spock is worried." The text below, on which Spock had labored, was incidental to the message. Reprinted in 700 newspapers worldwide, the ad was treated as news by *Time* and *Newsweek* and was widely reprinted as posters.[20] Meanwhile, the Student Peace Union attracted 4,000 students to Washington to lobby and rally against the resumption of testing. When the U.S. government went ahead with its Pacific tests, that raised the salience of the issue still further. SANE received help from new professional chapters—in August from Graphic Artists for SANE, which designed a popular poster, and a few months later from Dentists for SANE, which publicized the effects of strontium 90 released in atmospheric tests.

Then, in October, Kennedy confronted Khrushchev over the installation of Soviet nuclear missiles in Cuba, and the threat of nuclear war became terrifyingly real. A few pacifists demonstrated in Washington, 10,000 people rallied in New York, and peace groups urged that the conflict be mediated by the United Nations. It was resolved on a bilateral basis instead, as both superpowers backed off warily. Peace groups returned to their work on behalf of a comprehensive test ban.

While they did so, Norman Cousins initiated a contact that led instead

For this 1961 New York City demonstration against nuclear weapons testing, the radical pacifist Committee for Non-Violent Action, with what became known as the "peace symbol," joined ranks with the liberal pacifist and internationalist Committee for a SANE Nuclear Policy, with its ad featuring well-known baby doctor Benjamin Spock. *Swarthmore College Peace Collection*

to a limited test ban treaty. With the encouragement of Secretary of State Dean Rusk, he flew to Russia for a candid talk with Khrushchev. The American conveyed his government's receptiveness to a test ban treaty and also assured the Soviet premier that the organized peace movement would mobilize support behind an agreement. Upon his return, Cousins was able to assure Kennedy that Khrushchev would respond positively to a diplomatic overture, which the president included in a major address at the American University in June. Negotiations got under way quickly, and by the end of July 1963 a partial test ban treaty was signed. [21]

The administration welcomed help in winning public support for the treaty, since it was well short of the two-thirds of the Senate votes required for ratification. It advised Cousins to convene an ad hoc committee for that purpose, however, so that the effort would have the broadest possible base. Although SANE and other peace groups worked on their own, they also participated in an ad hoc Citizens Committee for a Nuclear Test Treaty. Gradually but firmly, public opinion swung behind the campaign, and on 24 September the treaty carried in an 80 to 19 Senate vote.

The Test Ban Campaign in Retrospect

For peace activists the 1963 treaty was partial in several respects. It permitted underground atomic testing, and therefore it was an instrument with which to manage a continued arms race. In fact, it made deterrence theory all the more publicly acceptable. [22] For that reason, it was supported by many advocates of further military buildup. Certainly, it was not the step toward reversing the arms race that had been envisioned by the campaign for a comprehensive ban. Just when the disarmament issue had achieved maximum salience for the public, it was preempted by arms control.

Moreover, the very Cold War confrontation of 1961–62 that gave the issue such large import had provoked SANE, the AFSC, and related groups to broaden their agendas. The challenge was raised explicitly in a special meeting of SANE's national board in June 1961. Sandford Gottlieb and H. Stuart Hughes, among others, held that the organization had to address the foreign policy crises that were driving the arms race, whereas Donald Keys and Homer Jack argued for a single-issue focus. Finally, Keys suggested that crises such as the Bay of Pigs could be used as "teachable moments" with which to relate general foreign policy and nuclear weapons. That became the rubric under which SANE fashioned position papers on Berlin and the Cuban missile crisis. [23]

The fact that Spock and Hughes succeeded Cousins and Pickett as cochairmen in 1962 accented the organization's attention to broad foreign policy questions. Meeting after treaty ratification, the large annual conference of 1963 identified its priorities as economic conversion from military to civilian production (long advocated as a goal by economist Seymour Melman), opposition to expanded civil defense programs, and political action in the 1964 election. Gottlieb pursued the political mandate in a coalition Peace Politics Clearing House. In the election year the national conference endorsed a merger with United World Federalists, but this was forestalled when SANE protested military involvement in Vietnam, because the UWF shied away from specific political issues. Thus, in the course of the test ban campaign, SANE modified its single-issue program, and this both impelled and enabled it to endure.

Endurance itself became an objective for peace groups as the testing issue receded in public consciousness. Women Strike for Peace stagnated. The Student Peace Union rapidly lost membership and income, and it dissolved in June 1964. Radical pacifists in CNVA were keenly frustrated, concluding that the peace movement had been co-opted by the partial treaty. [24] Within four years CNVA merged with the War Resisters League. SANE estimated that it had about 25,000 members, but many of them were nominal. Internal estimates assumed that there were 5 to 10 core activists for each of SANE's 150 chapters (a plateau reached in 1959), or a network of between 750 and 1,500 peace activists, but many of them became inactive following the treaty ratification. Estimates of the total number in the peace movement of 1963 ranged from 85,000 persons to 150,000 families. [25] Either figure represented outreach more than activism. Neither figure weighed the pervasive sense that the test ban campaign was essentially over, a feeling that many peace advocates shared with the general public.

There is an ahistorical quality to the movement's self-evaluation in 1963, and even to the record of decline in the following two years, because it fails to account for the changes produced since 1957. At the outset of the test ban campaign, not only was the peace movement dormant, it was located in two groups on the margin of American politics: world federalists and absolute pacifists. SANE enabled absolute pacifists, especially those associated with the AFSC, to cooperate actively with nuclear pacifists—essentially liberals like Reinhold Niebuhr who had become disillusioned with the so-called realism of the arms race. This coalition reached a broad public on the specific issue of atmospheric testing. It educated the public about the effects of radioactive fallout. In the process, it forced the government to acknowledge dangers that it had masked, and it elicited an apparent consensus against atmospheric testing that seemed to extend to nuclear war.

SANE did not quite create the antitesting movement, of course; it largely responded to grass-roots anxiety (as did the Student Peace Union and Women Strike for Peace), and it mobilized that feeling to work for a comprehensive test ban. Despite a serious rift over the exclusion of alleged Communists, and in part because of that controversy, national SANE developed stronger relationships with its local chapters. From an ad hoc coalition, it grew to be an ever more formal organization with a professional national staff and federated local chapters able to mobilize grass-roots participation. In the crisis-ridden Kennedy years, it coupled its emphasis on the test ban issue with a constructive critique of foreign policy that was attractive to liberals who lacked other venues for dissent. Perhaps conscious of that constituency, by 1964 peace advocates were attempting to put pressure on the electoral system.

Coupled with SANE from the beginning, the Committee for Non-Violent Action offered a way for radical pacifists to apply direct action tactics to the arms issue. The existence of a separate organization may have minimized the effect of the Dodd affair on the coalition as a whole, since CNVA incorporated those most critical on SANE's policy of exclusionism. Actions on the high seas, at missile bases, and in walking from San Francisco to Moscow may have helped to dramatize the issue of the arms race and to link it with the issue of atmospheric testing: that is difficult to assess. The government did not bend before that small-scale confrontation, but between 1955 and 1963 direct action and the mass protest of foreign policy did become more accepted by the media and public. In large measure, that acceptance was a spinoff from the civil rights movement and the drama of large-scale nonviolent confrontation there. Indeed, civil rights often overshadowed the test ban campaign. Martin Luther King's Southern Christian Leadership Conference had a budget at least five times that of SANE at its peak, and it had a full-time staff over eight times larger. Although the civil rights movement helped the peace movement by legitimating dissent, therefore, it vied with the test ban campaign for public attention and resources.

The fortunes of peace advocates varied with the salience of the testing issue. They rose in 1957 with publicity about the harmful effects of fallout, only to fall with a self-imposed moratorium on testing in 1959. They rose again with the Cold War crises of 1961–62, the resumption of testing, and the Cuban missile crisis, only to fall with the ratification of a partial test ban treaty. Insofar as it could obtain negotiations or a treaty, the government affected the issue's import, and therefore the effectiveness of the peace movement. Peace advocates were left to react to events they could not control.

A central message of the test ban coalition was that the Cold War arms race itself was out of control. The AFSC had made that point in an important statement of 1955, *Speak Truth to Power*. Modern weapons offered security at the price of unacceptable harm, the AFSC said, and the arms race increased insecurity at the cost of individual freedom. The liberal intellectuals who met at Bear Mountain five years later agreed: relying on deterrence for security was an illusory "malaise." The arms race was a "time bomb under our vaunted security," wrote Reinhold Neibuhr.[26] The test ban campaign was strongest when events seemed to confirm that point. Its historic significance was that it linked pacifists with liberals who began to question the terms of Cold War internationalism.

Chapter Six

Vietnam and the Antiwar Movement, 1965–1975

The American peace movement was reconstituted around the nuclear testing issue. In the two years after the partial test ban treaty of 1963, it coalesced into an antiwar movement that became the focal point of American politics for most of a decade. In the process, its character changed.[1]

Peace advocates approached the Vietnam War in their accustomed role of witnessing to a minority position. Between 1965 and 1967 they attempted to inform and arouse the public as they had done with regard to nuclear fallout. Very quickly, however, they found that the war realigned elements within the antiwar movement and attracted other disaffected groups to it. Threading their way through the swirling politics and culture of the period, activists tried to harness widespread opposition to the war as they challenged the policy of two presidential administrations. At stake was the public opinion necessary to sustain the war effort.

That contest was most intense between 1968 and 1971. It was conducted both within the political system and outside of it. The war was challenged most visibly in the streets, most dramatically in confrontation. There the antiwar movement acquired its dominant public image as politically and culturally radical. Probably for that reason, it was not accepted by the public, despite the fact that the American people themselves withdrew their support for the war on a massive scale.

By 1972 opposition to the war was firmly located within the political system, notably in Democratic party leadership, and the weight of ele-

The first draft card burning, at New York City's Union Square on 6 November 1965, was a form of radical pacifist protest against the Vietnam War. Resistance to the draft broadened to include mass burning of draft cards with adult support and provided a fulcrum for opposition to the war. *Swarthmore College Peace Collection; copyright Diana Davies*

ments within the movement had shifted to liberal antiwar organizations. They formed a pressure group that became increasingly cohesive up to the end of war in Vietnam. The more they focused on political issues and worked within the system, though, the less visible they were. The radical image of protest endured, masking the extent to which the antiwar movement had permeated American society.

Emerging Currents of Dissent, 1955–1964

American intervention in Vietnam was criticized before it turned into full-scale war. Military involvement was opposed by the Pentagon in the mid-1950s when the United States succeeded France in attempting to thwart the nationalization of Vietnam under Ho Chi Minh and his communist cadres.[2] At that time, President Eisenhower adopted the goal that defined U.S. policy for the next 20 years: to build and sustain a sovereign, viable, and anticommunist state in the South. In an effort to make South

Vietnam viable, large amounts of economic aid and expertise were provided; to insure its sovereignty, the South Vietnamese army was trained and equipped; to assure an anticommunist government, the Ngo Dinh Diem regime was supported even though it alienated many of its own people. By 1963 the Asian country was reeling from the combined insurgence of noncommunist dissenters and communists reinforced from the North. Crisis mounted sharply that year when the regime brutally repressed Buddhists. The Kennedy administration began to reevaluate its policy for Vietnam, but in the fall it endorsed a coup d'état by the Vietnamese army that overthrew and then murdered Diem. A month later Kennedy was assassinated.

The new president, Lyndon Johnson, reaffirmed America's commitment to Saigon and authorized U.S. military support. In the summer of 1964 he ordered a limited air strike against North Vietnamese port facilities. The president acted in response to a reported attack on a U.S. destroyer in the Gulf of Tonkin (a report later revealed to be spurious), but he was also consciously projecting an image of restrained firmness for the election campaign. It worked. Johnson won congressional authorization for unspecified future military action—the Gulf of Tonkin resolution—and he won the election. His critics had no clearly defined policy to challenge and nowhere else to turn. As 1964 drew to an end, only insiders knew that the policy of intervention would soon sharpen to the razor point of war.

Although Vietnam was hardly noticed in America before the 1963 Buddhist crisis, there were already voices of dissent—from a few academics, foreign correspondents, commentators, and political leaders. Criticism of American intervention also came from the groups that had conducted the test ban campaign.[3] The Friends Committee on National Legislation even opened a clearinghouse to provide legislators and civic leaders with information on Vietnam. By the end of 1964 most of the arguments that would be used against the war had been made.

There were essentially four of them. The first was a calculation of feasibility, or the limits of force. It was argued that the United States could not create a representative and responsible government from the outside, and that an open commitment to South Vietnam would overtax America's worldwide resources. As Walter Lippmann put it, "the price of a military victory in the Vietnamese war is higher than American vital interests can justify."[4] A second point was that intervention would undermine regional stability by solidifying Ho Chi Minh's dependence on China and risking Chinese intervention. A third criticism was that supporting a repressive government in Vietnam violated American ideals and, in view of domestic crises, priorities. Fourth, in a related sense it was argued that the destructiveness of an all-out guerilla war would be worse than communist rule, and that it would be immoral to fight to the last Vietnamese for an essentially American interest. The elements of this anti-interventionist rationale shifted in the course of the war—moral concerns became increasingly central to dissent, and a fifth, anti-imperialist line was added by the radical left—but a coherent argument was in place at the outset.

The elements of an antiwar movement were in place, too, by 1965. Initial opposition to military escalation came from independent critics and from the groups that had conducted the the test ban campaign. The composition of the peace movement was shifting, however, and some of its elements acquired new weight as it became an antiwar movement. These constituencies included women, blacks, students and the New Left.

Women were already organized for peace action in the WILPF and the more activist-oriented Women Strike for Peace. A current of self-conscious feminism was surfacing in the early 1960s, though, and some women began to mobilize for equal rights legislation and its enforcement. Others moved into civil rights and student rights campaigns, where they not only developed organizing skills but also experienced male chauvinism from erstwhile reformers. The result was to sharpen the new feminist sensibility, which was carried into the antiwar movement.

Young people became a major constituency for activism when a wave of sit-ins resulted in the formation in 1960 of the predominantly black Student Nonviolent Coordinating Committee. SNCC offered a pool of antiwar activism when the Vietnam War was perceived to bear disproportionately on black and poor Americans. Even before the war, youthful white reformers had gone into the South, where they were baptized into social action and, often, repression. Their example challenged students who remained on campus and spilled over to student rights campaigns. The campaigns personalized politics for students, provided issues around which they could be mobilized beyond specific campuses, and created nuclei of self-conscious activists in student organizations.

Spreading civil rights campaigns authenticated radical pacifism as a form of social action. The experiments in nonviolence of CORE and the FOR, augmented by the Southern Christian Leadership Conference, were mainstreamed in the early 1960s. That was explicitly the point of forming the SNCC. As Gandhi was Americanized in the South, radical pacifism was repositioned in the peace movement, and just at that point the war in Vietnam offered it new scope. The war also provided a focal point for what A. J. Muste called the "third camp" position, a view critical of both the United States and the Soviet Union for extending the Cold War to thwart liberation movements in the third world. The third-camp position brought anti-imperialism to bear on Vietnam and, along with the personal politics of nonviolent action, aligned radical pacifists with another emerging constituency in American life: the New Left.

In the mid-1950s there had emerged a fresh critique of American society. Liberal authors like Arthur M. Schlesinger, Jr., Daniel Bell, and John Kenneth Galbraith sought a more just and plural society through consensual politics. The new liberalism imbued Americans for Democratic Action (ADA), a political grouping in the Democratic party, and it was epitomized by John F. Kennedy. To the left—a self-designated New Left—were authors such as sociologist C. Wright Mills, historian William Appleton Williams, and social philosophers Herbert Marcuse and Paul Goodman. They were impatient with the threadbare rhetoric of the 1930s Old Left, which had declined to a few thousand faithful Marxists mainly in the Communist party, the Socialist Workers Party, and the League for Industrial Democracy. But New Left leaders were also dissatisfied with liberal reform, for they located social injustice in the very structure and culture of the United States. Blending psychology and culture, they reinforced a kind of personal politics, whether in social action or intentional life-styles. Their inquiry into the quality of American life spawned several new journals and engaged student leaders, particularly as civil rights campaigns and fresh attention to poverty revealed deepseated injustice. The New Left found its organized expression in SDS.

Although Students for a Democratic Society was started in 1960 as the youth wing of the League for Industrial Democracy, it soon outgrew its parent organization. In June 1962 a few recruits gathered at a labor camp near Port Huron, Michigan, where they adopted a "manifesto" largely drafted by Tom Hayden, SDS field secretary and formerly the editor of the University of Michigan student newspaper. His "Port Huron Statement" was a synthesis of contemporary social criticism. It held that the problems of America and the world could be solved only through "participatory democracy": individuals and nations had to be liberated—enabled to participate in the decisions that affected them. Hayden and several other SDS members headed to urban ghettos to act out their ideas and empower people. The hallmark of early New Left activism was to put social change at the level of the individual in the community and to create alternative structures of power there.

That approach helped radical pacifists to relate to the New Left students. David Dellinger, among others radicalized by their experience in CPS camps during World War II, had come to envision a nonviolent social revolution in which "the problems of changing society and of changing ourselves are inseparable." In order to promote that vision, he and several WRL members had founded *Liberation* magazine (1955). The journal carried articles by many of the authors that fed the thinking of the New Left. "What matters to us," wrote Muste, "is what happens to the individual human being—here and now."[5] That was more of an ambience than an ideology, more a style of action than a prescriptive theory.

It was characteristic of the original SDS, the radical pacifism of *Liberation,* the early SNCC, and the new feminism. Taken together, and with the remnants of the Old Left, these elements had become defined by 1965. In the new political environment created by the war they were attracted to the antiwar movement, where their radical thrust was sharpened and weighed against the liberal orientation of the major peace groups.

The several SDS leaders who gathered in New York on 30 December 1964 were less concerned about Vietnam than with their community organizing projects and a major contest at the University of California for the right of students to engage in social activism (the Free Speech Movement). Nonetheless, they spent several hours with journalist I. F. Stone, who had come from Washington to discuss Vietnam. Stone persuaded them to accept leadership on that issue, and they agreed to sponsor a demonstration for American withdrawal. The date was to be Easter weekend 1965. Unknowingly, they set up the first confluence of antiwar currents.

An Antiwar Movement in Formation, Winter 1965 – Summer 1967

By late 1965 the Johnson administration estimated that South Vietnam was incapable of checking the Vietcong, as communist guerilla forces were called. It laid plans to intervene with massive air power. An attack on American troops at Pleiku provided the excuse, and on 24 February 1965 the United States began the sustained bombing of North Vietnam— Operation Rolling Thunder. The object was to cut off supplies to the south and to show so much muscle that the communists would disengage. Instead, they stiffened as bombing mounted and U.S. troops were deployed during the spring. By early summer large units of Vietcong were defeating South Vietnamese forces. U.S. strategy shifted. Instead of defending secure areas, Americans sought out and engaged communist units. At the end of July, President Johnson announced that U.S. troop strength in Vietnam would be raised to 120,000 and that the draft would be increased. This "really is war," he acknowledged. Indeed, by the end of the year 1,636 Americans had been killed in action.[6]

The American public accepted escalation, although with doubt and confusion over its purpose, and then rallied behind the full-scale war effort. By September a Louis Harris poll gave the president a 67 percent approval rating, which continued to climb as people viewed the war on television. A small minority of them wanted to carry the ground war directly into North Vietnam, and a like number favored a negotiated withdrawal from the conflict. The large majority in the center offered the president a passive base of support.

Tenuous Alignments   During the period of escalation, opposition was largely spontaneous and divided, but with all-out war there were serious efforts to form an antiwar coalition. Division persisted, however, and it sharpened differences between radical and liberal leaders as they tried to give direction to a largely grass-roots antiwar movement.

Liberal dissent was voiced first by a few members of the foreign policy establishment, the peace groups, and the intellectual community. In the Senate Mike Mansfield, Frank Church, George McGovern, Ernest Gruening, and Wayne Morse objected to escalation, while activists canvassed and lobbied on behalf of the WILPF, WSP, AFSC, FCNL, SANE, and ADA. In Detroit an anguished WILPF member, Alice Herz, burned herself to death as Vietnamese Buddhists had done two years before.

A second wave of liberal dissent was initiated at the University of Michigan, where on 18 April 1965 several faculty members organized an overnight teach-in on Vietnam. Student response was electric. Thirty-five campuses held teach-ins within a week, at least 120 by the end of the school year. Students and faculties were divided, some of them vociferously supporting the war, but the administration was so worried that it tried to organize students covertly. The teach-ins legitimated debate and identified a source of authority on foreign policy and Indochina that offered an alternative to the government. That was the basis of the "credibility gap" that plagued both presidents Johnson and Nixon.

Parallel to the teach-ins, dissent surfaced among religious and cultural leaders. The FOR helped to form an Interreligious Committee on Vietnam, which produced mailings and ads, convened Christian and Jewish

The first major demonstration against the Vietnam War, sponsored by Students for a Democratic Society, brought some 20,000 people to the capital on 17 April 1965. It was the largest peace demonstration in Washington up until that time, but opposition escalated along with the war so that a half million protesters turned out for a demonstration in that city four years later. *Swarthmore College Peace Collection; copyright Diana Davies*

clergy in Washington to lobby for peace, and dispatched a team that established direct links with Buddhists in Vietnam. Editors of the prestigious *New York Review of Books* circulated a petition against Johnson's escalation policy. Poet Robert Lowell refused an invitation to a White House Festival of the Arts, and two authors who did attend the event circulated an antiwar petition there. The president was miffed: "Some of them insult me by staying away," he complained, "and some of them insult me by coming."[7]

By that time, the SDS demonstration had offered a venue for national protest. On 17 April 1965 an estimated crowd of 20,000 turned out for the largest peace demonstration held in the capital to that time. The press was impressed by its size and character. Its New Left tone was conveyed in the singing of Judy Collins and Joan Baez and in speeches by I. F. Stone, historian Staughton Lynd, SNCC leader Robert Parris Moses, and SDS president Paul Potter. Vietnam policy was "the symptom of a deeper malaise," Potter said, and he called for America's "radical reconstruction."[8] That was the Port Huron program, after all, and in a strategy conference after the rally the SDS leaders elected to stay with their original program of campus reform and community organizing. Having put together the first major protest demonstration, they left a vacuum of leadership in what became a series of frustrating attempts to align elements of the left wing of the antiwar movement.

The distinction between liberal and radical approaches sharpened as the war escalated. To some extent it was defined by tactical issues of exclusionism and the demand for immediate withdrawal from Vietnam. Exclusionism referred to the strategy of limiting antiwar coalitions to politically acceptable constituencies—specifically to exclude communists. It reflected bitter experience with radical infighting in the 1930s and with McCarthyism in the 1950s, but it did not make any sense to the leaders of the New Left. The issue separated emerging radical protest from liberal dissent. Liberals differed from radicals also over whether to call for a negotiated settlement or immediate withdrawal. Beyond political tactics, they divided on basic social philosophy. For radicals, the heart of the problem was the unjust distribution of power in America and its extension as imperialism; for liberals it was the war itself. Norman Thomas was as committed to reform as anyone in the country, but he denied that peace required "radical transformation."[9] Radicals, on the contrary, insisted that the war offered an issue around which to mobilize a broad coalition of aggrieved groups and restructure society. Pacifist groups mirrored the strain in the movement because, although predominantly liberal, they included radical pacifists receptive to the New Left orientation of political radicals.

Seeking to align disaffected minorities, a small radical coalition attracted about 2,000 people to Washington in August for an Assembly of Unrepresented People. They held workshops on various social problems and marched to the Capitol, where some 350 antiwar protesters were arrested. Out of the assembly there emerged a tenuous National Coordinating Committee to End the War in Vietnam (NCCEWVN). Its only real program was to plan an October demonstration timed to coincide with international rallies against the war, but its formation reflected the radical attempt to form a coalition of social change movements on the periphery of American politics, by contrast with the liberal thrust to the center.

As the radical wing of the movement became increasingly active and visible, it was accommodated in the interest of presenting the broadest possible antiwar coalition. That accomodation became clear in the prep-

arations for the "International Days of Protest" in October. A strong coalition group, the Fifth Avenue Peace Parade Committee, was created
by individuals from New York City groups ranging from the Old Left to
the radical pacifists of the CNVA, WRL, and the *Liberation* collective,
and to liberals of SANE, WSP, and AFSC. The New York committee
skirted the issue of exclusionism by voluntary participation and local decision making. It also bypassed the issue of immediate withdrawal by
adopting the slogan "Stop the War in Vietnam NOW." SANE modified its
policy of exclusionism by encouraging local chapters to participate in the
nationwide demonstrations, and the result was a loosely coordinated protest by about 100,000 people in 80 cities and several nations.

The next month, SANE attracted 30,000 demonstrators to Washington in an effort to engage "the broadest possible participation" in "responsible criticism."[10] Sanford Gottlieb coordinated the rally. He
discouraged any actions that might alienate the political center, and yet
he sought broad representation. Radicals were excluded from the speakers' list, but the NCCEWVN was invited to participate. In fact it attracted
perhaps 1,500 people from 100 local and national antiwar and civil rights
groups to a convention it scheduled around the SANE demonstration.
The radical conference was riven with rancorous factionalism over priorities, tactics, and leadership.[11] People who came for serious discussion
of social problems and war were perplexed and dismayed.

The International Days of Protest, the Fifth Avenue Peace Parade
Committee, the SANE rally, and the NCCEWVN convention—all reflected the diversity of antiwar constituencies, the impulse for coalition,
and the difficulty of achieving it in the face of widespread public support
for the war effort and hostility to protesters.

Gathering Constituencies   During 1966 nodes of antiwar opposition multiplied within a still overwhelmingly prowar nation. The most
important of them was the religious constituency that organized as
Clergy and Laity Concerned (CALC) between January and April, with
William Sloane Coffin, Jr., as executive secretary.[12] This organization
gave the antiwar movement access to a network of religious leaders in
local communities. Small antiwar constituencies were organized among
labor leaders, social workers, the cultural elite, and a few military veterans. Opposition to the war began to crystallize also in Americans for
Democratic Action. The ADA leadership was keenly aware that an un-
popular war could derail the liberal reforms it supported, and yet it was
dependent on Johnson to attain them.

Trying to challenge the war without attacking the president, liberals turned to local politics. SANE set up a National Voters Peace Pledge Campaign to win votes for peace candidates in the November election, working through the summer along with the ADA, AFSC, and FCNL. The electoral action of 1966 engaged New York lawyer Allard Lowenstein to mobilize extensive contacts from years of activism in civil rights and student work. With ADA staff member Curtis Gans, Lowenstein became convinced that war policy was vulnerable at the grass-roots level. Together they began to lay the political base for a campaign to "Dump Johnson" as their party's 1968 presidential candidate.

While liberals worked into local politics, radical activists planning new demonstrations encountered the decentralized nature of antiwar sentiment. The NCCEWVN was mistrusted on all sides, and therefore the "Second International Days of Protest" in April was organized by local coalitions such as the Fifth Avenue Peace Parade Committee. Veterans assumed significant leadership in Philadelphia, clergy in Cincinnati. Perhaps 100,000 people participated in rallies in 80 to 100 cities in America and abroad. In the following months there were futile attempts to forge a cohesive antiwar coalition. The best that could be done was to schedule concurrent rallies by local groups in a November "experiment in united timing." Those actions were diverse and modest, involving only about 20,000 people nationwide. The march in New York gave visibility to a new constituency—the counterculture.

Counterculture was a loose term that embraced life-styles ranging from devotees of LSD and Eastern mysticism to a youth cult caught up in the fad of long hair and outlandish costumes. The common denominator was rock music and permissive attitudes toward personal behavior, sex, and drugs. In one form, the counterculture was a dropout, not only from mainstream America but from attempts to reform it. In another form it was the vision of an alternative and more authentic life-style, and it was often difficult to distinguish what was simply a change in social norms from what was an intentional challenge to prevailing values. By late 1966 a lighthearted, so-called hippie version had emerged, which reveled in absurdity without quite losing touch with social reality. This was the counterculture of poet Alan Ginsberg on the West Coast and of the bohemians who attached themselves playfully to the New York march. The media and political opponents of the movement promptly attached the counterculture image to the antiwar movement: to protest was to be a hippie.[13]

Organized draft resistance offered a more serious constituency. Conscientious objection to war and military service predated the antiwar movement, of course, but only the Vietnam War produced a highly organized network of young draft resisters and adult supporters. The reasons for rejecting conscription ranged from personal ambition and security to principled opposition to militarism or Indochina policy. Whatever the motivation, the import was the same: a sizable number of young men concluded that this war at least had no claim on them. "Not with my life you don't," they said. Counseling services on the ethical and legal aspects of conscientious objection expanded enormously as draft calls increased. Often sponsored by pacifist organizations such as the FOR, AFSC, and Catholic Peace Fellowship or by churches, counseling involved numerous sympathetic lawyers, ministers, and citizens.[14] An extensive program was developed by women in local WSP chapters who understood the advantage of associating motherly figures with conscientious objectors.

Beyond counseling individuals, there was resistance to conscription itself. Not only did the draft symbolize the war, it epitomized injustice because it was weighed disproportionately against black, poor, and less educated men. Independent "We Won't Go" groups were organized throughout the country. A conference of 500 activists early in December 1966 adopted draft resistance as a basic antiwar strategy. This was endorsed by the national convention of SDS two weeks later and then by the more representative Student Mobilization Committee (1966). The organization of draft resistance increased the weight of radical pacifists in the antiwar movement and added a constituency of men for whom even avoiding conscription could be interpreted as antiwar activism.

Dissatisfaction with the war spread during the winter of 1967, and new constituencies of protest were organized along professional lines. They included physicians, former Peace Corps workers, artists, authors, labor unions, the Federation of American Scientists, and Business Executives Move for a Vietnam Peace (BEM). Other sectors were represented too. Students, for example, were organized in the Student Mobilization Committee. Women's organizations with political platforms, like the WILPF and WSP, were supplemented by Another Mother for Peace, with its simple appeal to stop the sacrifice of mothers' sons. The single most important acquisition that season was Martin Luther King, Jr., for he brought along his stature as the 1964 Nobel Peace Prize winner and his civil rights associations. Moreover, with his record of both direct nonviolent action and political reform, King bridged the radical and liberal wings of the antiwar movement. Although he was criticized by conservative civil rights leaders, he gave a fresh impetus to the 1967 Spring Mobilization.

National Campaigns   Impelled by multiplying constituencies and a sense of urgency, activists coordinated plans for national demonstrations in the spring of 1967. They replaced the NCCEWVN with a more cohesive Spring Mobilization Committee. They reached out to antiwar liberals, adapting their platform to include a bombing halt, a ceasefire initiated by the United States, negotiations, and "phased withdrawal" of American troops. The FOR, SANE, CALC, and WSP endorsed participation by local chapters in the Spring Mobilization.

The point of mass demonstrations was to dramatize a broad, united opposition to the war. In terms of organizations, that cohesiveness did not exist. Antiwar groups were divided, sometimes sharply, by issues such as immediate withdrawal from Vietnam and by movement politics. There were marked differences and tensions between national and local levels of most groups and among the local chapters of some. And there was a large, undefined mass of citizens who had strong reservations to the war but were not affiliated with any national antiwar group. To the extent that opposition to the war was coherent, it existed in the undifferentiated anxiety that was spreading throughout the country. A major demonstration such as the Spring Mobilization was designed, therefore, to attract people whose energy it could not really direct; it provided the decentralized, heterogeneous movement with a focal point for public outreach.

Even organizing such an event required enormous energy and resources. Its image, often phrased in terms of a slogan or title such as "Spring Mobilization to End the War in Vietnam" had to be negotiated among sponsoring groups. There were practical tasks: funding had to be secured; permits obtained; arrangements worked out with local authorities; speakers and entertainers selected and provided for; publicity distributed; media cultivated; people transported, accommodated, and provisioned. Marshals had to be trained to direct the crowd, deal with emergencies, and intercede between demonstrators and hecklers (antiwar protesters had been attacked by then, and racial violence was roiling throughout the country: Martin Luther King, Jr., warned that several cities were virtual "powder kegs").[15] Given such formidable tasks, the style of organizing itself could become a divisive issue.

Nonetheless, the spring rallies were massive and effectively conducted. At least 200,000 people walked from the United Nations building to New York's Central Park; 50,000 marched in San Francisco.[16] The crowds included old and young, men and women, blacks and American Indians, hippies and businessmen, contingents of military veterans and 150 conscientious objectors who burned their draft cards in a public ceremony. There were no untoward events, and the demonstrations conveyed the image of diverse and growing opposition to the war.

The next month a meeting of antiwar groups settled on three parallel strategies: Vietnam Summer, Negotiations Now!, and draft resistance. The first project was a direct thrust to the grass roots. Coordinated by a former national secretary of SDS and the executive director of CALC, a loose network of students recruited part-time local volunteers to canvas, petition, teach, and generally raise community consciousness about the war. Although hampered by inconsistent staff, ideological differences, and public apathy, the project stimulated local organizing. Negotiations Now!, on the other hand, was promoted by SANE, ADA, and prestigious liberals to rally the politically literate public through newspaper ads and petitions to the president. The third strategy of the summer was draft resistance. With support from the FOR, AFSC, and some local chapters of SANE, draft counseling was stepped up and a Draft Resistance Clearinghouse was formed. We Won't Go groups spread. A national network calling itself "the Resistance" was organized through the efforts of David Harris, former student body president at Stanford, and his Berkeley friend, Lennie Heller. They invited resisters across the nation to turn in their draft cards on 16 October 1967. Men above draft age and women sympathizers signed "A Call to Resist Illegitimate Authority," explicitly making themselves complicit with eligible young men.

Although in retrospect it seems clear that the Spring Mobilization and the summer projects of 1967 were relating to a growing public disaffection with the war, antiwar forces felt ever more frustrated and isolated. There were several reasons for this. For one thing, patience was difficult for activists who were immediately and often totally consumed by the war issue and the moral conflict it represented. Oppressed by public apathy and resistance, they found it difficult to wait for a turn in the slow tide of popular opinion. Moreover, the war was debated in the context of domestic crises. Racial anger and recrimination erupted in violence throughout the South and in northern cities where, for example, 43 people died in Detroit riots that required thousands of soldiers to quell. With American institutions seeming to break down, it was hard to trust them to reverse the war. Finally, polarization within the country as a whole was replicated within the antiwar movement. Although keenly aware of the importance of a united front, activists experienced unending factionalism.

A loose antiwar coalition—the Movement—had been forged between the inauguration of Operation Rolling Thunder in the winter of 1965 and the conclusion of Vietnam Summer in 1967. While its member groups staged impressive demonstrations and its constituency broadened, the war intensified and the administration's commitment solidified. Although antiwar groups were able to cooperate on specific and sometimes large-scale projects, their energy and confidence was sapped by internal divisions over strategy and goals. The dominant groups were centrally organized, but they were trying to mobilize a movement whose real force and initiative were decentralized and inchoate. The pervasive tensions of the movement's formative period were sharply exposed in the turbulent year beginning in the fall of 1967.

The Movement in Turmoil, Fall 1967–Fall 1968

Logical Contradictions   For a year beginning in the fall of 1967, the nation rode a rollercoaster of emotions, as hope alternated with anxiety, political participation with confrontation. Urban and racial crises contributed to it, but everything was war related in one way or another. In general, confrontation increased to the extent that the political system seemed to be unresponsive, although splintering factions in radical antiwar constituencies also generated extremism. Nothing seemed to work out as intended, whether by the Johnson administration or by antiwar activists.

It seemed perfectly logical to the radical left that a coalition of disaffected minorities could both end the war and transform society. That was the logic of the National Conference for a New Politics, which held a convention in Chicago early in September. Its sponsors hoped to combine street action with electoral politics. Instead, the meeting turned into a chaotic scramble to assuage a demanding black caucus. Vietnam was even dismissed as a "local" and temporary issue. The convention collapsed. The illogic of it all made cooperation with radicals problematic for many leaders in SANE and spurred a reorganization that, with leadership from liberal historian H. Stuart Hughes, led to a clear focus on electoral work.

To the National Mobilization Committee (Mobe), which had taken over from the Spring Mobilization, it seemed quite logical that a major autumn demonstration should be held in Washington to dramatize national protest. Acting for the Mobe, David Dellinger turned to California activist Jerry Rubin for leadership. Rubin brought with him the counterculture style. He insisted on making the Pentagon itself the target of an October march to "Confront the Warmakers," promising to levitate the building and exorcise it of war demons. That kind of talk was good media; but it reinforced the image of the radical coalition as a fringe group, and liberal groups pulled back. A logical compromise offered participants a choice of actions ranging from a mass rally on the Mall to nonviolent civil disobedience at the Pentagon.

As the national rally approached, tension was heightened by the national draft card turn-in on 16 October. More than a thousand young men participated directly in formal ceremonies, and they were seconded by older supporters. When nonviolent demonstrators were arrested in Oakland, California, several thousand people tried to shut down an army induction center and the response of police led to a riot. There was violence also in Madison, Wisconsin. Under these circumstances, groups including SANE and SDS declined to endorse the Washington demonstration. Nonetheless, on the morning of 20 October some 100,000 people rallied peaceably on the Mall to protest the war. In the afternoon, about half of them marched across the Potomac to the Pentagon, where, despite careful planning for nonviolent action, a small number of militants provoked troops to respond in force. Tear gas, arrests, and beatings left marchers in disarray. The incident unfairly tarnished the whole rally with an image of willful confrontation that contributed to a backlash against antiwar protest. Isolated incidents of militant provocation the following month reinforced public hostility.

Although many Americans mistrusted protest, they also had deep-seated doubts about the war. This feeling showed up in many ways, an elusive but palpable desire to be out of Vietnam. What is more, Lowenstein's and Gans's attempt to "Dump Johnson" finally turned up a challenger for the Democratic nomination in Senator Eugene McCarthy. Even before the Minnesotan declared, President Johnson consulted with a group of senior consultants, the so-called Wise Men. They confirmed that there was serious "domestic disquiet" as a result of "the prospect of endless inconclusive fighting." They urged him to emphasize accomplishment for the short term, and to design a military strategy that would steadily decrease in cost over the long haul. The people needed to believe that the corner had been turned in Vietnam, they said.[17] The political thrust of this advice was to sell the war, not to evaluate it.

The administration acted on that logic. It arranged for favorable news releases, assembled a citizens committee to rally the people, and brought U.S. ambassador to South Vietnam Henry Cabot Lodge and General William Westmoreland home to shore up confidence. The president himself undertook a round-the-world public relations tour, exclaiming on his return that the enemy had "met his master in the field."[18] Meanwhile, the administration hardened its response to dissent, saying that the antiwar movement was controlled by communists. They knew better because the Federal Bureau of Investigation and the Central Intelligence Agency had kept activists under close surveillance, penetrating their groups with informers and harassing protesters with illegal tactics. The director of the CIA told the president that the agency had "no significant evidence" of communist "direction of the U.S. peace movement or its leaders."[19] Johnson refused to release the report. In the logic of rallying the political center, it was useful to keep dissenters on the margin.

The center broke when Vietcong troops attacked American bases and South Vietnamese cities on 30 January 1968—Tet, the lunar new year. Communist troops were thrown back in savage fighting that resulted in huge civilian loses, although a major battle raged around the isolated U.S. base at Khe Sanh well into March. General Westmoreland claimed a victory, but the public saw Vietcong strength and tenacity instead. Popular "disquiet" found an outlet in the New Hampshire presidential primary, where McCarthy made an unexpectedly strong showing against Johnson. Shortly afterward Senator Robert Kennedy of Massachusetts joined the race. The president ordered his secretary of defense to review the military situation, and he reconvened the Wise Men. Military and political advice was equally sobering: the war could not be won without a major escalation of cost, which the people would not accept. In a dramatic address on 31 March Johnson, promising to put a ceiling on the war effort and open peace negotiations, withdrew from the presidential race for the sake of national unity.

Events were overtaking all rational calculations, and four days later Martin Luther King, Jr., was gunned down. The nation ricocheted between order and disorder. Riots in over 100 cities led to the death of 46 people and the arrest of 200,000. There was a record number of protests on college campuses, mostly over local issues and occasionally violent. In Vietnam, where deteriorating army morale threatened the command structure, a two-week U.S. offensive cost 1,100 lives. Fragmentation in the society was reflected in radical left. There was a huge gap between the new national leadership of SDS, caught up in challenging established institutions, and the membership, whose activism was mostly conventional in style.

The 1968 Election Campaign   Indeed, as the McCarthy and Kennedy primary campaigns became a major vehicle of the antiwar movement in the spring of 1968, large numbers of young people signed on. Vice President Hubert Humphrey was admired for his liberal record, but he was mistrusted as an administration candidate. McCarthy had been endorsed by SANE and ADA even before the New Hampshire primary. He and Kennedy attracted support from all the major antiwar groups and enlisted their memberships. They also attracted political constituencies that although resentful of the war, had not associated with the antiwar movement. The two challengers were equally paired by June, when Kennedy was fatally shot and the spirit went out of the campaign.

Singer Phil Ochs had explained earlier, "if you feel you have been living in an unreal world for the last couple of years, it is particularly because this power structure has refused to listen to reason."[20] Whimsically dramatizing that attitude, Jerry Rubin and some friends designated themselves as yippies and promised to play out their counterculture version of reality at the Democratic national convention in Chicago.[21] On a more serious note, an antiwar demonstration at Chicago appealed to David Dellinger, Tom Hayden, and his friend Rennie Davis as a way of forcing the issue on the Democratic party. Left to run the Mobe when most of its constituent groups moved into the election campaign, they laid plans for a rally. Mayor Richard Daley's political machine refused permits and was altogether intimidating. When the demonstration was called anyway, the stage was set for confrontation the last week in August.

An air of unreality in Chicago was heightened by yippie pranksters. It was no joke to Daley's police. Five days of skirmishing with demonstrators reached a brutal crescendo when battle flooded the lakefront area downtown. Within the convention hall the efforts of Kennedy and McCarthy forces to get a strong antiwar plank in the party platform were stymied, and Humphrey was nominated. Stunned, the nation watched the conflict at the convention and in the streets. Most of the public endorsed Daley's heavy-handed rule, despite the fact that an official review panel later ruled it a "police riot."

Militant actions, some of them violent, followed the explosion in Chicago like aftershocks, as political radicals became all the more isolated. Large numbers of antiwar activists who had worked for Kennedy and

McCarthy despaired of the political system. Humphrey suffered from that cynicism, and although he began to close the gap as the election approached, he lost a very close race to Richard Nixon. His defeat paved the way for the Democratic leadership in the Congress to wage a more aggressive campaign against the war, given a Republican president. In the sense that antiwar pressure found an outlet in the legislature, and despite outward appearances, the political system was opening to dissent.

The Movement in Transition, Winter 1969–Spring 1971

The Fall Offensive   Nixon had campaigned on a promise to bring "peace with honor." While the nation waited to learn what that implied, the antiwar movement was reorganized. The Mobe was shunted aside by new groupings. Liberal peace advocates aligned with the Kennedy-McCarthy wing of the Democratic party in a nominal Coalition for National Priorities. Pacifists, with a heightened sense of the importance of nonviolent discipline and careful coordination, formed a tight network called the National Action Group (NAG, 1969). [22] A reconstituted Student Mobilization Committee cooperated with the SWP and GI-Civilian Anti-war Action Conference in anticipation of demonstrations in the spring of 1969. Those rallies were local, modest affairs under an overall slogan that appealed to the movement itself: "Resistance and Renewal."

Nixon prompted action when he revealed his peace plans in May. Although he promised a gradual reduction in troop strength, he assured the country that the North Vietnamese were on the verge of collapse and insisted that peace would come with the honor of fulfilling the original goal of a sovereign, anticommunist South Vietnam. The president's speech revived dormant opposition in the Congress and prompted the antiwar movement to design two coalition efforts aimed at the fall: the moratorium and the mobilization.

The moratorium was fashioned by several young activists fresh from the 1968 presidential campaign and active in liberal Democratic politics. [23] The idea was deceptively simple. People would be asked to set aside one day in a month for a moratorium on business as usual in order to reflect on the war in any way they felt appropriate. The plan was geared to the decentralized, grass-roots nature of antiwar sentiment, and it required no haggling over terms among sponsoring groups. Assured of initial funding from antiwar liberals, the Vietnam Moratorium Committee (VMC) set up an office in Washington and began to organize for October.

They worked mainly with student leaders in the summer, but then the idea began to take hold among liberal groups, intellectuals, civil rights and religious leaders, and organized labor. It was endorsed by 24 Democratic senators. CIA informers infiltrated the paid staff of 31 (there were also 7,500 field workers) and warned the agency that the moratorium was "shaping up to be the most widely supported peace action in American history."[24] That prospect worried Nixon, who had secretly threatened North Vietnam with overwhelming force if it did not negotiate on his terms by November. An outpouring of antiwar sentiment would weaken the credibility of his threat.

The outpouring came on 15 October. It was nationwide, massive, diverse in form, locally based, and representative of all public sectors. In rallies of from 10 to 100,000 people, an estimated quarter of a million ordinary citizens and elected officials, housewives and entertainers, business people and workers, expressed their desire to be out of Vietnam and to move on with a more cohesive America. The deeply patriotic tone of that desire was captured by the media.

At first the president's threat to North Vietnam seemed to be nullified. An aide recalled that Nixon "was as bitter and disappointed" as he ever saw him. The White House took the offensive, disparaging the moratorium's organizers and encouraging counterdemonstrations for an "Americanism" that supported the war effort. The campaign was capped by a televised speech on 3 November in which the president dismissed critics as a minority of defeatists, promised to turn the war over to the South Vietnamese, and called for support from "the great silent majority of citizens."[25] Polls suggested that he had that support. Congressional legislation to require withdrawal was put on hold. Antiwar activists could scarcely believe that six months of effort had evaporated overnight. A planned moratorium for 15 November was in jeopardy, and so was the second thrust of the 1969 antiwar movement, the national mobilization scheduled for the same date.

That demonstration was the product of another attempt to align an antiwar coalition of the left. Leaders in the AFSC and SWP had called a meeting in July, carefully choosing the participants so as to exclude militant radicals. Although they had a broad social agenda, they agreed that the war was "the Pivotal Issue."[26] Creating a New Mobilization Committee (New Mobe), they designated 13–15 November for mass demonstrations in Washington and San Francisco to demand immediate withdrawal from Vietnam. Nixon's counteroffensive raised the stake of a successful demonstration and increased pressure on the New Mobe and

VMC to coordinate their efforts. The result was dramatic and controlled. Nearly a half million people from all walks of life confronted the war with clarity and seriousness appropriate to the ongoing tragedy.

The 15 November mobilization was the largest protest demonstration in American history to that time, but it had no appreciable impact on the public. Americans polled were overwhelmingly tired of the war, half of them regarding it as morally indefensible. And yet most of them also objected to antiwar demonstrations. It was difficult to penetrate that paradox. One explanation is the public thirst for domestic order. Controversy was exacerbated by protest, whereas it was defused by the president's policy of Vietnamization—turning the fighting over to South Vietnamese and withdrawing American troops. In any case, the disparity in public attitudes perplexed and frustrated antiwar critics.

Regrouping   Many activists felt washed out and turned to other causes or to the business of reordering their own lives. Those who remained active found that the mobilization had drained the movement of funds on even the local level. The New Mobe disintegrated, pulled apart by competing extremists from the movement's fringe. The Vietnam Moratorium Committee faded out. By the spring of 1970 there were three definable elements in the organized antiwar movement: political liberals, veterans, and pacifists. Each of them evolved in ways that set the stage for a dramatic series of protests a year later.

Antiwar liberals shifted much of the energy that had animated the moratorium into electoral politics and congressional lobbying. Groups such as SANE and CALC combined with ADA Democrats to assist selected antiwar candidates. Their plans were interrupted on 30 April when Nixon announced that he had sent American troops into Cambodia, provoking a wave of protests, overwhelmingly spontaneous and locally initiated. At Kent State University, Ohio National Guard troops fired on students who were not even demonstrating at the time, killing four and sending shock waves across the nation's campuses. Other killings followed at Jackson State University in Mississippi. A million and a half students left classes, and some university systems had to close down. The remnants of the New Mobe hastily arranged a demonstration of over 100,000 people in Washington, but the rally lacked a clear focus. For all of its immensity, the nationwide protest was ephemeral. The spring crisis contributed to the political thrust of antiwar liberals, though, because it generated a strong demand for congressional action.

Nixon withdrew the troops from Cambodia and continued Vietnamization, but he faced legislators determined to set a definite date for withdrawal from Vietnam. Antiwar liberals mobilized public support for that legislation, and they also fielded thousands of students to work for peace candidates. By midsummer about 40 national organizations were involved in coordinated electoral efforts. The administration stepped up its surveillance and harassment of critics and ostentatiously wrapped itself in the American flag. In September it beat back Senate legislation for a cutoff date. The next month Nixon took to the campaign trail on behalf of his supporters. Voting was indecisive as a test of war policy, although several activists were elected to Congress.

There emerged a broad coalition in support of congressional efforts to set a definite withdrawal date. The initiative came from SANE, CALC, the FOR, and Protestant and Jewish leaders, and soon they were joined by the AFSC, ADA, Common Cause, and about 20 religious groups. A designated date to end the war was even endorsed by the Democratic national committee. After months of careful building, the project was launched in February 1971 as the Set the Date Now Campaign. By then antiwar liberals had developed a cohesive coalition around a specific program.

Meanwhile, antiwar veterans became better organized, notably in Vietnam Veterans Against the War (VVAW). They brought credibility and fresh vitality to the movement, along with sobering realism. In September 1970 they dramatized the war with a mock search-and-destroy action in New Jersey and Pennsylvania. Then they cooperated with civilian activists to show that atrocities like the well-publicized massacre of civilians at My Lai were not exceptional events. CALC had raised the issue of war crimes before, but the veterans were speaking from firsthand experience. A December hearing in Washington resulted in 300 pages of lurid testimony and a formal request from several officers for a court of inquiry into war crimes. By then First Lieutenant William Calley was on trial for his role at My Lai. VVAW activists argued that guilt lay with the war itself and the command responsible for it, not with individual soldiers. They drove their point home with an inquiry early in February, in which veterans depicted a pattern of atrocities and coverups. By that time the VVAW was looking for a larger field of action.

Pacifists, although still aligned in the National Action Group, were slower to develop a coherent antiwar program than either political liberals or veterans. By the fall of 1970 they had evolved a project for a People's Peace Treaty. The idea was to take a draft peace treaty directly to the public in order to inform discussion and generate pressure on Congress for withdrawal. The project was endorsed by CALC, WSP, and SANE, and in February 1971 the People's Coalition for Peace and Justice was established to coordinate it. Meanwhile, the National Student Association had sent a delegation of students to North and South Vietnam to discuss its own version of a people's treaty. In February, however, the student treaty project was attached to an older proposal for mass civil disobedience: an action on the first of May would threaten to close down Washington if the treaty were not adopted by the government.[27] This so-called MayDay project caused consternation in the People's Coalition, since mass civil disobedience had not been approved by the fragile coalition. Confounding the whole scene, a National Peace Action Coalition had been formed in the wake of the Kent State killings to plan large spring demonstrations on the theme "Out Now!"

Thus, by midwinter 1971 each of several antiwar constituencies had evolved its own tactic: antiwar liberals and Set the Date Now, veteran protesters fresh from their war crimes hearings, a tenuous left-wing coalition of radical pacifists built around the People's Peace Treaty, the MayDay group threatening mass civil disobedience, and the National Peace Action Coalition planning a single-issue demonstration. A small group of pacifists bridged pervasive mistrust and recrimination to work out terms by which the various tactics could be sequenced. This made it possible for activists to participate in one of several forms of protest. It seemed to be the only alternative to chaos and confrontation.

The sequence of spring actions opened on 26 March with an appeal to Set the Date Now from church leaders who had met with all the parties to the peace negotiations in Paris. Sponsored mainly by the FOR, AFSC, and CALC, the appeal was promoted by religious groups through Easter weekend. Early in April there were multi-issue rallies around the country, coordinated by the People's Coalition with support from civil rights and poverty groups and using $1 million worth of donated advertising in a campaign to "unsell the Vietnam war."

Beginning on 18 April, the VVAW mobilized veterans in Washington, where they held a memorial service, staged mock search-and-destroy operations, and testified before the Senate Foreign Relations Committee. At the end of the week 700 of them demonstrated at the Capitol, identifying themselves by name and angrily flinging away their medals and ribbons. Against the powerful symbolism of that action, between 200,000 and 500,000 people demonstrated on 24 April (as well as some 125,000 in San Francisco) in a rally that was well-managed, orderly, and impressive. For several days afterward, activists lobbied for a specified

Mass demonstrations in Washington, D.C., and San Francisco were held on 24 April 1971 despite Vietnamization and the withdrawal of U.S. troops. They were part of a series of April Actions that involved religious, civic-reform, and antiwar veteran constituencies and culminated in the MayDay civil disobedience action. By this time the nation and the movement reflected a changed life-style: compare the appearance of these demonstrators with those of 1965. *Swarthmore College Peace Collection; courtesy of Theodore B. Hetzel*

end to the war, and the People's Peace Treaty was introduced into Congress as a House resolution.

The program of mass civil disobedience, designed to tie up Washington traffic and dramatize the connection between war and social disorder, was deliberately placed last in the sequence in order to separate the MayDay group from people coming only for the antiwar rally and to permit training for nonviolent confrontation. Washington police and military forces made preemptive strikes on the demonstrators, though, and 7,000 people were summarily arrested and briefly incarcerated. The government's response was directed from the White House, where Nixon encouraged his aides to "bust" the protesters. Media coverage fused the impression of rioting with the fact of the earlier demonstration, doubtless reinforcing the image of defiant confrontation. In fact, the sequenced actions in the spring of 1971 reflected disciplined protest and sophistication in managing factionalism and political actions.

Although the people could not be aroused against the war, they could not be mobilized for it either. Government policy reflected that fact. The draft was abandoned, for example, because of mismanagement in the face of widespread citizen resistance. Vietnamization was in part a recognition of deteriorating morale and outright war resistance among the troops, and it was also a concession to war weariness at home: Vietnam policy had become a matter of executive discretion, not a national cause. Under these circumstances, activists became ever more oriented to the tactics of persuasion and congressional pressure. The movement became less visible as it flowed more fully through mainstream politics.

Movement in the Political System, Winter 1972–Spring 1975

The perimeters of dissent in 1972 were set by the presidential election of that year. The main Democratic contender, George McGovern, declared early for prompt withdrawal of American forces by a set date. Antiwar groups endorsed that approach, and they developed a campaign against the air war, which Nixon had extended to Cambodia and Laos. The bombing there had been conducted in secret, without congressional authorization, so that the Campaign to End the Air War challenged not only military policy but also executive accountability and credibility. The campaign was organized by the liberal pacifists of the National Action Group. It included research and direct action against munitions makers such as Honeywell, but it was intended primarily to generate pressure for congressional action.

Just as the Campaign to End the Air War got under way, North Vietnam launched a powerful offensive that sent South Vietnamese troops reeling. Nixon intensified the air war, carrying it to the North Vietnamese capital of Hanoi. Spontaneous protest around the country was channeled to the Congress by the antiwar groups. Although congressional opposition stiffened, Nixon responded to a communist advance in May by increasing the bombing still further and ordering the mining of North Vietnamese ports and rivers. Another round of protest ensued, but it was defused when the Soviets welcomed Nixon to Moscow for arms negotiations and later when peace talks were resumed in Paris. Together with his earlier détente with China, Nixon's Moscow card gave him a strong suit as he headed into the electoral campaign of midsummer.

Antiwar groups supported the McGovern ticket and put their resources at its disposal. Even former radical Tom Hayden came out of a self-enforced isolation to help form the Indochina Peace Campaign, which he aimed at the political mainstream. For McGovern, abandoned by conservative elements of the Democratic party and traditionally supportive newspapers, it was an uphill campaign. Nixon exploited every weakness, even authorizing illegal tactics like burglarizing the Democratic headquarters at the Watergate complex in Washington, which he managed to cover up temporarily. Meanwhile, Secretary of State Henry Kissinger quietly negotiated a settlement with the North Vietnamese. When the deal became public at the end of October, it undercut the already flagging McGovern campaign. It also made Nixon's victory a mandate for peace.

Accordingly, the president was under more pressure than ever to end the war. This was especially serious because South Vietnamese president Nguyen Van Thieu initially rejected the peace settlement, concluding that it would effectively scuttle his regime. Nixon increased the pressure on him to comply and launched a devastating bombing campaign on Hanoi in December. The Congress made clear its determination to cut off the war once and for all, but by the time the president was inaugurated on 23 January, all parties had acceded to a peace accord. It was signed four days later.

The so-called Christmas bombing of 1972 was the catalyst for the last and most cohesive antiwar coalition, the Coalition to Stop Funding the War (CSFW). Formed by representatives of SANE, ADA, the National Education Association, and ten religious peace groups, the CSFW was originally designed to bring pressure on Congress to cut off funding when it appeared that Nixon's October initiative had stalled. By the time of the peace accord, the coalition had raised significant funds and organized a network of offices in sensitive congressional districts. It had early support from McGovern's office, the United Auto Workers, and the WILPF, and it quickly expanded to about 40 organizations, including the AFSC, CALC, BEM, and WRL.

The new coalition continued after the 1973 peace accord. Nixon was continuing the air war in Cambodia, and he had pledged support to the Thieu regime. Activists directed their efforts to cutting off indirect intervention. They mobilized pressure on Congress to end the bombing in Cambodia and aid to Thieu, while they publicized repression in South Vietnam and the plight of political prisoners there. They achieved some success. The Congress finally stopped the air war in Cambodia in mid-August, and it continually reduced the level of assistance to South Vietnam. The CSFW worked informally with the Indochina Peace Campaign and pacifist groups until in October it obtained the full cooperation and shared resources of 15 national organizations.

The force of congressional opposition rose during 1973 as Nixon became enmeshed in the Watergate scandal. At stake were the constitutional questions of presidential accountability and credibility. Antiwar activists avoided the issues of Watergate and even impeachment, but they couched their campaign against the air war and aid to Thieu in constitutional terms. By May 1974 the president was deeply implicated in Watergate. Impeachment proceedings were begun, and three months later Nixon resigned. The CSFW remained in place to challenge aid for the Thieu regime when it was requested by the new president, Gerald Ford.

A major North Vietnamese offensive in December made the military assistance issue critical. South Vietnamese troops pulled back and then retreated headlong. Ford requested aid, but the consensus in Congress was that assistance was a futile gesture. That sentiment was shared by a large majority of the American people, and it was represented on Capitol Hill by peace groups that massed 2,000 activists for political action and their last antiwar rally, the 25–27 January 1975 Assembly to Save the Peace. Within months South Vietnam collapsed. Americans were evacuated from Hanoi on 30 April as North Vietnamese forces converged on the city. For the United States the war was officially over, the goal of a sovereign and anticommunist state in the South abandoned at the cost of over 56,000 American and over 1 million Vietnamese lives.

The Movement Assessed

For a decade the antiwar movement kept the prospect of failure before the American public as an option that had to be faced. That was its main achievement. Informing and arousing the public to the war issues, it accepted the negative role of claiming that the national war effort was futile, ill-conceived, and morally wrong. In the process, it engaged two strong presidents in a contest for popular and then congressional support. Antiwar protest did not prolong the war: the Johnson and Nixon administrations did that by pursuing the elusive goal of a sovereign South Vietnam. The antiwar movement did not end the war: the American people did that by withdrawing passive support for it. The movement did force the issue, however, and it did so in three ways. First, it generated alternative sources of authority on Vietnam policy, clarifying the political and moral issues involved. Second, it mobilized enough opposition to set perimeters on war policy that were exceeded, by Nixon especially, only in violation of presidential accountability. Third, it added to the social cost of the war by the very controversy it engendered.

There never was a single antiwar movement, of course. There were shifting sets of leaders and constituencies throughout the decade. Improvisational and varied, they reacted to events more than they created opportunities for influence. In a broad sense and on the national level, they were divided between liberal and radical approaches. Liberals tended to concentrate on the war issue, mobilizing the political center of the country and channeling dissent into the system. Radicals hoped to align disaffected minorities in a coalition that would confront and transform American society. The radical approach acquired considerable force between 1967 and 1971 as it subsumed other social causes. Its confrontational approach was accentuated by the fact that the political system seemed unresponsive to dissent. The liberal approach was critical in defining the war issues in 1965–67, and it acquired force from 1968 to 1975 as radical extremism played itself out and the political system opened up, notably through Democratic party politics.

To describe the antiwar movement as two wings is deceptive, however. Even the most cohesive radical group, the Socialist Workers Party, had to work through coalitions because of its small membership and its preference for mass demonstrations. The SDS abandoned any pretense of antiwar leadership in 1965, and it was thoroughly fragmented by extremism. Indeed, most of the disaffected minorities on which radicals relied were fractured by internal division. Advocates of black power disrupted the civil rights movement, for example; women who experienced male chauvinism in civil rights and antiwar groups turned to women's liberation; and militant ideologues and counterculture devotees fragmented various radical groups. Leaders in those groups changed rapidly and were often distanced from the constituencies they professed to represent. Only the powerful moral challenge of the war wielded disparate radicals together, and then only occasionally and for specific purposes.

Liberals, on the other hand, were based in the relatively cohesive peace groups existing at the beginning of the war, to which CALC was added. Each of those groups had its own set of constituencies and agendas, and each had to weigh those against the advantages and disadvantages of cooperating with others. The cost could be significant when cooperation involved radical groups with confrontational styles and political positions that were offensive to members of liberal groups, their elite contacts, or to the general public. Each peace group also experienced competition between its national staff and local chapters for funds, time, and priorities. Adding confusion to dilemma, groups such as the AFSC, FOR, and WILPF included both liberal and radical pacifists, so that their own leaderships, although united on the principle of nonviolence and opposition to the war, were divided on questions of political strategy and position.

The movement, for all its multiplicity of leadership and organized constituencies, tried to mobilize the American people against a war conducted by their elected leaders. In fact, however, antiwar sentiment was organized independently where people lived and worked as people themselves became disillusioned with the war and impelled to do something about it. There at the grass-roots level was also a passive public that sullenly withdrew its support from the political leadership or simply turned to other matters. If this large, undifferentiated public resented the war, it valued social order and authority. Accordingly, antiwar organizations, which were mostly centralized on the national level, were faced with the problem of mobilizing public sentiment, which was highly decentralized and even suspicious of organized protest.

Antiwar activism altered the peace movement in several respects. Activists dealt with the problem of exclusionism by giving flexibility to local branches and individuals and by offering them a range of options. They developed innovative forms of protest, from street theater to civil disobedience. They learned to manage mass demonstrations with discipline and attention to the media. They advertised. They engaged in the political process at both the electoral and congressional levels, working within Democratic party politics. They called into question the basic tenets of the Cold War, which underlay Vietnam policy and challenged the priority of military security over social welfare. They adapted to a decentralized base of organization, which led to forms of networking in place of the directive style of earlier campaigns. Throughout, the political environment was charged with emotion, anxiety, and frustration. Nothing was clear at the time. In retrospect, the significance of antiwar protest was its profound effect not only on foreign policy but also on the peace movement itself.

Chapter Seven

The Second Campaign against Nuclear Arms, 1975–1987

The antiwar movement had been reduced to its core peace organizations as the United States withdrew from Vietnam. Even during the war, however, peace advocates had addressed the larger issues of the Cold War, especially the spiraling arms race and its effect on the quality of American life. SANE and related groups challenged the development of new nuclear weapons through 1979, when it became a salient public issue and led to the Nuclear Weapons Freeze Campaign, which grew spectacularly for three years. Indeed, the campaign was so dramatic that it was widely but wrongly taken to be the whole of the peace movement. The second coalition against nuclear arms was initiated by some of the same groups that sponsored the first one, but they worked in a new environment.

The political confrontation and polarities of the Vietnam War had obscured changes in the context of political activism. There had been a pervasive sense of citizen participation not only in the antiwar movement but also in civil rights, women's rights and roles, student life and governance, cultural norms, environmental issues, and consumer protection. Although the rhetoric of participatory democracy had been best articulated by the New Left until it succumbed to ideological extremism, the substance of participation had not at all been limited to the left. Middle America had become involved in a wide range of antiwar and reforming actions that had generated new social movement organizations. Participation in decision making had acquired fresh precedents and constituencies, reinforced by the wartime experience of challenging established

146

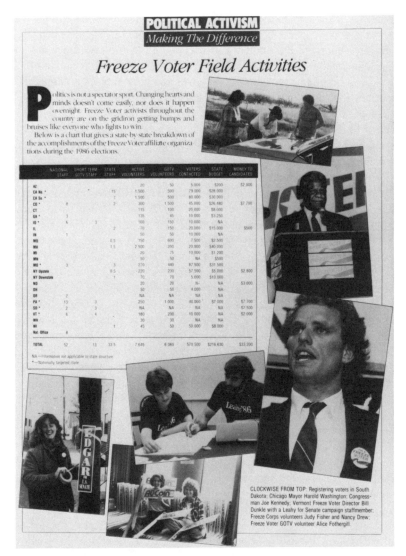

"Politics is not a spectator sport" begins the text of this page from the *Freeze Voter Report and Prospectus, 1986–88*. These pictures depict the political activism of a grass-roots movement and include former mayor of Chicago Harold Washington, Vermont Freeze Voter Director Bill Dunkle, and Freeze volunteers. The chart in the center gives a state-by-state comparison of the staff, volunteers, voters contacted, budget, and campaign funds raised. Compare this image of the movement with that conveyed by the program of the 1907 Arbitration and Peace Congress.

authority. Beyond the cynicism of the radical left there had emerged a pervasive skepticism about received tradition and official assertion. Alternative sources of authority had contributed to the credibility gap of the Johnson and Nixon administrations. Foreign and military affairs had been researched at the grass-roots level and in private or academic institutes. The antiwar movement had made its own contacts overseas and attempted a form of people's diplomacy. Now, in the 1970s, activists began to move into positions of civic responsibility on all political levels, bringing a vitality out of proportion to their numbers, while the Congress reasserted its constitutional role in foreign affairs.

The peace movement that emerged from the Vietnam War included the core pacifist groups (the FOR, AFSC, and WRL) and denominational fellowships such as Pax Christi, USA. There was a strong pacifist and transnational orientation also in the WILPF and CALC. The liberal internationalist tradition was represented in SANE and profession-based organizations such as Physicians for Social Responsibility (1961), the Council for a Livable World (CLW, 1962), and the Union of Concerned Scientists (UCS, 1968). SANE broadened its agenda and called itself "A Citizen's Organization for a Sane World." Its executive director, Sanford Gottlieb, helped to create a Coalition for a New Foreign and Military Policy (1969), which reached beyond traditional peace constituencies. Activism was reinforced by organized research. Peace researchers and educators explored conflict resolution as a social process and in a global context, and they had international connections. Indeed, the war stimulated efforts to teach about peace and conflict resolution in formal institutions and informal settings such as churches.[1]

Peace advocates reviewed their antiwar experience and reached a general consensus by 1972: the movement had been frustrated by ideological factionalism and extremism; it had not functioned effectively as a coalition of disaffected minorities; it had known the difficulty of channeling spontaneous grass-roots sentiment into political action; it had learned the importance of addressing the public in acceptable language and national symbols; it had experienced the power of the media and advertising; and it had emerged more than ever committed to work within the political system on specific issues.[2] The postwar peace movement understood that all issues were interrelated—peace and justice at home, order and revolution abroad, militarism and environment everywhere—but also that political effectiveness required attainable priorities around which to mobilize public support. Chastened activists prepared to address the world beyond Indochina.

The Vietnam War had modified, but had not dislodged, containment policy. According to the so-called Nixon Doctrine, the nation would sharply limit intervention abroad, but would maintain its overall capacity to restrict Soviet influence. President Jimmy Carter, for all his emphasis on human rights and interdependence, never questioned military containment. That policy rested in a frightening measure on nuclear weapons and arms control.

The 1963 partial test ban treaty had only moved atomic testing underground. The development of ever more sophisticated atomic weapons accelerated. By 1966 the United States had a triad of 1,054 intercontinental and 656 submarine-launched ballistic missiles and about 600 strategic bombers.[3] The Soviets lagged badly in numbers and technology. By 1970 the United States was deploying MIRVs, missiles whose multiple warheads could be targeted independently. The Soviet Union began to convert its land-based missiles into MIRVs in 1975, its sea-based ones four years later. By that time a Strategic Arms Limitation Agreement (SALT I) was in effect between the two superpowers, together with several other treaties limiting the conditions of testing and the overall number of delivery weapons. SALT I established ceilings on strategic delivery vehicles within which each power could build and modernize: both sides valued some form of arms control.[4]

Arms control involved weapons treaties and the process of negotiating them. It aimed at a rough balance of strategic forces designed to deter each country from initiating a first strike on the other. It did not stem the proliferation of nuclear warheads or new weapons systems, and it did not imply disarmament. It assumed on the contrary that, in the absence of fundamental change in the Soviet Union, geopolitical conflict and the race for technological advantage in nuclear weapons were inevitable. Arms control was a vital, if limited, instrument of management—a loose harness for a runaway horse that could not be stopped. Within the foreign policy establishment there emerged a small bureaucracy whose goal was to negotiate agreements that might gradually reign in the nuclear horse. The weapons race and arms control together changed the terms on which peace advocates addressed foreign policy in the 1980s.

Origins of the Freeze

The connection between the first and second coalition against nuclear arms was clearest in SANE and the AFSC. Even though the 1963 partial test ban treaty and the Vietnam War deprived nuclear weapons of political salience, SANE leaders did not abandon their original goal. They and CALC staff lobbied hard against the development of an antiballistic missile system (ABM) in 1969, insisting that it was too expensive and would destabilize deterrence. The AFSC and FOR joined the ABM campaign, which was directed especially toward localities where missiles would be deployed. The Union of Concerned Scientists also challenged the ABM, expanding from the Massachusetts Institute of Technology into a national organization as its members popularized scientific analysis, lobbied, and testified on Capitol Hill. The campaign probably contributed to the ratification of the ABM and SALT I treaties. In 1972 a successful campaign against the B-1 bomber program was conducted by the AFSC, allied with CALC, SANE, and some 40 national peace, feminist, environmental, labor, and religious groups.[5] When President Ford later pressed for a $100 billion military budget, leaders from SANE, WSP, and Businessmen Move for Peace participated in a pro-disarmament rally in the capital, and the WRL conducted a walk for disarmament and social justice from Vancouver to Washington, D.C.

Memberships in all peace groups declined after the Vietnam War, and SANE bottomed out at about 6,000 in 1976, when it was operating with a large deficit.[6] Gottlieb left the organization that April after having directed it for a decade. The staff limped along until October, when the position of executive director went to David Cortright, founder of GIs United against the War in Vietnam and subsequently a specialist in military affairs. Funding, membership, and activity increased. SANE lobbied for congressional legislation to divert spending from military to "human" needs. It enlisted the leadership of the Democratic party and organized labor, and it cooperated with the newly formed Jobs for Peace, which conducted local referenda on the proposal.

Antinuclear activism mushroomed across the country in the 1970s, but it was aimed mainly at atomic power.[7] The UCS turned to environmental dangers and became an effective lobby. Environmental organizations such as Friends of the Earth and the Sierra Club were enrolled, although the campaign against nuclear power was decentralized in perhaps 1,000 groups. Localizing the campaign was a deliberate strategy, designed both to target popular concerns at specific sites and to maintain local control through cohesive "affinity groups." Some of them engaged in direct action on the model of the Clamshell Alliance, which entered a nuclear facility at Seabrook, New Hampshire, where civil disobedience in 1977 resulted in 1,414 arrests.[8] The AFSC sponsored demonstrations at a Rocky Flats, Colorado, weapons facility that grew to 15,000 participants in 1979.[9] By then the UCS had returned to its original emphasis, with an appeal for ratification of SALT II that was signed by thousands of scientists and other professionals. The time was ripe for a coalition around the combined issues of nuclear arms and atomic power.

The Mobilization for Survival (MFS, 1978) was that coalition. It linked some 280 local, regional, and national groups with religious, peace, feminist, or environmental constituencies.[10] Its leadership was representative of activism from the test ban campaign through the Vietnam War. The coalition sponsored a rally of 20,000 at the First Special Session on Disarmament of the U.N. General Assembly (June 1978) and several antinuclear protests; but it was divided over the conflicting priorities of environmentalists and peace advocates and, among the latter, over preferences for incremental arms control or disarmament.

Concern over nuclear arms grew in 1979. It engaged religious leaders ranging from Catholic bishops to the National Association of Evangelicals. It stimulated the revival of the dormant Physicians for Social Responsibility through the efforts of founder Bernard Lown and charismatic physician Helen Caldicott. SANE cultivated local opposition to a new missile, the MX, in the western states where the mobile weapon was to be deployed. Working with the AFSC and the UCS, SANE also campaigned for ratification of the SALT II arms control treaty, which President Carter signed in June. The AFSC and CALC proposed a three-year unilateral moratorium on new weapons systems. The MFS proposed to curtail the production of both nuclear power and arms. A resolution for a bilateral freeze on the deployment of nuclear weapons was introduced into the Senate by Mark Hatfield, and the idea was developed in an article by Richard Barnett. Arms specialist Randall Forsberg urged a bilateral freeze on the production, testing, and deployment of all nuclear weapons. In sum, the arms race provided a focus around which the peace movement regrouped in 1979, but it did not become significant to the public until late in the year.

Disparate events suddenly converged to produce an ominous sense of threat. Nicaraguan dictator Anastasio Debayle Samosa, long supported by the United States, was overthrown in July. Three months later, revolutionaries occupied the U.S. embassy in Iran and held a large number of Americans hostage. Soviet troops rolled into Afghanistan in December. President Carter hardened U.S. policy. He defined the Persian Gulf as an area of vital interest within the U.S. defense perimeter. He boycotted the 1980 Olympic games to be held in Moscow, withdrew SALT II, escalated defense spending, created a "rapid deployment force," and pushed the new Trident II nuclear submarine and the MX missile (both capable of taking out Soviet ICBMs and, therefore, potentially first-strike weapons). He articulated a nuclear arms policy that went beyond deterrence to actual use in connection with conventional warfare. Most important, U.S. pressure induced NATO's two-track decision at the end of December.

The issue before NATO was whether or not to deploy a new generation of intermediate-range nuclear weapons (the cruise and Pershing II missiles) to offset Soviet ones (SS-20s and SS-22s). Opinion over the new so-called "Euromissiles" was divided in NATO countries, and a compromise was reached. On one track, NATO pushed arms negotiations with the Soviets. On a second, it agreed to go ahead with missile deployment pending Soviet withdrawal of its intermediate force. This dual approach provided time for the organization of massive antimissile demonstrations in Europe, which, in turn, inspired American opponents of an arms buildup.

The effect of the foreign crises of 1979–80 and of the administration's response to them was to raise anxiety and to polarize opinion in the United States. Large numbers of Americans identified threat with communism, specifically the Soviet Union. That view had been consistent in U.S. public opinion throughout the Cold War, and it was effectively exploited by the well-funded Committee on the Present Danger (formed in the 1950s but revived in 1976 to oppose SALT II). Some of its members had held positions in government. All of them believed that the United States should be prepared to fight and win a nuclear war with the Soviet Union, which, they argued, was inherently aggressive and had achieved nuclear superiority. They disdained arms control, much more disarmament. The committee found in Ronald Reagan a presidential candidate who could dramatize anti-Soviet anxiety as a national cause. On the other hand, large numbers of Americans felt threatened by atomic war itself. That anxiety too had been latent in public opinion throughout the Cold War. Given the crises of 1979—80, it provided the basis for a second coalition against nuclear weapons.

The campaign can perhaps be dated from Randall Forsberg's presentation of the idea of a bilateral, verifiable freeze on nuclear weapons development to the convention of the Mobilization for Survival in December 1979. Forsberg was a defense analyst with seven years of experience at the Stockholm International Peace Research Institute, which specialized in military issues. She was a hardheaded political realist with an abiding moral concern. She argued that a comprehensive freeze could thwart a new generation of nuclear weapons systems, that only a bilateral approach could disentangle the threat of nuclear war from mistrust of the Soviet Union, and that in any case a freeze campaign could mobilize large numbers of people and generate real debate. She understood it to be a first step that might help to reorder world priorities. In order to concentrate on the freeze, Forsberg left the Massachusetts Institute of Technology to direct her own Institute for Defense and Disarmament Studies.

The Freeze Campaign, 1980–1982

The freeze proposal was first adopted by the pacifist and morally concerned wing of the peace movement. Early in 1980 it was considered at meetings that included AFSC, CALC, and FOR staff. An Ad Hoc Task Force for a Nuclear Weapons Freeze was created in order to establish an organizational base while Forsberg honed her *Call to Halt the Nuclear Arms Race,* stressing the technical practicality, political import, and economic advantages of a mutual freeze. The AFSC distributed 5,000 copies of the *Call to Halt* in midspring as endorsements came from peace societies including CALC, the FOR, WILPF, Pax Christi USA, and the Coalition for a New Foreign and Military Policy. Arms control–oriented groups stayed aloof for the time being, reluctant to associate with organizations on record for disarmament.

The AFSC tried to force the freeze into politics by lobbying delegates to the Republican and Democratic national conventions that summer. Although neither the parties nor the candidates endorsed the proposal, 40 percent of the Democratic delegates supported it, and the organizing work itself contributed to the growing network of freeze activists. The Republicans nominated Reagan and took the offensive, depicting Carter as having weakened the nation's military posture. Carter lost the election against the background of economic problems and the still unresolved hostage crisis, and the Democrats lost control of the Senate.

In western Massachusetts there was an aside in the November voting that contributed to the local thrust of the freeze campaign. There former antiwar activist Randall Kehler and the Traprock Peace Center, which he had founded in 1979 in Deerfield, put the freeze proposal on the November ballot in three state senate districts. They thus enlisted public participation in military and foreign policy, areas of decision making normally reserved to distant experts. With help from the AFSC, Massachusetts activists signed up hundreds of volunteers and secured endorsements from local business people and politicians. The freeze won in 59 of 62 town referenda.[11] Reagan won a clear majority in the region too: sentiment did not readily translate into politics, it seemed. Increasingly in the next two years policymakers and the media treated the freeze as a symbol of public concern rather than as a serious proposal.

A Symbolic Campaign The Nuclear Weapons Freeze Campaign (NWFC) was consolidated early in 1981. Forsberg used her institute and her personal identification with the freeze as leverage among experienced peace advocates through the winter. Questions of strategy and organization were deferred to the campaign's national conference in March, when over 300 activists from peace, religious, and environmental groups gathered at Georgetown University. After intense debate, they adopted Forsberg's model—a single-issue campaign that, unlike the B-1 and MX campaigns, would elicit mainstream leadership and not depend on the peace movement. Local organizing was to build a strong grassroots base of national debate and pressure that eventually would lead to a policy decision for the freeze. The process was expected to take three to five years. The freeze itself was to be "a dramatic, simple, moderate, but still effective proposal to mobilize the middle class, to give them hope and to bring them actively into the ranks of those who oppose the arms race."[12]

The NWFC linked virtually autonomous local groups through a national clearinghouse whose function was to inform and inspire. In a clear symbol of populism and decentralism it was agreed to locate the clearinghouse in Saint Louis, Missouri, far from the traditional eastern venues of peace advocacy. Campaign policy was vested in an annual conference where every congressional district was equally represented, although a large national committee and a small executive committee provided interim supervision of the clearinghouse. In practice, the loosely affiliated local branches and national organizations followed their own lines, whether concentrating on the freeze or relating it to other priorities such as economic conversion, intervention in Central America or the Middle East, nonviolent direct action, draft registration, or specific new weapons systems. The freeze was valued by everyone for its symbolic value, but it did not command the full resources of constituent groups with other goals.

As the conference delegates fanned out across the country, the national leadership secured official endorsements, notably from new peace organizations of lawyers, educators, business executives, nurses, technicians, musicians, and other occupation groups. The single most important professional organization, Physicians for Social Responsibility (PSR), was not new, and its membership exceeded 10,000.[13]

Local organizing followed the lines of the Traprock campaign. Activists circulated public petitions and got endorsements of the freeze from civic bodies and even several state legislatures. Their efforts were favorably covered in local media. Public support was widespread according to July polls, and it increased after Reagan announced plans to produce a neutron bomb (designed for maximum lethality with minimal destruction). SANE mobilized a coalition of 24 peace, religious, and environmental groups in response. With Soviet cardiologist Evgeny Chazov, PSR founder Bernard Lown established International Physicians for the Prevention of Nuclear War (it won the 1985 Nobel Peace Prize). Helen Caldicott initiated Women's Action for Nuclear Disarmament. In October the NWFC clearinghouse was finally moved from Boston to Saint Louis, with Randall Kehler as director. According to the *Freeze Newsletter,* the campaign was then active in 40 states and had petitions signed by over 250,000 people and endorsements from 40 national organizations and 19 members of Congress. "So much is happening so fast," the newsletter added, "that it has been impossible for the Clearinghouse to monitor all activities." The NWFC claimed a working force of 20,000 activists, overwhelmingly volunteers.[14]

In fact, there had been two waves of voluntarism. Initially they came from established peace, environmental, and community organizing groups. That network mobilized a second wave of local volunteers, who quickly formed new local bodies, often freeze chapters. It proved unexpectedly easy to recruit the second wave, which seems to have come largely from the Vietnam generation of the 1960s and early 1970s. If that is the case, it helps to account for the bias for participant control and against centralized leadership in the early freeze movement.[15] In any case, the campaign had generated an activist constituency from which a new leadership was becoming established on local, state, and national levels. It must have seemed that the strategy of building a broad popular base was working.

Until November 1981 the national media paid scant attention to the campaign. Then 300,000 West Germans mobilized for an antinuclear demonstration in Bonn. About 1,300 women from the Women's Pentagon Action demonstrated at the Pentagon and employed civil disobedience with help from the AFSC and the MFS. The Union of Concerned Scientists and other groups sponsored a major Convocation on the Threat of Nuclear War and teach-ins on over 150 American campuses. SANE arranged for European peace leaders to meet with congressional and State Department aides and to have press and television interviews. By the end of the year the media were covering antinuclear activism, indiscriminately associating all of it with the freeze campaign. The NWFC adroitly encouraged that impression as momentum picked up through the spring of 1982.

In February journalist Jonathan Schell detailed the consequences of nuclear war—the extinction of human life—in a series of *New Yorker* articles. The next month 157 town meetings in Vermont endorsed the freeze, and a fresh round of demonstrations rocked several European cities. March also saw the initial conviction of the Plowshares Eight, a group that had broken into a General Electric plant at King of Prussia, Pennyslvania, the previous September, smashed the tips of two Minutemen missiles, and poured blood over equipment. Media coverage was guaranteed by the drama of the action, the involvement of antiwar activists Daniel and Philip Berrigan, the fact that former attorney general Ramsey Clark served as defense counsel, and the harshness of the 3–10 year sentences meted out. Their conviction enhanced visibility of the Berrigans as speakers while their case was under appeal.[16] Acts of civil disobedience multiplied. The media associated them with the freeze campaign, which, however, discouraged that impression and made no effort to relate direct action to campaign strategy.

Schell's *The Fate of the Earth* was published as a book in April and became a best-seller. Its message was brought home to hundreds of communities and campuses as activists from Ground Zero laid out the destruction that would result from nuclear explosions at specific sites. About the same time, over half of the nation's Catholic bishops as well as Protestant and Jewish bodies, SANE and Common Cause endorsed the freeze. By the spring of 1982, freeze resolutions were approved by "309 New England town meetings, 320 city councils from coast to coast, 56 county councils, one or both houses in eleven state legislatures, and 109 national and international organizations, including the U.N. General Assembly."[17] The campaign flowed into June and the largest demonstration in American history.

It was held in New York City on 12 June 1982, in conjunction with the Second Special Session on Disarmament of the U.N. General Assembly. Perhaps 1 million people began marching near the United Nations at midday. The orderly, even celebratory demonstrators from every walk of life were still filing into Central Park at dusk. Rallies were held in other cities, Pasadena's drawing about 100,000 people. The demonstrations

The Nuclear Freeze Campaign attracted the largest demonstration in American history, when perhaps a million people marched through New York City on 12 June 1982. In the crowd shown here on 42nd Street virtually all segments of the population are represented in a politically active, grass-roots movement. *Photo by Steve Cagan/Impact Visuals*

were coordinated by a steering committee of 13 groups, of which the NWFC was only one sponsor, but in 1982 the media associated all anti-nuclear activism with the freeze and interpreted concern over nuclear war as "a relatively wholesome fad that was hardly political."[18]

In the capital, on the other hand, the campaign was valued precisely for its political potential. Not that the freeze itself was regarded as a significant legislative step; rather, it was perceived as a powerful symbol that could align mainstream Americans against Reagan's policies. Sometimes that translated into political ambition, as it did for Representative Edward Markey and Senator Edward Kennedy. The freeze also translated into a defense of the whole arms control approach. Although there was continuity in the military policies of Carter and Reagan, there were two significant differences. The first was rhetorical: the Reagan administration was belligerently anti-Soviet and cavalier in its discussion of nuclear war. That provided a catalyst for the public freeze campaign. The second difference was administrative. Reagan replaced the arms control experts with members of the Committee on the Present Danger, who were hostile to the whole concept. Lacking access to policy-making, the arms control community and its legislative supporters turned to the freeze. Said Representative Les Aspin, "If we had a President who was genuinely interested in arms control . . . we would need no [freeze] resolution at all."[19] What is more, Reagan's huge military budget and its accompanying waste generated hostility among both the socially deprived and the business community.[20] For many reasons, then, the freeze had political appeal as an anti-Reagan symbol.

A Political Campaign   The NWFC had intended to build a stronger grass-roots base and a solid core of bipartisan legislators before moving its proposal into the Congress. It did not work that way. In March Kennedy and Mark Hatfield sponsored a freeze resolution in the Senate while Edward Markey and Jonathan Bingham introduced one in the House. Their version of the freeze was carefully tested against arms control expertise and political possibility, and it modified the original. In large measure the freeze became the prisoner of the political process. The legislative focus minimized internationalism in the campaign, as Pam Solo has observed, both in the sense of inhibiting fundamental questions about Cold War policy and in distancing the American movement from its European counterparts.[21]

That long-range view was obscured as the freeze imploded in the legislative chambers and reverberated beyond them. People on Capitol Hill found it necessary to become informed and take positions on arms control issues. The Kennedy and Markey offices made the freeze a top priority, generating hitherto inaccessible endorsements, publicity, and funds for the movement.[22] Markey's resolution was barely defeated (200 to 204) when it came up for a test vote on a substitute amendment in August, but the narrow loss only incited the freeze coalition to stronger political efforts. Political action committees (PACs) for SANE and the Council for a Livable World channeled funds to selected candidates. The NWFC pressed forward with its referenda campaigns, winning endorsements from over 800 local bodies and 17 state legislatures by October. In the November election freeze resolutions carried 9 of 10 states and 34 of 35 cities where they were on the ballot, and they had some effect on congressional races. [23] The NWFC had moved into the political arena more quickly than it had planned. The media followed the shift, interpreting legislation as the whole game.

The initial responses of the Reagan administration were inept. Teams sent to debate the issues in the field had little impact. Red-baiting was ineffective, although it may have reinforced the NWFC's moderation and bilateral emphasis. In May, feeling real political pressure, Reagan offered his own proposal for a strategic arms reduction treaty—START. It was patently nonnegotiable and did not appear to have immediate results, but it helped to set the terms of the legislative debate to which the freeze had become committed.

Although freeze leaders felt unprepared for a political test on the national level, they accepted it in the hope that it would increase campaign visibility and funding. It did. The NWFC raised $450,000 in 1982 (up from $50,000 in 1981), and the distribution of funds was significant. Eighty percent came from foundations and major individual donors, which reinforced pressure for a moderate and single-issue campaign.[24] California millionaire Harold Willens acquired considerable influence, for example, introducing professional organization and advertising. Large-scale funding also enabled the campaign's national office to add specialized staff positions and to provide training to local and state groups. Those were becoming professionalized and were reluctant to release funds (they contributed hardly more than 1 percent of the 1983 national budget of $1.33 million),[25] and the new activists they attracted were interested in the freeze itself. Accordingly, the distribution of funding reinforced the independence of the NWFC on national, state, and local levels and strengthened the single-issue thrust of the whole campaign. This in turn distanced peace groups with multi-issue agendas. The NWFC was becoming less a coalition than a federation of state and local groups with a somewhat independent national office whose leadership interacted with other peace organizations.

The legislative contest dominated the third national NWFC conference in February 1983. The national leadership maintained tight control, avoiding legislation that would bind the president on the grounds that it could not be passed, insisting on a bilateral treaty, and rejecting the introduction of collateral issues. In March a "Citizens Lobby" of 5,000 activists presented their elected representatives with freeze petitions bearing over 800,000 signatures. Shortly afterward, the House Foreign Affairs Committee reported out a nonbinding freeze resolution. Amended to apply for only two years if there were no missile reductions in that time, the resolution passed on 4 May with a 286 to 149 vote. Three weeks later the House approved funds for the production of the MX missile. It had given a symbolic recognition to the national mood, but it had not concretely challenged defense policy (the Senate even tabled the Kennedy-Hatfield resolution).

Beyond the Freeze, 1983–1987

Although the freeze campaign was subjected to a "virtual blackout" by the mass media following the House vote, it continued to grow at the state and local levels through 1985.[26] The NWFC's original emphasis on its grass-roots base was reinforced by its experience on Capitol Hill. Further legislative work required a change in the composition of the Congress, which could be accomplished only at local levels. That required funds, but contributions from foundations and large donors were falling (there was a drop of about 85 percent between 1983 and 1987). The national staff tried to compensate for its lack of a national dues-paying membership by creating its own PAC, Freeze Voter. Electoral work also required effective activists. The NWFC started training programs aimed at the approaching congressional elections. This strategy only reinforced the decentralized organization of the campaign, as did the national news media's flagging attention. There were fissures over questions of leadership and power within the NWFC, and pressure to broaden the campaign's agenda. Fending off the latter in the interest of a minimal consensus, the NWFC defined itself yet more narrowly and lost disaffected groups. There was also pressure to make the national committee more responsive to local and state branches and less to other national peace organizations.

Those organizations had grown during the freeze campaign. The membership of PSR increased from a few hundred to 30,000, CLW's to 80,000, and subscriptions to the *Bulletin of the Atomic Scientists* nearly doubled. SANE experienced a renaissance, doubling its staff and membership between 1981 and 1984 to 20 and 75,000 persons respectively. It owned its offices and produced numerous publications and a radio program. It had a political action committee (SANE PAC), two full-time lobbyists, and a nationwide Rapid Response Network of people who agreed to mobilize immediate support for pending legislation. It fielded 50 full-time activists for door-to-door canvassing and four field organizers to assist its 45 chapters. Its national office housed an Arms Control Computer Network, which provided facilities and access to a peace constituency for itself, PSR, NWFC, CLW, the Coalition for a New Foreign and Military Policy, Friends of the Earth, and Greenpeace.[27] The peace movement, with its new organizational technology, was addressing numerous issues besides freeze legislation, notably the MX and Euromissiles, economic and environmental consequences of arms spending, and U.S. intervention in Central America. Those problems required political solutions. Accordingly the coalition mobilized for the 1984 election.

Viewing the election as a direct challenge to Reagan's overall policies, peace organizations endorsed Democratic candidate Walter Mondale. They concentrated on the Democratic party platform, which adopted strong planks on arms control. Helen Caldicott and some other activists cast the national campaign in apocalyptic terms, but peace advocates increasingly concentrated on congressional races as it became clear that Mondale's personality and campaign were weak by comparison with Reagan's and that his economic program was alienating potential contributors and voters. Thousands of volunteers were recruited, trained, and fielded. Political action committees set up by the NWFC, CLW, the Women's Action for Nuclear Disarmament, SANE, and other peace groups generated some $6 million for campaigns. SANE, the NWFC, and CLW created a joint committee, which retained a consulting firm to produce radio and TV ads on the dangers of nuclear arms and Reagan's proposed space-based weapons system. Election activity helped both the NWFC and SANE to expand, the latter to 100,000 dues-paying members.[28]

President Reagan's overwhelming victory in November was offset by the fact that congressional support for arms control was retained. There was even some slight gain in the Senate. Although the movement's impact on the election cannot be calculated with certainty, it appeared to have marginal importance and was acknowledged by some successful candidates. [29] Nevertheless, the president's reelection defined a political agenda: the public and the Congress would have to be further mobilized against continuing pressure for new weapons systems and interventionism in a continuing cold war.

Peace advocates reorganized. SANE prepared to build a broad coalition of peace and other public advocacy groups. The NWFC, no longer a coalition, attempted to become a membership organization. Meanwhile, there were negotiations to merge the two. In many respects they seemed to be complementary. The NWFC had active state and local chapters, but lacked a viable national office. SANE's strong national office was supported by a large dues-paying membership, but its chapter structure was limited. Underlying the structural differences there was a difference in organizational culture: "many of the SANE leaders had been active in the organization for a long time, some since its inception, and . . . saw the Freeze as too narrow and technology-focused. Freeze activists were strongly influenced by the New Left's emphasis on participation, and viewed SANE's structure as somewhat elitist."[30]

SANE/Freeze merged in 1987. The designation of William Sloane Coffin, Jr., as president was crucial. Coffin had roots in both the pre-Vietnam peace and civil rights movement and a reputation as an antiwar activist, and he brought a pastoral style to administration that facilitated the final merger. It was agreed that policy would be set for the new organization by an annual national congress representative of congressional districts, and that interim policy and administrative decisions would be vested in a board whose directors represented state chapters or were elected at large. A thousand delegates to the first national congress of SANE/Freeze, in November, approved the structure and adopted long-term goals: a nuclear freeze leading to disarmament in both atomic and conventional weapons; a change in foreign policy from intervention to the protection of human rights and promotion of socioeconomic development; a cut in military spending and conversion to a civilian economy meeting human needs; and an improvement in international relations. The common premise of those objectives was that national security involves the common freedom of peoples from the threats of war, social injustice, and environmental degradation. On that basis, SANE/Freeze hoped to write a new chapter in the history of American peace movements.

There was a general sense in 1987 that a chapter had been concluded. Many peace advocates and observers alike entitled it "The Nuclear Freeze," assuming that it had been the story of a noble failure. As a serious policy proposal, the freeze was indeed beaten back. It was subverted by its opponents and co-opted by its political supporters. The effort to implement it had failed. What more could be said?

Understood as a symbolic program to arouse public awareness, Forsberg's proposal was an effective tool that cut through layers of technical obfuscation to reveal the naked terror of nuclear warfare. For millions of Americans the program clarified the fact that the nuclear arms race threatened the national security it was supposed to protect. That clarity was translated into referenda, petitions, endorsements, and activism on an unprecedented scale. For the first time, the fear of nuclear war was articulated more forcefully than the long-standing fear of Soviet communism.

Even understood as a serious proposal, the freeze contributed to the resurgence of arms control as a part of defense policy.[31] In the Congress, it provided a focal point around which the arms control community rallied. It was an instrument for the education of numerous legislators who had regarded defense issues only perfunctorily or technically. It generated numerous counterproposals for treaties and contributed to legislative constraints on specific weapons systems such as the MX missile. As an issue, and especially as it was tied to electoral politics, the freeze excited national activism and elicited broad support. Arms control became a Democratic program. Its base in the decision-making process was so strong that the administration's only effective response was to adopt the rhetoric and posture of negotiated restraint.

Understood as a campaign, therefore, the freeze was part of a broader peace movement. It was located at the interface of arms control and disarmament, so that it permitted a tenuous coalition between liberal internationalists and pacifists. It contributed to the significant growth of organizations with other priorities and to the formation of new peace constituencies. It infused the movement, even if briefly, with financial and political resources. It provided a media context for civil disobedience such as the Plowshares action. It pursued tactics such as pressure group and electoral politics with techniques such as direct mailing, canvassing, and advertising. It created fresh links among peace and civic groups. The functional effect of the campaign on the movement was obscured, however, as the NWFC evolved into a single-issue campaign and then into an organization, and as the freeze was interpreted by partisans, opponents, and the media as the essence of arms control and the substance of the peace movement. It was neither. It was but one of several contending constraints on the arms race, which was in turn but one of many contesting national issues; it was the most visible part of the second coalition against nuclear arms.[32]

During the campaign the perimeters of peace advocacy changed again in terms of both organization and policy issues. The environmentalism and new feminism of the 1970s emerged as strong social-change movements with explicit policy concerns: ecological crises and the right to abortion. Poverty and homelessness mounted too, and there was a nagging apprehension that civil rights were being discounted. The constituencies alive to those causes were still aligned with the peace movement in a general way, but by the end of the decade their own agendas had been sharpened. The peace organizations themselves were affected by changing priorities, especially in two areas of foreign policy.

The Reagan administration escalated opposition to revolutionary change in Central America. It engineered and armed a counterrevolutionary force of Contras to challenge the Sandinista government in Nicaragua, and it channeled aid to besieged military regimes in El Salvador and Guatemala. The next chapter of the peace movement rapidly wrote itself, as a plethora of organizations emerged to challenge administration policy, intervene directly against human rights abuses in Central America, and respond to the plight of people there. On a political level, they marshaled support for congressional actions that in the late 1980s cut off funds for the Contras and challenged administration policy in the region. At the end of the decade Nicaraguans elected a government to which the United States had pledged support, and the United Nations undertook to negotiate the crisis in El Salvador. Misery still blanketed Central America, but public concern for the area diminished in the United States.

Those events took place in the context of an even more far-reaching change. From 1985 on, Mikhail Gorbachev's new leadership restructured the political system of the Soviet Union, redirected its economy, and recast its foreign policy. After a period of wary diplomacy, the Reagan administration opened negotiations that led in 1988 to an epochal treaty dismantling a whole class of intermediate-range nuclear missiles. START talks on strategic missiles resumed and were continued in the George Bush administration. Communist regimes throughout Eastern Europe tumbled in the wake of Gorbachev's initiatives, and leaders in the American foreign policy establishment spoke openly of the end of the Cold War. That perception, together with a huge federal deficit, propelled cuts in military spending. Soviet leaders themselves began to interpret national security in terms of common, even global interests. Under these circumstances, peace groups like SANE/Freeze were challenged to reassess their programs once more. Indeed, the American people were challenged to redefine their world role.

Conclusion

The American Peace Movement

The peace movement began in prophesy.* Early peace advocates were moral evangelists who elevated values derived from Christian and enlightenment tradition into national standards. They were a prophetic minority in an age when war "was almost universally considered an acceptable, perhaps an inevitable, and for many people a desirable way of settling international differences."[1]

The stance of a witnessing and prophetic minority became deeply imbedded in the movement, and also in friendly and hostile assessments of it:

The peace subculture speaks of forbearance within a culture that has flowered in conquest . . . of reconciliation within a society that works better at distributing weapons than wealth . . . of supranational authority among a highly nationalistic people who dislike all authority . . . of a just global order to governing officials anxious for pre-eminence and profit. Accepting their distance from the country's dominant power values and realities, members of the peace subculture have consequently resolved to serve as the most vocal critics of power as traditionally pursued and applied.[2]

---

*Because this chapter examines patterns of change in the peace movement during the period of time covered in the preceding chapters, it is cast in the past tense. It is by no means to be considered a postmortem, however; the movement is still very much alive and continuing to change.

The notes for this chapter contain references to the general literature on social movements.

Nobody will expect pacifists to be active supporters of nuclear deterrence, or the use of force against terrorists, or even of military aid to weak regimes facing the threat of foreign-sponsored subversion. But neither should they obstruct all such policies that the democratically elected government of the United States pursues. . . . When the pacifist's conscience does not allow him to support policies that utilize the threat of force, the proper course for him is to remain silent.[3]

Those judgments are too stereotypic of American society and too pristine as regards the peace movement. A dissenting minority it was, but not merely an alienated prophetic one. On the contrary, it evolved into an innovative social movement that engaged the mainstream, informing and mobilizing citizens to act in their foreign affairs.[4]

Historically, the peace effort was an attempt to persuade the American people to abandon war for other instruments of foreign policy. Its advocacy for a presumed public interest related it to social movements such as those for environmental quality and consumer's rights. Like them, it was affected by the interests and perspectives of its constituencies but was held together over time mainly by a social vision. As with all public interest movements, assessments of success or failure must be tempered by the fact that ultimate responsibility for public policy lies with the people themselves.

Since most social movement theory deals with collective action that is a form of protest, it is important to recognize the dual nature of what was both a *peace* and an *antiwar* movement. At various times it included organized advocacy, witness, dissent, protest, and resistance. It worked within a political system whose authority it sometimes challenged sharply. Its member groups alternately aligned, divided, or even clashed with one another, so that it was itself a testing ground for competing approaches to peace.

The movement has had great longevity. Much peace advocacy was relatively informal—the work of countless individuals who wrote, spoke, and acted on behalf of peace, or witnessed against war if only in solitary refusal to participate in it. Still, a great deal of effort went into formal organization. At some points peace groups aligned for campaigns in which they dared to define the terms of foreign policy debate and contested the government for public support. At those times there was a recognizable social movement that enlisted people outside its own constituencies. In the Vietnam War and the freeze campaign, it became a mass movement that attracted spontaneous involvement from public sectors. The periodic extension of organizations into political campaigns created the impression of a succession of peace movements. The dissipation of each campaign in turn contributed to the image of recurring failure. On closer inspection, though, there was continuous organization and evolution at the core of this episodic movement.[5]

How Have Peace Advocates Interacted with One Another?

People and Ideas At first glance, peace advocates were irreconcilably diverse: clergy and business leaders, educators and politicians, scientists and poets, Quakers and Catholics, young people and old, singular and organizational, cautious and daring. One common denominator was that they were overwhelmingly from the educated middle or professional class. Even within the socialist, labor, and civil rights movements it was the educated leadership that mainly responded to peace proposals or opposed specific wars. The sources of movement leadership roughly followed the course of education and professionalism in American society: from clergy and lawyers to business people in the nineteenth century, for example, to social workers, journalists, political reformers, students and women in the twentieth. From the 1960s on, peace and antiwar advocates often organized on professional lines. Those categories of leadership were cumulative rather than successive.[6] Peace advocates were distinguished, then, by having disposable time and informed perception. Even uneducated persons might refuse military service on the basis of, say, religious principle, but only people familiar with national and international systems and with the history of war and peace were positioned to understand the social implications of war and advocate alternatives to it.[7]

A second common denominator of peace advocacy consisted of a set of ideologies (in the broad sense of orienting perspectives). These also were generally cumulative in the movement, and each of them underwent its own evolution. Each appealed, although not at all exclusively, to a distinctive constituency of peace advocates.

The traditions of religious, absolute pacifism and of humanitarian, moral reform prevailed in the first half of the nineteenth century. Their thrust was to decry mass violence, or war, and to promote social harmony. The Garrisonians identified violence with repression, and were led to a terrible dilemma in the Civil War. Others introduced a strong note of internationalism as they sought alternatives to war through international organization and law or through popular associations across national boundaries. Internationalism became the dominant ideology of peace reform from the Civil War to World War I, and it took the form especially of international law or treaties for arbitration, conciliation, and unfettered economic expansion. Since it was designed essentially to preserve the existing order of states against the excesses of militarism and the disruption of major wars, it can be called conservative internationalism. The motivating ideologies of absolute pacifism and moral reform continued through this period, the latter emerging strongly in education and religious ecumenism just before World War I.

Internationalists found their positions clarified by World War I, which most of them supported. Insofar as some of them envisioned changes in international order that would modify national sovereignty through international law or collective security, they introduced a distinctly liberal internationalist tradition. Beginning with the campaign for American neutrality, meanwhile, progressive notions of reform were related to absolute pacifism to emphasize the relationships of war and arbitrary power, peace and justice. The result was the formation of several groups that carried a reform-oriented, or liberal, pacifism into the postwar period. Those groups also assumed the necessity for a fundamental modification of the sovereign state system, so that they shared the ideology of liberal internationalism and extended it to a transnational world view.

In the interwar years, liberal pacifists and both wings of internationalists learned to mobilize public support on political issues, a development that climaxed in the neutrality coalition of the mid-1930s, the Emergency Peace Campaign. At that point, liberal pacifists (along with traditional religious pacifists) were separated from those liberal internationalists who organized to support intervention in the European war. During World War II liberal internationalists mounted a strong campaign for a United Nations that would modify the state system through collective security arrangements. Liberal pacifists supported this effort even as they elevated transnational values, defended the right of conscientious objection, challenged mass violence, and extended humanitarian service.

Following World War II liberal internationalism was briefly extended to world federalism, although the polarization of the world led to a dominant form of internationalism that was identified with U.S. Cold War policy, military security, and intervention abroad. That ideology was questioned during the test ban campaign and began to break down during the Vietnam War, as groups like SANE carried a revived form of liberal internationalism into the antinuclear campaign of the 1980s. Meanwhile, liberal pacifism was supplemented by organized radical activism and by an intense moral emphasis that crested during the Vietnam War. Although radical activism became subdued, the tenets of liberal pacifism remained strong and were applied to the issues of nuclear weapons and intervention in Central America. The freeze campaign was part of an international mass movement seeming to herald a global consciousness that could amount to transnationalism.[8]

The metamorphosis of ideologies was largely a result of changes in America's world context and in ways of thinking that went beyond foreign policy issues. It pervaded the movement and defined the lines on which peace advocates interacted. Ideas and values, more than class or social characteristics, determined the lines of peace reform.[9]

Values and Goals To some extent peace organizations reflected constituent interests—the pacifists' concern for the right of conscientious objection, for example, or the international lawyers' interest in arbitration—but they were part of a social movement only insofar as they had larger goals. In their general approach to peace they included "polity" and "community" internationalists, to use the distinction Sondra Herman applied to the Progressive Era.[10]

In her sense, an emphasis on policy characterized conservative, liberal, and Cold War internationalists. All of them sought peace through arrangements between nations, which were understood to be the basic units of international society. They valued American institutions as a model for the world, and they preferred to work within the foreign policy establishment. They valued power, and although they preferred alternatives to war, most of them endorsed force when it seemed necessary to maintain order. They tended to organize around single issues and for short-term goals. Polity internationalists helped to orient the peace movement to national and international institutions. Their access to power elites carried the illusion of influence and sometimes made them a conduit from the government to the public.

An emphasis on community, on the other hand, was characteristic of liberal pacifists. They regarded war as an instrument that was not only destructive but victimizing because it perpetuated unjust structures of power with violence. They worked within the political system, but sought to mobilize public pressure on policy-making. Although they engaged in specific policy campaigns, they responded to multiple issues and were organized for long-term goals. The community they envisioned was "an organic, natural entity embracing all the peoples of the world and pervaded by the spirit of fellowship."[10] They were in this measure transnational and value oriented.

This liberal-pacifist wing of the movement was community oriented in another sense: its groups were bonded together by the influence and heritage of individuals. That is the sense with which antiwar and civil rights activist James Bevel greeted the loss of A. J. Muste in 1967: "People working together, people creating; people trying to get people together so we can end the war: that's A. J. He isn't dead."[11] The importance of individual leaders and activists cannot be overemphasized, even though it is obscured in organizational history. The leaders with the most staying power were those who were grounded in a religious faith and had a sense of humor. Activist commitment often was fixed by a transforming personal experience. Often set apart from their fellow citizens by fidelity to ideals, these were self-consciously "people who dare."[12]

Polity and community were relative emphases in the movement. Often they overlapped, as they did before World War I, from 1920 to about 1937, in the campaign for the United Nations, in the coalitions against nuclear weapons, and with difficulty in the Vietnam War. Sometimes they clashed, as they did over intervention in both world wars. Always they affected one another, making the overall movement a microcosm of foreign policy debate.

Beyond specific policy objectives, all elements of the movement affirmed the values they attributed to peace itself (whether international order, world government, social justice, a religious ideal, or personal and social harmony). Organizations that lasted more than a generation were held together by long-term goals shared by their leaders and activist core. The liberal pacifist groups endured the longest, and they were named for the values they espoused: the Fellowship of *Reconciliation,* the American Friends *Service* Committee, the Women's International League for *Peace and Freedom.* They imbued social process with their values. "There is no way to peace," they said; "peace is the way."[13]

Value-oriented peace organizations tended to be centralized and stable over time. Many of the leaders and core activists knew one another and learned to manage differences within an accepted set of rules, whether constitutional or behavioral. Each group represented an organizational consensus based on shared values, after all, and it operated on a minimal but clearly defined set of resources—funds, leadership, and constituency. Conversely, these groups were particularly vulnerable to frustration insofar as they assessed intragroup and political dynamics against their demanding ideals.

The less visibility that peace groups had, the less they faced the pressure of being defined externally by public norms or popular expectations of achievement. If they were little noticed, they were nonetheless important because they formed the critical core from which political campaigns were generated. They were alert to policy issues. They were the storehouses for the movement's heritage and goals, and the "halfway houses" for the ideals, experience, skills, and often the initial staff and funding from which broad campaigns could be generated.[14] They had access to the resources that were needed in order to mobilize a peace or antiwar campaign.

Campaigns and Coalitions   Peace groups of all persuasions were politically active insofar as they promoted specific policy objectives. For the most part, and in the absence of an overt national crisis, they worked through the channels available to their own constituencies. At times, though, a core of leaders and activists sought to widen their influence. This occurred under two conditions: (1) when it appeared that a war or peace-related threat or opportunity was felt, even if vaguely, by the public at large, and (2) when there was an available issue through which value, apprehension, or hope could be translated into a foreign policy choice.[15] At those points, peace organizations aligned with one another and with other organizations to form peace campaigns.

In American history there were well-defined campaigns for arbitration treaties and against imperialism at the end of the nineteenth century, a campaign to mediate but abstain from the European war in 1914–18, campaigns for disarmament and a world court from 1921 to about 1932, the Emergency Peace Campaign of the mid-1930s, a campaign for the United Nations during World War II, the test ban effort of 1955–63, the antiwar movement of the Vietnam War, and the nuclear freeze campaign of 1979–83.[16] In those campaigns peace organizations mobilized their resources in order to activate their constituencies and influence the public and decision makers.[17] Some resources were internal to peace organization—funds, skills, organizational structures, and constituencies. Other resources were external—funding from outside sources like foundations, for example, and the allied skills and memberships of other social movement groups.

In order to maximize their resources, peace organizations attempted to work together in coalitions.[18] As a coalition was formed, interactions among member groups multiplied rapidly. This extended a common set of values and frames of reference within the movement, but it also magnified organizational tensions. Broad coalitions were possible only as they enabled groups to consolidate and activate their respective constituencies while reaching a broader public. They therefore involved inherent differences about the allocation of resources respectively to the political goals that aligned organizations and to the specific purposes that distinguished groups from one another. Accordingly, peace coalitions were delicately balanced between centripetal and centrifugal forces.

As a result, activists experienced at least two kinds of tensions. Some of them had to do with campaign organization: would it be centralized or decentralized, emphasize professional or grass-roots leadership? Other tensions had to do with campaign strategy: would it address the foreign policy elite or the broad public, stress peace as order or as change, have a broad or narrow focus, seek short-term reforms in policy or the long-term transformation of society? All of these questions were interrelated. From a movement perspective, they involved relative choices because a coalition could endure only by compromise, and each set of alternatives offered relative trade-offs. Peace and antiwar coalitions were threatened internally when leaders and groups interpreted those questions as either-or choices.

Organizational Tensions   Given the U.S. federal system, where power is broadly distributed, it was important both to mobilize people locally and to coordinate and focus them nationally. This meant that there was an inherent national-local tension in peace campaigns. In practical terms, it surfaced in questions of funding and decision making: would contributions raised on the local level be spent there or sent to a national office; would strategic decisions be made nationally or locally? There were advantages to each emphasis. More centralized coalitions (like the EPC) with a strong national office and staff could work more effectively with decision makers. They could recruit expertise and distribute consistent information. They enabled the movement to present a coherent image to the media and to focus attention on relevant issues. On the other hand, more decentralized organizations (like the NWFC) could more easily adapt to varied constituencies, recruit local activists, and form strong interpersonal bonds.

Historically, most peace *organizations* were centralized along a continuum of strong to weak hierarchical authority: from conservative through liberal internationalists and from liberal to radical pacifists (the WRL and CNVA reflected a distinctly antiauthoritarian bias). Peace *coalitions* varied widely: a national office aligning independent organizations (NCPW), a federation of preexisting peace groups with their own local contacts

(Emergency Peace Campaign), an informal alliance between national organizations with local branches (early SANE), a decentralized network of activists (CNVA), committees organizing projects sponsored by national or local groups or both (the Vietnam-era demonstrations), and a federated organization with a strong base in nearly autonomous local and state groups (NWFC).

Two new alternatives emerged in the 1980s. One was the design for SANE/Freeze: local organizing within a federal model that (1) permitted much autonomy for local or state chapters and incorporated them into the decision-making process, while (2) at the same time maintaining a strong centralized office. The second model was networking.[19] The coalition for Central America solidarity combined autonomous national organizations with specialized functions—lobbying, providing information, channeling humanitarian aid, sponsoring economic development, and mobilizing political pressure—with strong local groups of church people, farmers, academics, lawyers, and peace advocates who made their own foreign policies as they related directly to counterparts abroad. These groups were linked through communications and action networks (often by computer, phone, or direct mailing). The examples of SANE/Freeze and the Central America solidarity movement suggest that alternative models could be adapted to quite different constituencies and foreign policy opportunities. Always there was a tension between centralization and decentralization, between the interests and capacities of peace constituencies and the politics of decision making.

A closely related issue was whether peace groups and coalitions should organize more or less along the lines of professional or voluntary leadership.[20] Professional leadership had the obvious advantage of mobilizing skills on the national level, where foreign policy issues were decided. It could develop political sophistication and adapt to changes in political power and issues. It could make efficient use of finances and technology and was compatible with centralized organization. Leadership at the grass-roots level, by contrast, was compatible with decentralized organization. It offered vitality and innovation and could mobilize funding, voluntary activists, and political pressure on local, state, or regional levels.

The American peace movement had a long tradition of professional leadership. Internationalist associations of the early twentieth century (like the Carnegie Endowment for International Peace) often had paid staff and were supported by major donors. Liberal pacifist organizations such as the FOR and the AFSC developed fully staffed offices. The NCPW, WLIPF, and FCNL had paid staffs working on legislative issues.

The wide-ranging Emergency Peace Campaign of the 1930s was coordinated by staff members who were effective lobbyists, administrators, publicists, and fund-raisers. After the 1950s, SANE built an increasingly professional office. Although some scholars have argued that professional entrepreneurship is a cause of conservatism in social movements, nearly a century of American peace movement experience suggests that this is not necessarily so.[21] Rather, interaction between leaders and constituencies has determined orientations, priorities, and preferred strategies. Particularly in the Vietnam era, a strong bias toward individual participation entered the movement.

Thereafter, the role of professionalism itself changed. It made use of technologies such as issue-oriented research, direct mailing, phone networks, and computers. Also, it was combined with grass-roots organization. Direct mailing made it possible to tap large numbers of small donors, making movement organizations less dependent on large contributors. Computerized mailing and phone trees contributed to networking among autonomous groups. Moreover, professionals facilitated voluntary activism by training people in organizing techniques such as polling and neighborhood canvassing. Given the strong pressures for both professional and grass-roots organizing, peace groups were challenged to manage the interplay between these styles so as to minimize tension, maximize resources, and adapt to changing circumstances.

Strategic Tensions   It has been observed that social movements tend to replicate their targets, those which focus on national institutions tending to develop centralized, hierarchical, and professional structures.[22] A strategy that is institutional and seeks to influence the foreign policy establishment, for example, is likely to involve leaders from that elite and to emphasize political compromise and realism. A strategy whose goal is to empower people will involve grass-roots leadership. Not surprisingly, then, the structure of the peace movement—its organizations and coalitions—interacted with its strategy.

The fundamental strategic tension in movement coalitions was between specific reforms of foreign policy and the transformation of society and its world role. Often that tension was expressed as the difference between peace as order (as internationalists usually defined it) and peace as change for the sake of justice (as liberal and radical pacifists understood it). For the most part, change was subordinated to order, and social transformation was deferred to specific reforms; but occasionally tension became so sharp that it polarized the movement, as it did during the Vietnam War. Even then, however, coalitions were formed around minimal demands.

A strategy of short-term goals accommodated organizational interests, since groups in any coalition sought to endure beyond the campaign that aligned them. It also posed a double risk: the thrust of the movement could be weakened as it consolidated around a moderate center, and it could also be co-opted or defused if a limited objective was achieved (both things happened to the test ban and freeze campaigns). The difficulty was that coalitions could not get consensus on long-term goals of social transformation, which, in any case, could not have yielded the immediate results needed to maintain momentum. Therefore, they organized for short-range goals. Interestingly, during the Vietnam War (and to some extent in World War I) the government repressed peace and antiwar protest to such an extent that it transformed the long-term value of political participation into an immediate issue of civil rights.

Although peace organizations addressed a wide range of issues, coalitions were built around single issues. Constituent groups divided when they could no longer align on a specific objective. Thus, although Vietnam War radicals repeatedly tried to assemble disaffected minorities by offering or endorsing diverse social changes, they could not satisfy any minority group that its interest was really served by the coalition, which therefore addressed limited antiwar demands. That is to say, they distinguished the aims of the coalition from those of its member groups.

In sum, the interaction of peace groups with one another generated organizational and strategic tensions with strong pressures for centralization and professionalism and for the pursuit of moderate, short-term, single-issue goals. Still, throughout the century peace campaigns increasingly adapted professionalism to grass-roots organization, in keeping with a growing priority for citizen participation in the policy-formation process. And meanwhile, leading peace organizations infused the movement with values, notably transnational solidarity and nonviolent approaches to conflict.

How Have Peace Organizations Interacted with the Public and Decision Makers?

As used here, the term *public* refers to those people and institutions outside the movement's own constituency that it seeks to influence. An important part of this public is its *elite sector*—those individuals and institutions that have access to decision makers by virtue of their status and expertise. The broader public is politically inert in the sense that it has to be aroused to exercise its influence. This is the *public at large.* Potentially *allied citizen groups* enhance the ability of the peace movement to reach both the elite and at-large sectors of the public. Three mediating factors that are critical to the movement's public role are *issue salience,* the *media,* and *cultural symbols.* In all these respects, peace advocates have interacted with the public and not merely acted upon it.

Historically, peace advocates assumed that other social-movement organizations constituted natural allies. Believing that war and militarism are not in the interest of society, they expected support from public advocacy groups like environmentalists and special interests, especially labor and minorities. Peace groups traditionally aligned in peace campaigns with organizations representing labor, women, farmers, and blacks. From the 1950s on, they also enlisted coteries of activists who were organized *within* special-interest sectors—women, scientists, educators, students, physicians, and entertainers, for example. This reinforced centralized, professional organization and limited-issue, short-term strategy. Special interest and advocacy groups were not interested in an open-ended commitment to a political campaign. They required that objectives be clearly defined and coalitions be limited. They valued centralized organization, if only because it usually corresponded to their own structures. The elite sector of the public made similar demands. It preferred to work within an institutional framework, with professionals attuned to the process of political compromise, and with practical objectives. Thus, the broader the coalition, the more limited was its program.

In a kind of counterpoint, centralized and issue-specific organization helped coalitions to ward off groups that tried to co-opt or disrupt them. In particular, the experience of having been threatened by communist or communist-led front groups in the 1930s led some peace advocates to be anxious about communist influence in the 1960s. Although the danger of co-optation was exaggerated, the threat of disruption was real because no real coalition could long exist if it were dominated by a group that represented an extreme interest within it.

The *public at large* could be mobilized only for short periods of time and for limited, defined objectives—for reform, not transformation. Moreover, since most people followed the cues of leaders and groups that they respected, political positions could be legitimated by respected elite figures and institutions. Peace movement organization and strategy was therefore constrained by the very public that it sought to mobilize.

An important factor in this respect was *issue salience,* the extent to which an issue was understood by large numbers of people, was important to them, and offered them a clear policy choice. An issue had to have salience in this sense for both the elite and at-large sectors of the public, whether it was perceived in terms of threat (as in the cases of impending war and atmospheric testing) or as opportunity (as in the case of disarmament in the early 1920s and late 1980s). The public apathy so often rued by activists probably was a form of political realism in the face of issues that were perceived to be too complex or too ambiguous for a clear popular choice or too little susceptible to public influence. Overcoming apathy, whatever its source, required an issue with salience.

In part, that meant it required drama, since the *media* responded to those issues that could be framed as a story. The peace movement enlisted public support with stories such as Bertha von Suttner's *Lay Down Your Arms* (1889), Eric Remarque's *All Quiet on the Western Front* (1929), Nevil Shute's *On the Beach* (1955), and Jonathan Schell's *The Fate of the Earth* (1982), but drama became particularly important with the technology of film and television, where even the best news coverage was a form of entertainment. The visual media could carry a powerful message to the public, as it did with the video drama *The Day After* (1983). It could also compromise the foreign policy claims of government, as it did in the case of U.S policy in Vietnam and Central America. It could legitimate policy critics like Benjamin Spock and Martin Luther King, Jr. It carried the central message of protest demonstrations, which was the simple fact that they did occur.[23] Accordingly, the media was an important mobilization resource.

It was also a constraint on movement strategy because it largely created its stories. A case in point was its role during the Vietnam War.[24] Television coverage fixed the impression of a radical, demonstrative antiwar movement in the public mind at the time when that aspect of the movement was most visible (about 1967–71). It largely ignored those who worked conventionally within the system. Moreover, the media filled its own requirements for a story by creating leaders where they did not exist (thus, it interpreted the fragmented radical left through the image of individuals like Staughton Lynd or Jerry Rubin, whom it cast as leaders in a centralized social movement). Decentralized protest was most vulnerable to misrepresentation. The leadership of centralized organizations, by contrast, conformed to the expectations of the media and was more likely to have public relations skills, information and demands.

Related to the role of media was that of *cultural symbols*. From 1815 to the present, peace advocates have been pushed to the political margin by the use of symbols and myths that have identified militarism or war policy with national culture. Perhaps the movement's greatest vulnerability during the Vietnam War was its inability to distance itself from antisymbols that placed it on the political margin. Perhaps its greatest achievement has been to identify peace with national and global interest—most notably in the image of the planet Earth as seen from outer space, which was the first universal symbol in history. Peace advocates themselves, and certainly the public they addressed, always operated within the context of socially integrating cultural symbols, so that there was ever pressure to work with images and myths that had inherent acceptance.

In short, dependence on the elite and the public at large, allied special- and public-interest organizations, issue salience, media, and cultural symbols—all reinforced the tendency of movement coalitions toward centralized organization and discrete goals.

Peace movements also targeted foreign policy *decision makers,* and here they confronted the most powerful constraints of all.[25] In even relatively democratic governments the executive branch guards its primary role in foreign affairs. At the same time, however, foreign policy is more or less subject to public review by the legislature and to internal review by business leaders, academics, scientific consultants, public institutes, foundations, and voluntary associations of interested intellectuals. The foreign policy establishment in this sense grew significantly as the United States expanded its world role during and after World War II. Peace advocates have sought support from decision makers since the arbitration campaigns of the nineteen century. Sometimes, as in the effort to secure a United Nations, that alliance has been critical.

Attempts to mobilize support within the government and foreign policy establishment created further pressure for a peace movement to adopt centralized organization and limited, short-term goals. Such a structure and strategy paralleled political organization and the hierarchy of decision making, as well as of elitist associations, and it was well adapted to the process of practical compromise. Moreover, large portions of the foreign policy establishment could be alienated by an aggressive pursuit of social transformation or by a fundamental challenge to the organization of power. Indeed, when government was able to characterize the peace movement in those terms, it made protest itself an issue, as the Nixon administration did in 1969–71.

Although the strategy of limited, specific objectives was reinforced by the political process, it also made peace campaigns vulnerable to that process. Peace leaders frequently confused their access to decision makers with influence they did not have. Moreover, campaign issues were sometimes defused by government action. That occurred after 1939 when the Roosevelt administration found ways to aid Great Britain's war effort within the letter of neutrality legislation. It happened in 1963 when the partial test ban treaty eliminated atmospheric testing as a vital issue. Possibly the Reagan administration's START talks and Strategic Defense Initiative had a similar effect on the freeze. Alternatively, a peace campaign issue could be co-opted by its political friends, as when Senator Borah linked outlawry of war to the Kellogg-Briand Pact, and when congressional leadership passed a heavily modified freeze proposal. Those political expedients took the wind out of the movement's sails.

In summary, peace organizations became political when they engaged in campaigns to influence public policy. As they interacted with one another, with the public, and with the decision-making community, they formed coalitions and framed issues. The great weight of this process was on compromise, on relatively centralized organizations, and on limited, short-term goals. It has been suggested that the transnational vision of the peace movement diminished in the second half of the twentieth century, at least as it was conveyed to the public.[26] If that is so, it may be partly a consequence of the growing ability to build coalitions.

On the other hand, peace movements were constituted by organizations with long-term goals, or at least values. They were designed to confront decision makers, to challenge foreign policy, and to force decisions into the public arena. Otherwise there would not have been any point to the frustrating and energy-consuming task of forming campaigns out of organizations. Although the peace movement has been constrained by pressures for centralized organization and short-term objectives, therefore, it also has been propelled by long-term visions that include the decentralization of political power and the transformation of the international order. Those tensions were inherent insofar as the peace movement engaged in the political process.

How Has the Peace Movement Interacted with the Course of History?

An assessment of the movement can be only suggestive, since foreign policy is subject to a multitude of domestic and international influences, a large proportion of which are off the public record. Peace advocates have been among many contending economic and civic interests in the United States, and they were also part of a multinational movement. With these caveats, the failure of many peace campaigns to achieve their objectives can be understood as part of the political process. Instead of failures or success, therefore, it is perhaps better to consider contributions and roles. The movement's contributions have been prophetic, innovative, instructive, and democratic; its role has been both cumulative and dialectical.

Contributions   Peace advocates have been prophetic in their direst predictions about the consequences of war. They have been prophetic, too, in asserting that alternatives to social violence are possible, given purposeful choice. With that sense of possibility, they undertook to produce change in the society.

Even as a prophetic minority, the peace movement was consciously innovative, believing that it prefigured social values and norms.[27] That belief was rooted in assumptions of the early Christian community and its emulation in seventeenth-century England. Quakerism especially laced the American peace movement with the assumption that personal life-style and group forms had a political import insofar as they modeled a future community. From the Garrisonians to the New Left, individuals and groups attempted to act out behavior they associated with peace, whether in conscientious objection to militarism, humanitarian service across boundaries, or attempts to make power accountable to humane values. Although some persons responded to an essentially individual morality, a host of them expressed loyalty to a social ideal. Women like Jane Addams explicitly identified a viable community with what they took to be feminine roles, such as reconciling and nurturing. Their view was not so far from subsequent interpretations of security as the meeting of mutual human needs. Insofar as utopianism has a role in social innovation by opening up new cognitive frameworks, it was acted out by innumerable peace advocates.[28]

They were innovative, too, in quite practical ways. Virtually every existing instrument of avoiding war or moderating its effects was envisioned by peace advocates well before it became feasible or necessary for political leaders: the codification of international law and human rights and adjudication by an international court or commissions, treaties of arbitration and techniques of mediation and conciliation, the laws of war and the International Committee of the Red Cross, succor for displaced persons and other victims of war, international organization and collective security arrangements, disarmament, decolonialization, and international measures to make the world economy more accessible and stable. The precursors of these measures, and often the agencies that developed them, were related to the American and international peace movement.

Beyond the specific institutions of an increasingly global society, the peace movement contributed inventive ways of thinking. Its prophetic challenge to militant idealism was itself innovative, of course; but beyond this, peace advocates attempted to take the idealism out of war. A Polish-Russian entrepreneur, Jean de Bloch, made an epochal economic and technical analysis of modern warfare (1898); an English journalist, Norman Angell, described war as *The Great Illusion* (1909–10); an American historian, James Shotwell, directed the exhaustive *Economic and Social History of the World War* for the Carnegie Endowment (1919–35); and an American liberal pacifist, Kirby Page, insisted that war must be evaluated as a method, not an idea. With innumerable others, they concluded that war was no longer a viable extension of politics, nor imperialism a valid form of economics. They disseminated that view in their acccounts of the consequences of modern warfare, and they grounded their argument in empirical realism.

Conversely, peace advocates reformulated the problem of peace in terms of the process of social change and the accountability of power. That was a main reason for the attractiveness of Gandhi's example in the interwar period, and for the application of nonviolent direct action techniques in civil rights, antiwar, and antinuclear campaigns. It was a view not limited to pacifists. John Foster Dulles explored the practical relationship of *War, Peace, and Change* (1939) while he was active in the religious wing of the peace movement, and long before he became a cold-war internationalist and secretary of state. The peace research community that evolved in the 1960s developed practical methods of conflict resolution and theoretical studies of conflict and social systems.[29]

The dissemination of innovative thinking itself was a form of instructions, but peace advocates provided information in more concrete terms. From the Lake Mohonk conferences at the turn of the century to seminars on Vietnam early in the 1960s and the freeze campaign of the 1980s, there were signficant efforts to inform the foreign policy elite on specific issues. From the *Olive Leaves* of Elihu Burritt to the television ads of SANE there were attempts to inform the public at large. Peace advocates were directly responsible for popularizing otherwise inaccessible information on the Philippine-American War, the European phase of World War I, the international crises of the 1930s, the emerging United Nations, the effects of nuclear testing, the Vietnam War, and nuclear weapons. In several of these cases they provided material that was suppressed by their government. The result was to locate increased understanding and authority in the public sector. This was perhaps especially important when issues were shrouded in the cloak of bipartisan foreign policy. By unveiling them in the public arena, often against the resistance of decision makers, peace advocates participated in the political process and made it more democratic.

Role   The role of the peace movement in American history has been both cumulative and dialectical. The cumulative aspects have been unfairly neglected (even in this volume) because they have been apolitical and undramatic. They consisted of efforts to influence the way people think and act in regard to war, peace, and international relations, including organized efforts to influence educational instruction and the media, and programs for value-oriented international exchanges. Even the Cosmopolitan Clubs and Rotary exchanges were initially envisioned as peace programs. So, too, were the continuous attempts in this century to change the treatment of war and other nations in U.S. textbooks, and to teach peaceful values and ways of interacting. On a slightly different line, the international peace movement contributed symbols that achieved widespread and positive recognition, notably the once controversial "peace symbol," the perennial dove, and the annual Nobel Peace Prize.[30]

Instruments for resolving conflict and new ways of thinking about it helped to transform the international system. As they were institutionalized by governments, though, those social inventions were dissociated from their origins among peace advocates. The result was to denigrate the movement's function within the politcal system and to fix its adversarial role. But of course it was in fact a dissenting and contesting minority. In this respect, it was engaged in a dialectical process, for it was involved in the continuous resolution of more or less antagonistic interests and orientations.

The process began with the formation of peace organizations and coalitions. From doctrinal pacifism to direct nonviolent action, from narrowly based, elitist international arbitration and law to the broad antinuclear arms campaigns, from collective security programs to the idea of mutual security, each generation of peace advocates had to adapt its political effort to a new set of international issues and to distinctive political conditions. Each had to deal with several organizational and strategic tensions at once and, in fact, had to define the very issues it would address. In short, the historic peace movements engaged in a political process that involved inherent conflicts. Most frustrating of all, these conflicts, often disruptive and discouraging, could never be fully resolved. Every solution was a temporary expedient. Basic tensions surfaced again in new crises and different social structures. The lessons of one generation of peace advocates, even if remembered, were not simply a legacy for the next.[31] Each generation had to learn anew—to define itself in relation to questions of peace and public security.

In the process, all coalitions left within ongoing peace organizations some residue of social consciousness, social and political skills, and innovative ideas. They also generated latent constituencies for subsequent coalitions.[32] Occasionally, they even changed the terms of foreign policy debate.[33] They learned a good deal about mobilizing their own resources and reaching the public, about reciprocal political and economic influence, about international relations and conflict resolution—and all this in a century in which social, political, economic, and military institutions changed fundamentally. In the sense that peace advocates had to resolve policy and organizational issues for themselves, their movement was a microcosm of social change through conflict.

The process of forming successive peace coalitions was dialectical in a larger sense. The purpose of each peace organization was to dissent from war and advocate peace. But the point of peace *campaigns* was to mobilize other people against the leadership, ideas, and social structures that institutionalize warfare, if not also injustice: "People who dare to challenge authority are thus the basis of collective action, social movements, and cycles of protest."[34]

In this sense, even the most conservative, cautious peace coalition was confrontational in that it challenged conventional wisdom about war. The more liberal and radical coalitions also confronted the bureaucratic power that institutionalized conventional wisdom. Because they sought to transform politics, the primary point of attack for radicals was the structure or leadership of power. Because they sought to reform policy, the primary points of attack for liberals were issues. Strategically, there was a great difference between conservative, radical, and liberal peace advocates (who often were in conflict with one another) and that difference had great practical consequences. But the difference can be understood as strategic only when it is viewed as part of the process of political transformation.

The essence of that process was to mobilize people for action in the arena most closed to public participation—national security. Since that required people to make choices about national purpose in a world context, the most important resource that the peace movement mobilized was popular will. In this respect, the difference between conservative, radical, and liberal peace advocates was more than strategic. It was a matter of philosophy, a question of whether or not they were willing to subject their own evaluations of national security and purpose to popular decision. The public includes many sectors, of course, even the educated elite, and the politics of decision making vary from one time to another. But insofar as the peace movement both aroused the public and empowered it in the area of foreign policy, win or lose it confronted the exclusive power of decision makers. In that measure it was a cohesive if dialectical force in American history.

Perhaps recent European experience can clarify this point. Reviewing the large mobilizations against the new generation of nuclear missiles, two scholars concluded in 1985: "From the Soviet point of view, with Foreign Minister Gromyko in office for more than a quarter of a century, the Western countries may look like playing children who try another toy every day. This, of course, is an invitation to the Soviet Union to stimulate these children to concentrate on these toys even more and neglect the security interest. The peace movement's ideas are such toys."[35] It is perhaps too much to hold any authors to their view of the Soviet Union five years after Gorbachev took power, but it is instructive to notice what these writers missed.

Foreign Minister Andrey Gromyko was not the only person in the Eastern bloc who had observed the vigorous controversy over security that was provoked by Western peace activists. The politics of foreign policy–making in the West—the contest among independent parties and peace groups, and the vocal opposition to a new generation of missiles— all this was widely known east of the Elbe by many Germans and Czechs, and by informed Poles, Hungarians, and Russians. People who were not allowed to quote from their own constitutional guarantees of freedom of expression knew that on the other side of the border, perhaps only a few kilometers away, other people were debating the most basic issues of security. And these observers, precisely because they could only observe, understood that the most basic issue of security is the right and the will to participate in defining it. They could not challenge the policy of their states without changing their societies.

This is not a matter of "playing" with foreign policy issues. The peace movement in the United States has not been a toy. It has been a tool with which a dissenting minority has dared to provoke the society to redefine its purpose in the light of a changing world. It has been part of the process by which the American people, along with others on this endangered planet, have been challenged to form alternatives to war as an instrument of national policy and to institutionalize peace as a way of managing conflict without violence.

Chronology

1815 *New York Peace Society* and *Massachusetts Peace Society* are founded to appeal against war on religious and humanitarian grounds

1816 *London Peace Society* is created in England.

1828 *American Peace Society* is formed as a national association of peace advocates.

1838 *New England Non-Resistance Society* is founded to espouse nonviolent activism.

1843–1851 European peace conferences are held; an international campaign promotes arbitration of disputes.

1846 Mexican-American War. *League of Universal Brotherhood* is established as a transnational association.

1861–1865 Civil War. Resistance to military service develops among nonresistant sects.

1866 *Universal Peace Union* is founded as an advocate of nonresistance and social reform.

1867 *Peace Association of Friends* is established to advocate Quaker nonresistance.

1873 *International Law Association* is founded; arbitration campaign resumes.

1882 *National Arbitration League* is founded in the midst of rising campaigns for arbitration and international law.

1888 *International Parliamentary Union* is formed.

1899 First Hague Peace Conference.

1898–1899 Spanish-American War.

1899–1901 Philippine-American War. *Anti-Imperialist League* organizes antiimperialist campaign.

1907 Second Hague Peace Conference; *National Arbitration and Peace Congress* is held.

1907–1911 Peace organizations multiply, most of them made up of conservative internationalists seeking peace through understanding and accommodation, without fundamental changes in the state system: *New York Peace Society, American Association for International Conciliation, Cosmopolitan Clubs, American School Peace League, American Society of International Law, World Peace Foundation, Carnegie Endowment for International Peace,* and *Church Peace Union.*

1914 World War I begins in Europe; *Fellowship of Reconciliation,* a liberal pacifist group, and *Union of Democratic Control,* a democratic and internationalist group, are formed in Great Britain.

1915–1916 Most conservative internationalists avoid the issue of intervention, as new activist groups form in United States: *Women's Peace Party* undertakes a mediation campaign; *League to Enforce Peace* espouses liberal internationalism through a world organization; *Fellowship of Reconciliation* advoates liberal pacifism; and *American Union Against Militarism* initiates an antipreparedness campaign.

1916 *No Conscription Fellowship* is founded in Great Britain.

1917 United States enters war in Europe. New peace groups are organized: *Emergency Peace Federation* opposed intervention prior to war; *People's Council of America* advocates liberal peace terms in wartime; and *American Friends Service Committee* defends conscientious objectors and offers humanitarian service.

1919–1920 League of Nations controversy. *Women's International League for Peace and Freedom* and its U.S. section are founded to advocate transnational solutions for conflict.

1921 *National Council for Prevention of War* is formed to wage a disarmament campaign; *American Committee for Outlawry of War* is organized.

1922   *League of Nations Non-Partisan Association* of liberal internationalists is formed.

1924   World Court campaign. *War Resisters League* is founded by absolute pacifists, and *National Conference on the Cause and Cure of War* is created as a coalition of liberal internationalist women.

1928   Campaign for the Kellogg-Briand Pact to outlaw aggressive war.

1931–1932   Coordinated disarmament campaign is attempted, leading to *Emergency Peace Committee* and *National Peace Conference.*

1936–1937   *Emergency Peace Campaign* aligns liberal pacifists and internationalists, with a focus on the neutrality issue.

1939   World War II begins in Europe in September.

1939–1941   Differences between interventionists and neutralists sharpen with the organization of *Committee to Defend America by Aiding the Allies* and *Keep America Out of War Congress.*

1940   *Friends Committee on National Legislation* is established to defend conscientious objectors and promote humanitarian service; *Committee to Study Peace* and *Commission for a Just and durable Peace* are founded to promote internationalism in postwar planning.

1941   United States enters the war in December.

1942–1945   CORE promotes civil rights through nonviolent direct action; radical pacifism evolves among conscientious objectors; *United Nations Association* and other groups undertake a campaign for the United Nations.

1945   United States drops atomic bombs on Hiroshima and Nagasaki in August, ending war in the Pacific and inaugurating the nuclear age.

1946–1947   *Committee for Non-Violent Revolution* is formed by radical pacifists; *Federation of American Scientists* links nuclear pacifists; and *United World Federalists* promotes world federalism.

1948   Campaign against Universal Miltary Training.

1950 Korean War begins, consolidating Cold War internationalism.

1957 *Committee for a SANE Nuclear Policy* and *Committee for Non-Violent Action,* and in Great Britain *Campaign for Nuclear Disarmament,* are formed in a campaign to ban atmospheric testing of nuclear weapons.

1958–1962 Test-ban campaign spurs creation of new peace groups, including *Student SANE, Student Peace Union, Women Strike for Peace, Physicians for Social Responsibility,* and *Council for a Livable World*; and *Students for a Democratic Society* takes form.

1963 Partial test ban treaty signed, ending atmospheric testing of nuclear weapons

1965 Vietnam War begins, escalating through the spring; antiwar coalition grows with teach-ins, *Students for a Democratic Society*'s March on Washington, and International Days of Protest, among other events.

1966–1967 Antiwar constituencies multiply, with formation of *Clergy and Laity Concerned, National Voter Pledge, Another Mother for Peace, Business Executives Move, Vietnam Veterans Against the War,* and organized draft resistance, among others. National efforts in 1967 include Spring Mobilization, Negotiations Now! Vietnam Summer, national draft-card turn-in, and March on the Pentagon.

1968 Credibility of the war effort is challenged by communist Tet offensive; Martin Luther King, Jr., and Robert Kennedy are assassinated; Democratic National Convention in Chicago is disrupted with violence; and Richard Nixon is elected.

1969–1971 Antiwar movement is in transition, with formation of liberal pacifist *National Action Group,* politically liberal *Vietnam Moratorium Committee,* and radical *New Mobe.* October moratorium and November mobilization, 1969, are followed by Kent State killings, May 1970. Evolution of alternative strategies by *Set the Date Now, People's Coalition for Peace and Justice,* and others lead to coordinated demonstrations of April and May 1971.

1972   *Campaign to End the Air War* is organized; Democratic presidential campaign, with George McGovern as candidate, absorbs antiwar efforts.

1973–1975   U.S. signs peace accord with North Vietnam: *Coalition to Stop Funding the War* formed to challenge continuing air war and military aid to South Vietnam; Nixon resigns, Gerald Ford succeeding him as president in 1974; and South Vietnam falls in April 1975.

1977   *Mobilization for Survival* is founded as antinuclear coalition.

1978–1979   Campaigns against B-1 bomber and MX missile programs are conducted as Cold War intensifies, and NATO reaches its two-track decision on the deployment of new missiles.

1980   *Ad Hoc Task Force for a Nuclear Weapons Freeze Campaign* is formed, as the missile issue is dramatized by large-scale demonstrations in Europe and *European Nuclear Disarment* is formed there.

1981–1983   *Nuclear Weapons Freeze Campaign* organizes.

1987   SANE and freeze campaign merge.

Notes and References

Preface

1. Charles Tilly, "Social Movements and National Politics," in *Statemaking and Social Movements: Essays in History and Theory,* ed. Charles Bright and Susan Harding (Ann Arbor: University of Michigan Press, 1984), 313.

Introduction: Washington, November 1969

1. Sidney Tarrow, *Struggle, Politics, and Reform: Collective Action, Social Movements, and Cycles of Protest* (Ithaca, N.Y.: Cornell University Center for International Studies, 1989), 8.

1. The First Century of Peace Reform, 1815–1914

1. The phrase is the apt title of Charles DeBenedetti, *The Peace Reform in American History* (Bloomington: Indiana University Press, 1980).

2. The basic histories of the movement through the Civil War are Peter Brock, *Pacifism in the United State: From the Colonial Era to the First World War* (Princeton, N.J.: Princeton University Press, 1968), and *The Quaker Peace Testimony: 1660 to 1914* (York, England: Sessions Book Trust, 1990); Merle Curti, *The American Peace Crusade, 1815–1860* (Durham; N.C.: Duke University Press 1929).

3. The phrase is from the title of Dodge's 1809 pamphlet, *The Mediator's Kingdom Not of This World But Spiritual, Heavenly and Divine.*

4. David Low Dodge, *War Inconsistent with the Religion of Jesus Christ,* reprinted in *The First American Peace Movement,* ed. Peter Brock (New York: Garland Press, 1972), 120.

5. Noah Worcester, *A Solemn Review of the Custom of War,* in ibid., 22.

6. See Edson L. Whitney, *The American Peace Society* (Washington, D.C.: American Peace Society, 1928).

191

7. Worthington Chauncey Ford, ed., *Addresses on War by Charles Sumner*, (New York: Garland Press, 1971), 122.

8. London (1843), Brussels (1848), Paris (1849), Frankfurt (1850), London (1851).

9. Thomas Grimké, quoted in Brock, *Pacifism in the United States*, 494.

10. Ibid., 584.

11. "Announcement," quoted in Curti, *American Peace Crusade*, 145. See also Merle Curti, *The Learned Blacksmith: The Letters and Journals of Elihu Burritt* (New York: Wilson-Erickson, 1937).

12. See especially Frederick Merk, "Dissent in the Mexican War," in Samuel Eliot Morison et al., *Dissent in Three American Wars* (Cambridge: Harvard University Press, 1970), 35–63.

13. Brock, *Pacifism in the United States*, 691.

14. It is told most succintly but on the basis of original research in ibid., 713–866.

15. Love claimed 10,000 supporters, but Brock and Curti dismiss this as very exaggerated, Brock speculating that the figure included European peace societies and that in the United States there were no more than 400 active members and 4,000 sympathizers. Brock, *Pacifism in the United States*, 927.

16. The APA was not fully committed to this specific campaign, owing to reservations held by Charles Sumner and George Beckwith.

17. See Warren F. Kuehl, *Seeking World Order: The United States and International Organization to 1920* (Nashville: Vanderbilt University Press, 1969), 40–41.

18. Originally called the Association for the Reform and Codification of the Laws of Nations, the organization adopted the name International Law Association in 1895 (Merle Curti, *Peace or War: The American Struggle, 1636–1936* [New York: Norton, 1936], 101, and Kuehl, *Seeking World Order*, 30). Field was the only American to participate in the founding meeting, and he became president at its first anual assembly the next year.

19. See Calvin D. Davis, *The United States and the First Hague Peace Conference* (Ithaca, N.Y.: Cornell University Press, 1962) and *The United States and the Second Hague Peace Conference* (Durham, N.C.: Duke University Press, 1976).

20. Curti, *Peace or War*, 142.

21. Benjamin Trueblood, quoted in DeBenedetti, *Peace Reform*, 71.

22. Bryan's peace role then and later was complex. See Merle Curti, *Bryan and World Peace* (1931; reprint, New York: Garland Press, 1971) and Paolo E. Coletta, *William Jennings Bryan: Progressive Politician and Moral Statesman, 1909–1915*, vol. 2 (Lincoln: University of Nebraska Press, 1964).

23. For a careful analysis of this group see Robert L. Beisner, *Twelve against Empire: The Anti-Imperialists, 1898–1900* (New York: McGraw-Hill, 1968). See also E. Berkeley Tompkins, *Anti-Imperialism in the United States:*

The Great Debate, 1890–1920 (Philadelphia: University of Pennsylvania Press, 1970), and Daniel B. Schirmer, *Republic or Empire: American Resistance to the Philippine War* (Cambridge, Mass.: Schenkman, 1972).

24. Quotation from Schirmer, *Republic or Empire,* 151; see also Willard B. Gatewood, Jr., *Black Americans and the White Man's Burden, 1898–1903* (Urbana: University of Illinois Press, 1975).

25. Curti, *Peace or War,* 182.

26. DeBenedetti, *The Peace Reform,* 77.

27. Raymond Bridgman, *World Organization,* quoted in Kuehl, *Seeking World Order,* 64. Kuehl's work on this period of internationalsim is authoritative, and it is the primary basis of my account.

28. DeBenedetti, *The Peace Reform,* 79 (referring to the period 1901–14).

29. The WPF, originally named the International School of Peace, was conceived on the model of a European research university. On the WPF see Arthur N. Holcombe, *A Strategy of Peace in a Changing World* (Cambridge.: Harvard University Press, 1967), and Peter Filine, "The World Peace Foundation and Progressivism, 1910–1918," *New England Quarterly* 36 (December 1963): 478–501. On the CEIP see C. Roland Marchand, *The American Peace Movement and Social Reform, 1898–1918* (Princeton, N.J.: Princeton University Press, 1972); David Patterson, *Toward a Warless World: The Travail of the American Peace Movement, 1887–1914* (Bloomington: Indiana University Press, 1976); Michael A. Lutzker, "The Formation of the Carnegie Endowment for International Peace: A Study of the Establishment-Centered Peace Movement, 1910–1914," in *Building the Organizational Society,* ed. Jerry Israel (New York: Free Press, 1972); and Larry L. Fabian, *Andrew Carnegie's Peace Endowment* (Washington, D.C.: Carnegie Endowment 1985).

30. The social characteristics of these peace advocates are delineated especially in Sondra R. Herman, *Eleven against War: Studies in American Internationalist Thought, 1898–1921* (Stanford, Calif.: Hoover Institution Press, 1969); Marchand, *The American Peace Movement and Social Reform*; Patterson, *Toward a Warless World*; and David Patterson's updated "Citizen Peace Initiatives and American Political Culture" in *Peace Movements and Political Cultures,* ed. Charles Chatfield and Peter van den Dungen (Knoxville: University of Tennessee Press, 1988), 187–203. These works are usefully read in connection with Robert H. Wiebe, *The Search for Order, 1877–1920* (New York: Hill and Wang, 1967).

31. Patterson, *Toward a Warless World,* 149.

32. Ibid., 149–52; Marchand, *The American Peace Movement and Social Reform,* 129–34.

33. See ibid., x. This thesis is persuasively developed throughout the book.

34. The 28 original trustees of the CEIP included 9 lawyers, 6 financiers or businessmen, and 4 current or former university presidents (Ibid., 120–21).

35. This interpretation is based on Herman's analysis, reinforced by the

subsequent literature. Herman applies a distinction advanced by German sociologist Ferdinand Tönnies (1855–1936) to contrast the orientation of these internationalists to institutional reform with the emphasis on personal, community-based values that was characteristic of the peace advocates who entered the movement during World War I. For a selection of writings on this theme see Ferdinand Tönnies, *On Sociology,* ed. Werner J. Cahnman and Rudolf Heberle (Chicago: University of Chicago Press, 1971).

2. The "Protean" Peace Reform, 1914–1919

1. Marchand, *The American Peace Movement and Social Reform,* 387.
2. Wilson was "partly" responding to public opinion, but had his own qualms about entanglement (Patterson, *Toward a Warless World,* 223).
3. John B. Clark, quoted in Marchand, *The American Peace Movement and Social Reform,* 165.
4. James Scott, quoted in Patterson, *Toward a Warless World,* 238.
5. Elihu Root, quoted in ibid., 236.
6. Warren F. Kuehl, *Hamilton Holt: Journalist, Internationalist, Educator* (Gainesville: University Presses of Florida, 1960), 120.
7. The basic work on the LEP is Ruhl J. Bartlett, *The League to Enforce Peace* (Chapel Hill: University of North Carolina Press, 1944).
8. Marchand, *The American Peace Movement and Social Reform,* 169.
9. Progressive peace advocates are characterized in Herman, *Eleven against War*; Marchand, *The American Peace Movement and Social Reform*; and Patterson, *Toward a Warless World,* and are the initial focus of Charles Chatfield, *For Peace and Justice: Pacifism in America, 1914–1941* (Knoxville: University of Tennessee Press, 1971).
10. Fanny Garrison Villard, *A Real Peace Society,* printed copy of address of 21 September 1914, Women's Peace Society papers, Swarthmore College Peace Collection (SCPC). Villard wanted to organize a society of absolutely pacifist women, which did not emerge until after the war.
11. This double argument was observed in Marchand, *The American Peace Movement and Social Reform,* 201–4. Subsequent scholarship has significantly developed the terms of radical feminism in America and England. See, for example, Jo Vellocott, "Finding New Words and Creating New Methods," in Chatfield and van den Dungen, *Peace Movements and Political Cultures,* 106–24, and "Feminist Consciousness and the First World War," *History Workshop Journal* 23 (Spring 1987): 81–101.
12. Women's Peace Party, quoted in Marie Louise Degen, *The History of the Women's Peace Party* (Baltimore: Johns Hopkins University Press, 1939), 40.
13. See esp. Jane Addams et al., *Women at the Hague: The International Congress of Women and Its Results* (1915; reprint, New York: Garland Press, 1976).

14. Henry Ford, quoted in Barbara S. Kraft, *The Peace Ship: Henry Ford's Pacifist Adventure in the First World War* (New York: Macmillan, 1978), 67.

15. Quotations from ibid., 115.

16. Lillian Wald recounts the story of the AUAM in *Windows on Henry Street* (Boston: Little, Brown, 1934). See also Blanche Wiesen Cook, "Woodrow Wilson and the Anti-Militarists, 1914–1918" (Ph.D. diss., Johns Hopkins University, 1970).

17. See Blanche Wiesen Cook, *Crystal Eastman on Women and Revolution* (New York: Oxford University Press, 1978).

18. Borah's view was recorded in Charles Hallinan to the executive committee of the AUAM, 17 April 1918, AUAM papers, SCPC.

19. Crystal Eastman, "American Union against Militarism: Suggestions for 1916–17," October 1916, AUAM papers, SCPC. Although Eastman's words were recorded in October 1916, her view was reinforced by the Mexican incident.

20. John H. Holmes, quoted in "Swinging around the circle against Militarism," *Survey* 36 (22 April 1916): 95.

21. The history of the FOR is a central thread in Chatfield, *For Peace and Justice.*

22. David Starr Jordan to William Jennings Bryan, 1 April 1917, William Jennings Bryan papers, box 31, Library of Congress (LC).

23. David Starr Jordan, *Days of a Man* (New York: World Book, 1922), 2:735.

24. Quoted from *The Advocate of Peace*, May 1917, in Curti, *Peace or War*, 254–255.

25. Marchand's account of the People's Council is still best, but see also Frank L. Grubbs, Jr., *The Struggle for Labor Loyalty: Gompers, The A.F of L., and the Pacifists, 1917–1920* (Durham, N.C.: Duke University Press, 1968). Important accounts of socialists and the war are Merle Fainsod, *International Socialism and the World War* (New York: Octagon, 1966), and James Weinstein, *The Decline of Socialism in America, 1912–1925* (New York: Monthly Review, 1967).

26. See Donald Johnson, *The Challenge to American Freedoms: World War I and the Rise of the American Civil Liberties Union* (Lexington: University Press of Kentucky, 1963).

27. [Crystal Eastman], "Proposed Announcement for the Press," 24 September 1917, quoted in Marchand, *The American Peace Movement and Social Reform*, 254.

28. Ibid., 389. It is useful to read Marchand in connection with Roy Lubove, *The Professional Altruist: The Emergence of Social Work as a Career, 1880–1930* (Cambridge: Harvard University Press, 1965).

29. Sayre, Muste, and Page became key leaders in the FOR. For a sense of the importance of community to pacifists see esp. Addams, *Peace and Bread in Time of War* (1922; reprint, New York: Garland Press, 1971).

30. Letter, "To Members of the Fellowship," 23 April 1917, FOR papers, box 22, SCPC.

31. Kirby Page to Howard E. Sweet, 3 February 1918, Kirby Page papers, Southern California School of Theology, Claremont, Calif.

32. *Statement Concerning the Treatment of Conscientious Objectors* (Washington, D.C.: Government Printing Office [GPO], 1919), 9, 24–25; Selective Service System, *Conscientious Objection*, Special Monograph no. 11 (Washington, D.C.: GPO, 1950), 1: 49. See esp. Norman Thomas, *Is Conscience a Crime?* (New York: Vanguard, 1927), and Walter Kellogg, *The Conscientious Objector* (New York: Boni and Liveright, 1919).

33. Rufus Jones, *A Service of Love in War Time: The American Friends Relief Work in Europe, 1917–1919* (New York: Macmillan, 1920), 105.

34. On the AFSC see Lester Jones, *Quakers in Action* (New York: Macmillan, 1929), and Marie Hoxie Jones, *Swords into Plowshares: An Account of the American Friends Service Committee, 1917–1937* (New York: Macmillan, 1937).

35. Charles DeBenedetti, *Origins of the Modern American Peace Movement, 1915–1929* (Millwood, N.Y.: KTO, 1978), 8.

36. For an insightful analysis of the LEP program in comparison with Wilson's, see Kuehl, *Hamilton Holt*, 138–39, 146–50.

37. Hamilton Holt, quoted in ibid., 145.

38. The standard history of the WILPF remains Gertrude Bussey and Margaret Tims, *Women's International League for Peace and Freedom, 1915–1965* (London: Allen and Unwin, 1965).

39. Balch directed the Henry Street Settlement House in Boston and was active in the 1915 International Congress of Women. She received the Nobel Peace Prize in 1946, Addams in 1931. See Mercedes M. Randall, *Improper Bostonian: Emily Greene Balch* (Boston: Twayne, 1964).

3. Peace and Neutrality Campaigns, 1921–1941

1. My treatment of the peace movement in the 1920s closely follows DeBenedetti's *Origins of the Modern American Peace Movement*; the treatment of the 1930s is based largely on Chatfield, *For Peace and Justice*, and "Alternative Antiwar Strategies of the Thirties," in *Peace Movements in America*, ed. Charles Chatfield (New York: Schocken, 1973), 68–80, and on Robert Kleidman, "Organization and Mobilization in Modern American Peace Campaigns" (Ph.D. diss., University of Wisconsin, 1990), and "Opposing the Good War: Mobilization and Professionalism in the Emergency Peace Campaign," in *Research in Social Movements, Conflicts, and Change*, vol. 9, ed. Louis Kriesberg (Geenwich, Conn.: JAI Press, 1986), 177–200.

2. Carrie Foster, manuscript draft of a forthcoming book on the U.S. sec-

tion of the WILPF, 1915–46 (Syracuse, N.Y.: Syracuse University Press), 63, 89.

3. Ibid., 99–102.

4. See Harriet Hyman Alonso, *The Women's Peace Union and the Outlawry of War, 1921–1942* (Knoxville: University of Tennessee Press, 1989).

5. On the 1920s disarmament campaigns see esp. C. Leonard Hoag, *Preface to Preparedness: The Washington Disarmament Conference and Public Opinion* (Washington D.C.: American Council on Public Affairs, 1941), and Arthur A. Ekirch, Jr., *The Civilian and the Military* (New York: Oxford University Press, 1956).

6. Frederick Libby, *To End War: The Story of the National Council for Prevention of War* (Nyack, N.Y.: Fellowship, 1969), 13.

7. Detzer told her story in *Appointment on the Hill* (New York: Holt, 1948).

8. Shotwell's *Autobiography* (Indianapolis: Bobbs-Merrill, 1961) is a good source of his thought, but see also Harold Josephson, *James T. Shotwell and the Rise of Internationalism in America* (Rutherford, N.J.: Fairleigh Dickinson University Press, 1975).

9. DeBenedetti, *Origins of the Modern American Peace Movement,* 205.

10. Ibid., 209–10. For background see Robert H. Ferrell, *Peace in Their Time: The Origins of the Kellogg-Briand Pact* (New Haven, Conn.: Yale University Press, 1952).

11. For overviews of the neutrality controversy see esp. William Langer and Everitt Gleason, *The Challenge to Isolation: The World Crisis of 1937–40 and American Foreign Policy* (New York: Harper, 1952); Donald Drummond, *The Passing of American Neutrality, 1937–1941* (Ann Arbor: University of Michigan Press, 1955); Robert A. Divine, *The Reluctant Belligerent: American Entry into World War II* (New York: Wiley, 1965) and *The Illusion of Neutrality* (Chicago: University of Chicago Press, 1962); and, although it does not adequately distinguish neutral internationalism from isolationism, Manfred Jonas, *Isolationism in America, 1935–1941* (Ithaca, N.Y.: Cornell University Press, 1966).

12. Report of the general secretary to the trustees of the World Peace Foundation, 13 February 1935, Newton D. Baker papers, box 241, LC. On the LNA role in this period see esp. Robert D. Accinelli, "Militant Internationalists: The League of Nations Association, the Peace Movement, and U.S. Foreign Policy, 1934–1938," *Diplomatic History* 4 (Winter 1980) 1: 19–37.

13. "Buck Hills Falls," notes of the organizing conference of the EPC, by Miriam and E. Raymond Wilson, 4 December 1935, EPC Papers, box 1, SCPC.

14. See Mark L. Chadwin, *The Hawks of World War II* (Chapel Hill: University of North Carolina Press, 1968).

15. Report to the national executive committee 14–16, April 1938, Socialist Party of America papers, national office files, 1939, Duke University. On this period see esp. Wayne S. Cole, *American First: The Battle against Intervention, 1940–1941* (Madison: University of Wisconsin Press, 1953).

4. New Reference Points, 1941–1955

1. The calculation is from Lawrence Wittner, *Rebels against War: The American Peace Movement, 1933–1983* (Philadelphia: Temple University Press, 1984), 42. This is the standard source on pacifism from 1941 and is followed in this chapter. Also useful is DeBenedetti, *The Peace Reform,* chapter 7.

2. Jo Ann Ooiman Robinson, *Abraham Went Out: A Biography of A. J. Muste* (Philadelphia: Temple University Press, 1981), 76.

3. Wittner, *Rebels against War,* 32, 54.

4. See William D. Miller, *A Harsh and Dreadful Love: Dorothy Day and the Catholic Worker Movement* (New York: Liveright, 1973).

5. Clarence Pickett, *For More Than Bread* (Boston: Little, Brown, 1953), 105. Pickett is a good source on Quaker relief and legislative efforts related to World War II.

6. This emblem of Quaker service was adopted by relief workers after the 1870–71 Franco-Prussian War (Irwin Abrams, *The Nobel Peace Prize and the Laureates* [Boston: G. K. Hall, 1988], 149).

7. Gunnar Jahn, quoted in Pickett, *For More Than Bread,* 307.

8. Abrams, *The Nobel Peace Prize,* 150.

9. This campaign is recounted in Albert N. Keim and Grant M Stoltzfus, *The Politics of Conscience: The Historic Peace Churches and America at War, 1917–1955* (Scottdale, Pa.: Herald Press, 1988), 86–93.

10. The NSBRO was originally called the National Council for Religious Objectors. Its board included representatives of the Brethren Service Committee, Mennonite Central Committee, AFSC, FOR, and Methodist Commission on World Peace.

11. Of these, 4,665 were Mennonites, 1353 Brethren, 951 Friends, 673 Methodists, 409 Jehovah's Witnesses, and 449 unaffiliated (Pickett, *For More Than Bread,* 323–34).

12. Colonel Louis Kosch, quoted in Keim and Stoltzfus, *The Politics of Conscience,* 119.

13. "The Moral Equivalent of War" is the title of an essay by William James that urged that peacemaking be regarded as a challenge calling forth heroic qualities.

14. On the FCNL see E. Raymond Wilson's autobiographical *Uphill for Peace: Quaker Impact on Congress* (Richmond, Ind.: Friends United Press, 1975).

15. For the impact of Gandhian thought on American pacifism see esp. Charles Chatfield, *The Americanization of Gandhi: Images of the Mahatma* (New York: Garland Press, 1976).

16. Reports of youth field workers James Farmer, George Houser, and Bayard Rustin, minutes of the FOR, 28 November 1941, FOR papers, box 2, SCPC. On CORE see esp. August Meier and Elliott Rudwick, *CORE: A Study*

in the Civil Rights Movement, 1941–1968 (New York: Oxford University Press, 1973); James Farmer, *Freedom When?* (New York: Random House, 1965); and Bayard Rustin, *Down the Line* (Chicago: Quadrangle, 1971).

17. Although the organization was put on a national basis in 1943, with chapters in seven cities, it was then called the National Federation of Committees of Racial Equality. The name was changed the following year to Congress of Racial Equality.

18. Wittner, *Rebels against War,* 70–96, 152–59.

19. David Dellinger, quoted in ibid., 94.

20. Ibid., 154–55.

21. Ralph DiGia, quoted in ibid., 159.

22. Jim Peck, quoted in ibid., 92.

23. Robert A. Divine used the phrase "second chance" as the title for his excellent history of the campaign for the United Nations, drawing it from a 1945 speech by Arthur Sweetser (Divine, *Second Chance: The Triumph of Internationalism in America during World War II* [New York: Atheneum, 1967]). My account closely follows Divine's.

24. Two of the members of the Advisory Committee on Problems of Foreign Relations were not members of the State Department: Norman H. Davis, head of the American Red Cross, and George Rublee, a lawyer (ibid., 33).

25. Federal Union, Inc., was originally formed in 1939 as Inter-Democracy Federal Union. The shortened name was adopted in 1940. According to Divine, there were 60 chapters and numerous prominent supporters by early 1941 (ibid., 39).

26. The original name was the Commission to Study the Bases of a Just and Durable Peace. It was shortened in the spring of 1943 as the group shifted from study to advocacy.

27. The circumstances of Welles's resignation are not altogether clear, but Divine makes a strong case for Hull's role in it (Divine, *Second Chance,* 138–39).

28. These Gallup polls, cited in ibid., 68–69, were matched by other surveys of opinion.

29. *Changing World* (March 1943), quoted in ibid., 87.

30. Sponsors of the Non-Partisan Council included the LNA, UNA, Church Peace Union, Freedom House, and Carnegie Endowment for International Peace (ibid., 100).

31. Ibid., 110.

32. The disparity of power was recognized even in the General Assembly. The Soviet Union was given seats for the Ukraine and Lithuania, which were only nominally independent, in compensation for the Commonwealth nations of Great Britain and the Latin American dependencies of the United States.

33. Quoted in Foster manuscript history of WILPF, 752.

34. The term "collective security" became familiar only in the mid-1930s. It did not then necessarily denote the collective use of military force, although

by 1945 that was clearly implied. See DeBenedetti, *The Peace Reform*, 218, n. 31; Richard N. Current, "The United States and 'Collective Security': Notes on the History of an Idea," in *Isolation and Security: Ideas and Interests in Twentieth-century American Foreign Policy*, ed. Alexander DeConde (Durham, N. C.: Duke University Press, 1957); and Roland N. Stromberg, *Collective Security and American Foreign Policy: From the League of Nations to NATO* (New York: Praeger, 1963).

35. Divine, *Second Chance*, 183.

36. Truman, quoted in Wittner, *Rebels against War*, 131.

37. The "Franck Report" was named for James Franck, a physicist on the committee that produced it. Others included Leo Szilard and Eugene Rabinowitch, who were active in subsequent efforts to mobilize scientists for the international control of atomic weapons. On the postwar organization of scientists to influence policy see Wittner, *Rebels against War*, chapters 5–7; Alice Kimball Smith, *A Peril and a Hope: The Scientists' Movement in America, 1945–1947* (Chicago: University of Chicago Press, 1965); and Robert Gilpin, *American Scientists and Nuclear Weapons Policy* (Princeton, N.J.: Princeton University Press, 1962). Paul Boyer incorporates the scientist movement in his rich narrative *By the Bomb's Early Light: American Thought and Culture at the Dawn of the Atomic Age* (New York: Pantheon, 1985).

38. Albert Einstein, "The Real Problem Is in the Hearts of Men," *New York Times Magazine* (23 June 1946), 7, quoted in Wittner, *Rebels against War*, 166.

39. Wesley T. Wooley, *Alternatives to Anarchy: American Supernationalism since World War II* (Bloomington: Indiana University Press, 1988), 15. This is the best source on the evolution of world federalism in the United States, although Wittner's briefer account is also based on primary sources. See also Jon A. Yoder, "The United World Federalists: Liberals for Law and Order," in Chatfield, *Peace Movements in America*, 95–115.

40. The organizational details and membership figures for specific organizations are drawn from ibid., 36–37; the estimate for combined membership is Wittner's, *Rebels against War*, 170.

41. Wooley, *Alternatives to Anarchy*, 38, 53.

42. This strategy was initiated in 1941 by North Carolina lawyer Robert Lee Humber. Working independently, he secured legislative endorsements for some kind of world federation from 11 state legislatures by the time the UWF was organized in 1947 (ibid., 46–47).

43. Ibid., 50–51.

44. Cord Meyer, quoted in ibid., 58; Wooley quoted in ibid., 70.

45. Ibid., 121.

46. The evolution of a Cold War version of internationalism is traced in Wooley, *Alternatives to Anarchy*, and in Robert Booth Fowler, *Believing Skeptics: American Political Intellectuals, 1945–1964* (Westport, Conn.: Greenwood Press, 1978), esp. 121–48. The subject is developed with respect to decision

makers in John C. Donovan, *The Cold Warriors: A Policy-Making Elite* (Lexington, Mass.: D. C. Heath, 1974), and in the concluding chapter of Lloyd C. Gardner, *Architects of Illusion: Men and Ideas in American Foreign Policy, 1941–1949* (Chicago: Quadrangle, 1970). H. W. Brands, Jr., offers a case study of John Foster Dulles and Harold Stassen in *Cold Warriors: Eisenhower's Generation and American Foreign Policy* (New York: Columbia University Press, 1988). See also Harold Josephson, "The Search for a Lasting Peace: Internationalism and American Foreign Policy, 1920–1950" in Chatfield and van den Dungen, *Peace Movements and Political Cultures*, 204–21, and the symposium "Internationalism as a Current in the Peace Movement," in Chatfield, *Peace Movements in America*, 170–91.

    47. Albert Wohlstetter, "Strategy and the Natural Scientists," in *Scientists and National Policy-Making*, ed. Robert Gilpin and Christopher Wright (New York: Columbia University Press, 1964), 224–25. Bernard Brodie's "The Scientific Strategists" and other essays in the same book further develop the role of scientists in the defense establishment.

    48. Waldemar Nielsen, *The Big Foundations* (New York: Columbia University Press, 1972), 316. See also Mary Anna Culletin Colwell, "The Foundation Connection: Links among Foundations and Recipient Organizations," in Robert F. Arnove, *Philanthropy and Cultural Imperialism: The Foundations at Home and Abroad* (Boston: G. K. Hall, 1980), 413–52, and Edward H. Berman, *The Influence of the Carnegie, FOR, and Rockefeller Foundations on American Foreign Policy: The Ideology of Philanthropy* (Albany: State University of New York Press, 1983).

    49. Donovan makes a persuasive case in *The Cold Warriors* that an insulated elite with a coherent ideology dominated decision making from Secretary of War Henry Stimson, through secretaries of state Dean Acheson and John Foster Dulles, to the Kennedy and Johnson administrations.

5. The First Campaign against Nuclear Arms, 1955–1963

    1. See Robert Divine, *Blowing on the Wind: The Nuclear Test Ban Debate, 1954–1960* (New York: Oxford Univeristy Press, 1978), esp. 111–12.

    2. CNVA was originally called Non-Violent Action against Nuclear Weapons. The more familiar name, used in the text, was adopted following a reorganization in 1958–59.

    3. Lawrence Scott, quoted in Neil H. Katz, "Radical Pacifism and the Contemporary American Peace Movement: The Committee for Non-Violent Action, 1957–1967" (Ph.D. diss., University of Maryland, 1974), 32. This is the definitive study of the CNVA, but see also Katz's more accessible "In Defense of Losers: A Partisan Look at American Radical Pacifists," *New America: A Review* (Spring 1975) 2:2–10. The Catholic Worker Movement is set in its larger context

in Patricia McNeal, *The American Catholic Peace Movement* (New Brunswick, N.J.: Rutgers University Press, forthcoming 1992).

4. N. Katz, "Radical Pacifism," 216–17.

5. The basic secondary source is Milton Katz, *Ban the Bomb: A History of SANE, the Committee for a Sane Nuclear Policy, 1957–1983* (Westport, Conn.: Greenwood Press, 1986). The account in this chapter is based also on other secondary sources and primary sources in the papers of SANE, the AFSC, and related groups used to research Charles DeBenedetti, *An American Ordeal: The Antiwar Movement of the Vietnam Era* (Syracuse, N.Y.: Syracuse University Press, 1990).

6. Quotation from Lawrence Scott, in minutes of Provisional Committee, 21 June 1957, SANE Papers, series A, box 4, SCPC; the number of reprints cited is from M. Katz, *Ban the Bomb*, 29.

7. Report of the Pawling (N.Y.) Working Conference, SANE papers, series B, box 13, SCPC.

8. M. Katz, *Ban the Bomb*, 29. The distribution of SANE's constituency remained fairly constant through 1963.

9. Subsequently, the executive committee became a board of directors, and local representation on it was increased to one-half.

10. For example, most of SANE's $50,000 budget for fiscal year 1958–59 came from mail and individual solicitations and gifts; only $2,100 came from local committees (SANE budget document, SANE papers, series A, box 9, SCPC).

11. See especially Divine, *Blowing on the Wind*, 250. SANE's contributions are recounted in M. Katz, *Ban the Bomb*, 37–39.

12. Minutes of the Second Annual National Conference, 25–26 October 1959, SANE papers, series A, box 9, SCPC.

13. Gottlieb was a political scientist who had served as chair of SANE's Washington, D.C., chapter and was a member of the national board of directors.

14. "Standards for SANE Leadership," quoted in M. Katz, *Ban the Bomb*, 50.

15. Homer Jack became executive director, freeing Donald Keys to act as program director; Sandford Gottlieb was political-action director, and Ed Meyerding was development director.

16. "Summary, Third National Conference of the National Committee for a Sane Nuclear Policy, 14–16 October 1960, Chicago, "SANE papers, series A, box 9, SCPC.

17. Homer A. Jack, "New Frontier," *SANE-USA* (February 1961):2.

18. Lewis Coser et al., "The Committee of Correspondence: A Statement," May 1960, quoted in Charles DeBenedetti, *An American Ordeal*, 45. The Committee of Correspondence was an attempt to follow up the Bear Mountain Conference with a network of liberal intellectuals.

19. See Helen S. Hawkins et al., eds., *Toward a Livable World: Leo Szilard and the Crusade for Nuclear Arms Control* (Cambridge: MIT Press, 1987), 423–84, ix–xii.

20. Most of these actions and the Spock ad are described in M. Katz, *Ban the Bomb*, 66–75.

21. For accounts of this story see ibid., 81–84, and Norman Cousins, *The Improbable Triumvirate: John F. Kennedy, Pope John, Nikita Khrushchev* (New York: Norton, 1972). The negotiations from 1954 to 1963 are covered in Harold Karan Jacobson and Eric Stein, *Diplomates, Scientists, and Politicians: The United States and the Nuclear Test Ban Negotiations* (Ann Arbor: University of Michigan Press, 1966). Kennedy's speech is reprinted in full in *The Burden and the Glory: John F. Kennedy*, ed. Allan Nevins (New York: Harper and Row, 1964), 53–56.

22. See Boyer, *By the Bomb's Early Light*, and "From Activism to Apathy: The American People and Nuclear Weapons, 1963–1980," *Journal of American History* 70 (March 1984): 837–44.

23. "Minutes of Special Board Meeting—June 16–17, 1961—New Canaan, CT," SANE papers, series A, box 4, SCPC.

24. N. Katz, "Radical Pacifism," 186.

25. Charles Bolton, "A Program for the Future," *Nation*, 2 November 1963, 14; Homer Jack, "Next Steps in the American Peace Movement," SANE Washington logbook, 1963, SANE/Freeze National Office.

26. AFSC, *Speak Truth to Power: A Quaker Search for an Alternative to Violence* (Philadelphia:AFSC, 1955), 25; Reinhold Niebuhr, "Foreword," in Harrison Brown and James Real, *Community of Fear* (Santa Barbara, Calif.: Center for the Study of Democratic Institutions, 1960), 5.

6. Vietnam and the Antiwar Movement, 1965–1975

1. This chapter is based on DeBenedetti, *An American Ordeal*, and the sources used in researching it.

2. See Robert Buzzanco, "The American Military's Rationale against the Vietnam War," *Political Science Quarterly* 101, no. 4 (1986): 559–76.

3. Intervention was criticized in 1963–64 by SANE, WILPF, WSP, SPU, and SDS.

4. Walter Lippmann, "Mr. Kennedy on Viet-Nam," 5 September 1963, reel 10, Walter Lippmann papers, Yale University. This view was articulated well also by political scientist Hans Morgenthau.

5. David Dellinger, "The Here-and-Now Revolution," *Liberation* 1 (June 1956): 17–18; A. J. Muste, "Tract for the Times," *Liberation* 1 (March 1956): 6.

6. Of those casualties, 267 were killed before 1965. George D. Moss, *Vietnam: An American Ordeal* (Englewood Cliffs, N.J.: Prentice Hall, 1990), 378. Moss draws these statistics from Thomas C. Thayer, *War without Fronts: The American Experience in Vietnam* (Boulder, Colo.: Westview Press, 1985).

7. Quoted in Eric F. Goldman, *The Tragedy of Lyndon Johnson* (New York: Knopf, 1969), 450.

8. Paul Potter, "The 'Incredible' War," *National Guardian,* 24 April 1965, 5.

9. Norman Thomas, in "Vietnam and the Left: A Symposium," *Dissent* 12 (Autumn 1965): 396.

10. Sanford Gottlieb to Clark Kissinger, 31 August 1965, box 31, SDS Records, State Historical Society of Wisconsin Library.

11. From the perspective of the SWP, the Communist party predominated in the NCCEWVN. The executive secretary of the NCCEWVN, Frank Emspack, had close ties to the Communist party, but he seems to have attempted to run the national office at Madison, Wisconsin, as a genuine coalition. Given factional disputes, this was not possible. In any case, the role of the Communist party in the antiwar movement was relatively minor, and it was conservative in that the party preferred electoral strategy to demonstrative confrontations.

12. Originally called Clergy and Laymen Concerned about Viet Nam, the organization adopted its more familiar name, Clergy and Laity Concerned, in 1973. Its history is recounted in Mitchell K. Hall, *Because of Their Faith: CAL-CAV and Religious Opposition to the Vietnam War* (New York: Columbia University Press, 1990).

13. See David Farber, "The Counterculture and the Anti-War Movement," (paper delivered at the Vietnam Antiwar Movement Conference, University of Toledo, Ohio, 4–5 May 1990).

14. On a national level, counseling was coordinated especially by the Central Committee for Conscientious Objectors and by the National Service Board for Religious Objectors.

15. *New York Times,* 17 April 1967, 1.

16. It is impossible to arrive at accurate numbers. The New York press and police reported 200,000, but internal estimates of the organizers were twice that number. Conservative figures are used throughout this chapter, but absolute numbers for demonstrations are less significant than relative changes in them.

17. McGeorge Bundy, memorandum for the president, 10 November 1967, pp. 6–7, 1967 folder, box 2, MNF file, Lyndon Baines Johnson Presidential Library.

18. *Public Papers of the Presidents of the United States: Lyndon B. Johnson, 1967* (Washington, D.C.: GPO, 1968), 2:1186. For an excellent assessment of the effect of the antiwar movement on the executive branch, see Melvin Small, *Johnson, Nixon, and the Doves* (New Brunswick, N.J.: Rutgers University Press, 1988).

19. See Charles DeBenedetti, "A CIA Analysis of the Anti-Vietnam War Movement: October 1967," *Peace and Change* 9 (Spring 1983): 35–39.

20. Phil Ochs, "Have You Heard? The War Is Over!" *Village Voice,* 23 November 1967, 16, 38.

21. The Youth International Party (YIP) was the formal name of the group. It was something of a contradiction to give such a playful party a formal name,

but it was good media. The group itself was less an organization than an animating spirit.

22. Cooperating in the Coalition for National Priorities were peace advocates from SANE, CALC, ADA, BEM, FCNL, WILPF, WSP, AFSC, and FOR; in the National Action Group, from the AFSC, FOR, CALC, WILPF, and WRL (which absorbed CNVA in 1967).

23. These included Sam Brown, David Hawk, Marge Skilenkar, and David Mixner.

24. "Special Information Report (Special): 15 October 1969 Activities," 10 October 1969, CIA document released to Charles DeBenedetti.

25. Harry R. Haldeman and Joseph Dimong, *The Ends of Power* (New York: Times Books, 1978), 98; Nixon quoted from *Public Papers of the Presidents of the United States: Richard Nixon, 1969* (Washington, D.C.: GPO, 1970), 909.

26. Stewart Meacham, "Why Washington?—Why Now?" *New Mobilizer* 14 (August–September 1969): 5–6.

27. The project for mass civil disobedience arose in mid-1970. The project enlisted the tenuous, short-lived National Coalition against War, Racism, and Repression, and it was pressed especially by David Dellinger and Rennie Davis, leader of the May Day group.

7. The Second Campaign against Nuclear Arms, 1975–1987

1. National groups formed between 1965 and 1979 to promote peace through education or cultural interchange included the World without War Council (1967), World Conference on Religion and Peace (1968), Pax World Foundation (1970), Global Education Associates (1973), Global Learning, Inc. (1973), Friendship Force International (1977), and World Peacemakers (1978). The Conference (subsequently Council) on Peace Research in History was formed in 1964 and the Consortium for Peace Research, Education, and Development in 1964, the latter affiliated with the International Peace Research Association.

2. This consensus was explicit in the writing of organizational leaders. See DeBenedetti, *An American Ordeal*, 355–56.

3. Figures from Herbert Scoville, Jr., *MX: Prescription for Disaster* (Cambridge: MIT Press, 1981), extracted in *The Arms Race and Nuclear War*, ed. William M. Evan and Stephen Hilgartner (Englewood Cliffs, N.J.: Prentice-Hall, 1987), 68.

4. In general, "strategic" refers to weapons that can reach enemy territory, but in SALT I it was limited to intercontinental ballistic missiles (ICBMs), thus excluding forward-based intermediate-ranged missiles and strategic bombers. Since the limitation was on missiles, their MIRVing continued, with an enormous increase in the number of actual warheads on both sides.

5. The figure is from David S. Meyer, *A Winter of Discontent: The Nuclear Freeze and American Politics* (New York: Praeger, 1990), 144; see also

Pam Solo, *From Protest to Policy: Beyond the Freeze to Common Security* (Cambridge, Mass.: Ballinger Press, 1988), 29–30. Meyer's well-researched analysis relates the freeze campaign to social-movement theory and the politics of arms control. For SANE's work on nuclear arms issues, 1969–82, see M. Katz, *Ban the Bomb*, 129–52.

    6. Katz, *Ban the Bomb*, 137.

    7. See Jerome Price, *The Antinuclear Movement*, rev. ed. (Boston: Twayne, 1990).

    8. Figures cited in Meyer, *Winter of Discontent*, 145.

    9. Figures cited in Frances B. McCrea and Gerald E. Markle, *Minutes to Midnight: Nuclear Weapons Protest in America* (Newbury Park, Calif.: Sage, 1989), 93. Based on selected published sources, this analysis attempts to fit antinuclear campaigns into social movement theory.

    10. Figure cited in ibid., 93; on MFS see also Meyer, *Winter of Discontent*, 147–49, and Solo, *From Protest to Policy*, 31–34. Among the members of MFS were the AFSC, WILPF, CALC, and WRL.

    11. Solo, *From Protest to Policy*, 49–50.

    12. Randall Forsberg (November 1981) quoted in Meyer, *Winter of Discontent*, 162. Pam Solo gives an insightful participant's analysis of the internal dynamics of the freeze campaign in *From Protest to Policy*. I am particularly indebted, however, to Robert Kleidman for his organizational analysis.

    13. Figure in Kleidman, "Organization and Mobilization," 298.

    14. Quotation from *Freeze Newsletter*, October 1981, in Kleidman, "Organization and Mobilization," 300; the number of volunteers is reported as of January 1982, in "NWFC March 1983 Request for Funding," cited in ibid., 301. Kleidman notes that this is but a guess in view of the loose organization of the freeze. The figure is accepted in Solo, *From Protest to Policy*, 84.

    15. See Kleidman, "Organization and Mobilization," 298–99, for this analysis and esp. the sources of second-wave volunteerism.

    16. A new trial was granted on procedural grounds that, however, accepted the argument that the defendants were acting to prevent a "greater harm" as a legitimate defense. On media coverage see Meyer, *Winter of Discontent*, 199–201, 207, n. 14.

    17. M. Katz, *Ban the Bomb*, 149.

    18. Quotation from Meyer, *Winter of Discontent*, 130.

    19. Les Aspin, quoted in ibid., 223. My interpretation reflects Meyer's persuasive analysis of the political role of the arms control community.

    20. This was particularly important in leading important business interests to support the Democratic party on arms control. See Thomas Ferguson and Joel Rogers, *Right Turn: The Decline of the Democrats and the Future of American Politics* (New York: Hill and Wang, 1986), 146–54.

    21. Solo, *From Protest to Policy*, 111–14.

    22. For the impact of the freeze proposal on Congress, see Douglas C.

Waller, *Congress and the Nuclear Freeze: An Inside Look at the Politics of a Mass Movement* (Amherst: University of Massachusetts Press, 1987). Waller was a key aide to Markey.

23. The freeze was endorsed by over 150 national organizations by the year's end, and the NWFC had 650 local chapters. Figures from ibid., 156–66, 161; M. Katz, *Ban the Bomb,* 153; and McCrea and Markle, *Minutes to Midnight,* 112.

24. Figures cited in Kleidman, "Organization and Mobilization," 307. "Major donor" refers to gifts of over $1,000. The large foundations mentioned were MacArthur, Carnegie, Ford, Rockefeller, and W. Alton Jones. On the impact of large-scale funding see also Ferguson and Rogers, *Right Turn,* 151, and Meyer *Winter of Discontent,* 110–11.

25. Kleidman, "Organization and Mobilization," 318: "By the end of 1984, state and local Freeze offices had paid staff totalling 66.5 full-time equivalents, serving a total of 1,333 local groups."

26. Journalist Mark Hertsgaard, quoted in Kleidman, "Organization and Mobilization," 300.

27. Figures from Meyer, *Winter of Discontent,* 180; SANE programs described in M. Katz, *Ban the Bomb,* 154–56.

28. Dollar figure from Waller, *Congress and the Nuclear Freeze,* 294; SANE membership from M. Katz, *Ban the Bomb,* 163.

29. On election results see esp. Waller, *Congress and the Nuclear Freeze,* 296–97.

30. The quotation and the analysis of NWFC and SANE organizational cultures is from Kleidman, "Organization and Mobilization," 339.

31. Useful anthologies that treat the freeze concept seriously in relation to arms control are Steven E. Miller, ed., *The Nuclear Weapons Freeze and Arms Control* (Cambridge, Mass.: Ballinger Press, 1984), and Committee on International Security and Arms Control, National Academy of Sciences, *Nuclear Arms Control: Background and Issues* (Washington, D.C.: National Academy, 1985).

32. The richness of the larger coalition against nuclear arms is conveyed in terms of the lives of activists in Paul Rogat Loeb, *Hope in Hard Times: America's Peace Movement and the Reagan Era* (Lexington, Mass.: Lexington Books, 1987).

Conclusion: The American Peace Movement

1. Michael Howard, *The Causes of Wars and Other Essays* (London: Temple Smith, 1983), 9; Howard refers to the period before 1914.

2. DeBenedetti, *The Peace Reform,* 199.

3. Guenter Lewy, *Peace and Revolution: The Moral Crisis of American Pacifism* (Grand Rapids, Mich.: Eerdmans, 1988). For a critique of this book see

208   *The American Peace Movement*

Charles Chatfield, "Misplaced Crisis: Guenter Lewy's *Peace and Revolution,*" in *Peace Betrayed?,* ed. Michael Cromartie (Washington, D.C.: Ethics and Public Policy Center, 1990), 41–65.

4. It is understood in sociological theory that there can be no social movement without a dynamic interaction between a minority making public claims and the larger society it addresses.

5. The term "movement cycles" is used by Sidney Tarrow to refer to peaks and valleys (or perhaps better, extensions and contractions) of effort. Tarrow, *Struggle, Politics, and Reform,* esp. 44–45. Because the word *cycles* can also carry the sense of inevitable recurrence, I prefer, given the variation in contexts and issues, the word *episodic.*

6. McCrea and Markle, in *Minutes to Midnight* (esp. 29–37, 154–55) interpret the peace movement of the post–World War II era to validate theories associated with Jürgen Habermas and Alain Touraine that are predicated on the rise of a "new class" and of "new movements" carrying it into social action. I do not find the attempt convincing. Although Habermas and Touraine offer creative descriptions of postindustrial social structure, their theories do not explain social action and interaction and, in particular, beg the question of why such large numbers in the "new class" ranged themselves against the "new movements." See esp. Habermas, *The Theory of Communicative Action,* vol. 1 (Boston: Beacon Press, 1984); Touraine, *Post-Industrial Society: Tomorrow's Social History* (New York: Random House, 1971), and *The Voice and the Eye: An Analysis of Social Movements* (Cambridge: Cambridge University Press, 1981). For critiques of this school, see esp. essays in *From Structure to Action: Comparing Social Movement Research across Cultures,* ed. Bert Klandermans et al. (Greenwich, Conn.: JAI, 1988), and Tarrow, *Struggle, Politics, and Reform,* 57–69.

7. Arthur Meier argues that the prevalence of the intelligentsia in the movement is a result of "the worsening of their real living conditions under state-monopolistic rule" (Meier, "The Peace Movement: Some Questions Concerning Its Social Nature and Structure," *International Sociology* 3, no. 1 [March 1988]:84). What distinguishes this class, however, is its informed perception of a condition shared by others.

8. Ibid., 85–86.

9. The importance of values and beliefs in forming cohesion and solidarity within social movement groups was emphasized by Ralph Heberle in *Social Movements* (New York: Appleton, 1951), esp. 12–13. Charles Tilly defined a social movement as "a group of people identified by their attachment to some particular set of beliefs" in *From Mobilization to Revolution* (Reading, Mass.: Addison-Wesley, 1978), 9, and Joseph R. Gusfield attributes to Tilly the intent to designate beliefs "directed to change" ("Social Movements and Social Change: Perspectives of Linearity and Fluidity," in *Research in Social Movements, Conflicts and Change,* vol. 4, ed. Louis Kriesberg [Greenwich, Conn.: JAI Press, 1981], 319). This view modifies the notion of rational calculations of interest. It is a grounding

assumption in Tarrow's synthesis of the field, which views the collective life of movement subcultures as "the process through which people recognize their common interests and values and organize around them" (Tarrow, *Struggle, Politics, and Reform,* 13).

10. Herman, *Eleven against War,* 8.

11. James Bevel, quoted in Robinson, *Abraham Went Out,* 223.

12. The phrase is used in Tarrow, *Struggle, Politics, and Reform,* 8, 103.

13. Although this phrase was widely credited to A. J. Muste, it probably was coined by a French resistance leader of World War II (Robinson, *Abraham Went Out,* 228, n. 13). Each of the groups named also had short-term goals, of course, and the peace section of the AFSC was only one of several divisions that administered specific service projects.

14. The term "halfway house" is used in this sense by Aldon D. Morris in *The Origins of the Civil Rights Movement* (New York: Free Press, 1984).

15. "Movements appear when there are substantive issues and/or substantial constituencies not adequately integrated into the polity by existing linkage mechanisms" Meyer, *Winter of Discontent,* 8.

16. In Europe there were—apart from national movements—an at least incipient campaign to forestall war in the Balkans before World War I, efforts for disarmament in the 1920s, attempts to forge both neutrality and antifascist campaigns in the 1930s, the test ban campaign of the late 1950s, and the antinuclear movement of the early 1980s.

17. Resource mobilization theory is oriented to the terms on which social movements strengthen and use their resources. This approach arose in the 1970s as a self-conscious break with sociologists who had minimized the relationships between social movements, inequalities, and change. The diverse theorists in the tradition share several assumptions: that movement participation is rational; that social movements are extensions of institutionalized politics and represent attempts to alter unequal power relationships; that grievances generated by such relationships are widespread and that, therefore, specific movements can be interpreted only by changes in resources, organization, and opportunities for collective action. Resource mobilization research emphasizes the formal structures of organizations and their capacities to apply leadership, money, time, publicity, and commitment to the pursuit of group goals and social issues that affect opportunities for action. See esp. Anthony Oberschall, *Social Conflict and Social Movements* (Englewood Cliffs, N.J.: Prentice-Hall, 1973); William A. Gamson, *The Strategy of Social Protest* (Homewood, Ill.: Dorsey, 1975); John D. McCarthy and Mayer Zald, *The Trend of Social Movements in America: Professionalization and Resource Mobilization* (Morristown, N.J.: General Learning Press, 1973) and their classic "Resource Mobilization and Social Movements: A Partial Theory," *American Journal of Sociology* 82 (1977): 1212–41: and Charles Tilly, *From Mobilization to Revolution* (Reading, Mass.: Addison-Wesley, 1978).

18. The importance of coalition building was developed especially by An-

thony Oberschall in *Social Conflict and Social Movements* and, with specific reference to peace coalitions, by Charles Chatfield in "Pacifists and Their Publics: The Politics of a Peace Movement," *Midwest Journal of Political Science* 13, no. 2 (May 1969): 298–312.

19. Networking is interpreted as an organizational style in Luther P. Gerlach and Virginia H. Hine, *People, Power, Change: Movements of Social Transformation* (Indianapolis: Bobbs-Merrill, 1970).

20. The importance of moral entrepreneurs, or professional leaders in social movements, was developed especially in McCarthy and Zald, *The Trend of Social Movements in America.*

21. For an evaluation of the general literature in this regard, see Tarrow, *Struggle, Politics, and Reform,* 29.

22. See Gamson, *The Strategy of Social Protest.*

23. Joseph Gusfield argues that the media shape general movements by defining them, and that in the process they "refract" and "construct" perceived society ("Social Movements and Social Change," 327–28). Thus, the reported occurrence of a demonstration conveys an image of the society itself.

24. Todd Gitlin's *The Whole World Is Watching: Mass Media in the Making and Unmaking of the New Left* (Berkeley and Los Angeles: University of California Press, 1980) remains a classic study in this regard.

25. On the relationship of government and the political process to social movements generally, see Tarrow's use of the concept of political opportunity structure in *Struggle, Politics, and Reform,* esp. 25–34. Meyer, in *Winter of Discontent,* uses the term "political space." Peter K. Eisinger developed the notion of political opportunity structure in urban settings in "The Conditions of Protest Behavior in American Cities," *American Political Science Review* 67 (1973): 11–28; Craig Jenkins combined it with analysis of resource mobilization, movement strategies, consciousness, and grievances in his study of farmworkers, *The Politics of Insurgency* (New York: Columbia University Press, 1985); and Aldon Morris, in *Origins of the Civil Rights Movement,* achieved a similar synthesis regarding the civil rights movement.

26. This trend was noted in Charles DeBenedetti "American Peace Activism, 1945–1985," in Chatfield and van den Dungen, eds., *Peace* Movements and Political Cultures, 222–29.

27. The phrase "prefigurative politics" was coined to convey the New Left's assumption in the 1960s that personal life-style and group organizing style could affect the community of the future by modeling it. See Wini Breines, *Community and Organization in the New Left, 1962–1968* (New York: Praeger, 1982), and a brief summary of the position in Alice Echols, *Daring to Be Bad: Radical Feminism in America, 1967–1975* (Minneapolis: University of Minnesota Press, 1989), 16–17. Although I agree with Echols that the "prefigurative and personal politics of the Movement made '60s radicalism distinctive, setting it apart from politics as it has typically been practiced," I think it was not unique. It had much

in common with 17th-century English radicalism, Garrisonian thought, the romantic radicalism of the Progressive era, and many individual peace activists. One need only to note the "prefigurative" heroes of New Left historian Staughton Lynd.

28. Elise Boulding makes a strong case for the role of imagination as a gateway to social change, in *Building a Global Civic Culture: Education for an Interdependent World* (New York: Columbia Teachers College Press, 1989). The role of cognitive frameworks on cultural transformation is suggested by Michel Foucault in *The Order of Things* (New York: Vintage, 1973), among others.

29. See Carolyn Stephenson, *Peace Studies: The Evolution of Peace Research and Peace Education* (Honolulu: University of Hawaii Press, 1990) and *Alternative Methods for International Security* (Washington, D.C.: University Press of America, 1982).

30. See Abrams's authoritative *The Nobel Peace Prize and the Laureates.*

31. Robert Kleidman argues, from his close study of three peace campaigns, that there is little evidence of leaders consciously drawing lessons from previous experience. On the other hand, Charles DeBenedetti and I found extensive reassessment of the antiwar movement (DeBenedetti, *An American Ordeal,* esp. 355–57), and I have noted other rounds of self-evaluation in the 1930s and at the end of the 1980s. The longer record strongly suggests that, since successive campaigns are organized by ongoing organizations, leaders absorb and apply experience they may not articulate. The transmission of movement experience is a fruitful field for research.

32. Thus the loose Alliance for Our Common Future, formed to anticipate the 1990 election, was composed of almost 50 peace action and education groups dating from earlier periods.

33. See the "perspectives of linearity and fluidity" in Gusfield, "Social Movements and Social Change." Two concepts are particularly relevant. First, Gusfield argues that social movements open a vocabulary of ideas and action that generate "major paradigms of public discourse and discussion," which may be retained and applied as "crucial aspects of social and cultural change." Second, he points to the "reflexive character of movements." By this he means that public awareness of movements itself helps to institutionalize generalized change. See also Ralph Turner, "Collective Behavior and Resource Mobilization As Approaches to Social Movements: Issues and Continuities," in *Research in Social Movements, Conflict, and Change,* vol. 4, ed. Louis Kriesberg (Greenwich, Conn.: JAI Press, 1981), 1–24, and Gerlach and Hine, *People, Power, and Change.*

34. Tarrow, *Struggle, Politics and Reform,* 8.

35. Werner Kaltefleiter and Robert L. Pfaltzgraff, "Towards a Comparative Analysis of the Peace Movements," in *The Peace Movements in Europe and the United States,* ed. Kaltefleiter and Pfalzgraff (New York: St. Martin's Press, 1985), 204.

Further Reading

The large literature on the American peace movement is accessible through several finding aids. A comprehensive bibliography is Charles F. Howlett, *The American Peace Movement: References and Resources* (Boston: G. K. Hall, 1991). Useful bibliographical essays are Lawrence S. Wittner, "Peace Movements and Foreign Policy: The Challenge to Diplomatic Historians, "*Diplomatic History* 11 (Fall 1987): 355–70; Charles F. Howlett and Glen Zeitzer, *The American Peace Movement: History and Historiography* (Washington, D.C.: American Historical Association, 1985); and Charles DeBenedetti, "Peace History in the American Manner," *The History Teacher* 18 (November 1984): 75–110. Important reference works are Harold Josephson, ed., *Biographical Dictionary of Modern Peace Leaders* (Westport, Conn.: Greenwood Press, 1985) and Warren F. Kuehl, ed., *Biographical Dictionary of Internationalists* (Westport, Conn.: Greenwood Press, 1983), which are cross-referenced. The classic documents and writings of the European and American peace and antiwar movements are available in the Garland Library of War and Peace, edited by Blanche Wiesen Cook, Charles Chatfield, and Sandi Cooper (New York: Garland Press, 1971–79), a collection of over 300 titles reprinted with new introductions. A computer-generated bibliography, emphasizing the 1980s and keyed to coded categories but with a somewhat random distribution of titles, is John Lofland, et al., eds., *Peace Movement Organizations and Activists in the U.S.: An Analytic Bibliography* (New York: Haworth, 1990).

Biographies and autobiographies provide an interesting entrée to the field. They can be located in the bibliographic notes of the following books, which have been produced by the current generation of scholars and which offer a good introduction to the general reader.

General Works

Chatfield, Charles, ed. *Peace Movements in America*. New York: Schocken, 1973. An anthology of still useful essays, notably the symposium on internationalism.

Chatfield, Charles, and Peter van den Dungen, eds. *Peace Movements and Political Cultures*. Knoxville: University of Tennessee Press, 1988. An anthology of essays on European, Australian, American, and transnational peace movements, mainly in the twentieth century.

DeBenedetti, Charles. *The Peace Reform in American History*. Bloomington: Indiana University Press, 1980. A comprehensive survey of the movement through the Vietnam War. For this purpose it succeeds Merle Curti's classic *Peace or War: The American Struggle, 1636–1936* (New York: Norton, 1936), which nonetheless remains a classic in the field.

———, ed. *Peace Heroes in Twentieth-Century America*. Bloomington: Indiana University Press, 1986. Eight biographical studies, with an afterword by Merle Curti.

Specific Periods and Studies

Brock, Peter. *Freedom from Violence: Sectarian Non-Resistance from the Middle Ages to the Great War* (Toronto: University of Toronto Press, 1991), *Freedom from War: Nonsectarian Pacifism 1814–1914* (Toronto: University of Toronto Press), and *The Quaker Peace Testimony 1660 to 1914* (York, England: Sessions Brook Trust 1990). This trilogy supplants Brock's earlier *Pacifism in the United States* (1968) and *Pacifism in Europe* (1972) to 1914. His brief *Twentieth-Century Pacifism* (New York: Van Norstrand, 1970) is still useful.

Chambers, John W. II, ed. *The Eagle and the Dove: The American Peace Movement and United States Foreign Policy, 1900–1922*. New York: Garland Press, 1976; 2d ed., Syracuse, N.Y.: Syracuse University Press, 1991. A rich anthology of documents with a comprehensive introduction.

Chatfield, Charles. *For Peace and Justice: Pacifism in America, 1914–1941*. Knoxville: University of Tennessee Press, 1971. Follows the development of pacifism in the context of internationalism and foreign policy issues.

DeBenedetti, Charles. *An American Ordeal: The Antiwar Movement of the Vietnam Era*. Syracuse, N.Y.: Syracuse University Press, 1990. The first comprehensive history of this era based on archival sources.

———. *Origins of the Modern American Peace Movement, 1915–1929*. Millwood, N.Y.: KTO, 1978. Delineates organized internationalism and peace efforts in the 1920s.

Divine, Robert A. *Blowing on the Wind: The Nuclear Test Ban Debate, 1954–*

1960. New York: Oxford University Press, 1978. Depicts test ban campaigns in a national context.

————. *Second Chance: The Triumph of Internationalism in America during World War II*. New York: Atheneum, 1967. The definitive account of the campaign for a United Nations.

Herman, Sondra R. *Eleven against War: Studies in American Internationalist Thought, 1898–1921*. Stanford, Calif.: Hoover Institution Press, 1969. Treats peace advocates biographically in the context of intellectual history.

Katz, Milton. *Ban the Bomb: A History of SANE, the Committee for a Sane Nuclear Policy, 1957–1985*. New York: Greenwood Press, 1986. The standard organizational history.

Kraft, Barbara. *The Peace Ship: Henry Ford's Pacifist Adventure in the First World War*. New York: Macmillan, 1978. A lively and readable account of a specific peace project.

Kuehl, Warren F. *Seeking World Order: The United States and International Organization to 1920*. Nashville: Vanderbilt University Press, 1969. The standard study of early internationalism. It is usefully supplemented with Kuehl's biography *Hamilton Holt* (Gainesville: University Presses of Florida, 1960).

Marchand, Roland. *The American Peace Movement, 1887–1914*. Princeton, N.J.: Princeton University Press, 1972. A historical narrative that treats peace organizations with sociological insight.

McNeal, Patricia. *The American Catholic Peace Movement*. New Burnswick, N.J.: Rutgers University Press, forthcoming 1992. The first comprehensive history of peace advocacy in this religious tradition in its full range, from the "just war" tradition through radical pacifism.

Meyer, David S. *A Winter of Discontent: The Nuclear Freeze and American Politics*. New York: Praeger, 1990. A sound political history explicitly related to social movement theory.

Robinson, Jo Ann O. *Abraham Went Out: A Biography of A. J. Muste*. Philadelphia: Temple University Press, 1981. A readable, sympathetic, but scholarly treatment of a leading pacifist.

Wittner, Lawrence S. *Rebels against War: The American Peace movement, 1933–1983*. 2d ed. Philadelphia: Temple University Press 1984. A comprehensive, readable survey.

Wooley, Wesley T. *Alternatives to Anarchy: American Supernationalism since World War II*. Bloomington: Indiana University Press, 1988. Traces the metamorphosis of world federalism.

Zaroulis, Nancy, and Gerald Sullivan. *Who Spoke Up? American Protest against the War in Vietnam, 1963–1975*. Garden City, N.Y.: Doubleday, 1984. A dramatic narrative.

Index

ABM, 150
Abrams, Henry, 108
Acheson, Dean, 98
Addams, Jane, 25, 32, 33, 44, 48, 180
Afghanistan, 151
AFSC, 46, 49, 88, 105; and the
    Emergency Peace Campaign, 65,
    66; and liberal pacifism, 54–55, 58;
    and nuclear arms control, 106–7,
    109, 114, 115–16, 148–51, 152;
    Speak Truth to Power, 116; in the
    Vietnam War, 127, 130, 136, 138,
    139; in World War II, 75–78
Allen, Devere, 55, 67, 71, 81
Allen, Steve, 110
allied citizen groups, 176
American Civil Liberties Union (ACLU),
    55
American Friends Service Committee.
    See AFSC
American League to Limit Armaments,
    35
American Neutral Conference
    Committee, 34
American Peace and Arbitration League,
    25
American Peace School League, 21
American Peace Society. *See* APS
American Revolution, 2–3
American School Citizenship League, 40
American Society of International Law,
    21

American Union against Militarism. *See*
    AUAM
Americans for Democratic Action (ADA),
    121, 126–27, 134, 138
Angell, Norman: *The Great Illusion,* 181
antiballistic missile system. *See* ABM
anticommunism, 96. *See also* communism
    and communists
anti-imperialism: interlude of, 1898–
    1902, 16–18; and Vietnam, 121
Anti-Imperialist League, 17–18
anti-intervention, 39–40
antipreparedness, 32, 35–39
Anti-Preparedness Committee, 36
anti–Vietnam War movement, ix–xxvi,
    117–18: assessed, 143–45; and
    emerging currents of dissent, 118–
    22; formation of, 122–31; in the
    political system, 141–43; in
    transition, 135–41; in turmoil, 131–
    35
antiwar protest: in Civil War, 10–12; in
    Mexican War of 1846, 10; in
    Philippine-American War, 17–18; in
    Spanish-American War, 16–17; in
    World War I, 43–50; and the War of
    1812, 3; in World War II, 75–84. *See*
    also anti-imperialism; anti–Vietnam
    War movement; civil disobedience;
    conscientious objectors;
    nonresistance; pacifism and
    pacifists; radical pacifism

215

The Author

Charles Chatfield was born in Philadelphia and grew up mostly in Oak Park and Monmouth, Illinois, graduating from Monmouth College. He earned his M.A. and Ph.D. in history at Vanderbilt University. In 1961 he joined the faculty of Wittenberg University, where, except for appointments elsewhere as visiting professor, he has continued to teach. In the 1970s, as an officer of the Council of Peace Research in History and the Consortium on Peace Research, Education, and Development, he became active in international education. A series co-editor of the Garland Library on Peace and War, he has edited *Peace Movements in America* and has written *For Peace and Justice: Pacifism in America, 1914–1941*, as well as numerous articles. In the 1980s, as part of his efforts to link historians abroad who were researching peace movements, he coedited the international symposium *Peace Movements and Political Cultures*. Toward the end of the decade, he completed Charles DeBenedetti's unfinished *An American Ordeal: The Antiwar Movement of the Vietnam Era*. He is currently codirecting a collaborative Soviet-American project, "Ideas of Peace in History."